AF521744

Conversations with KOSTABI

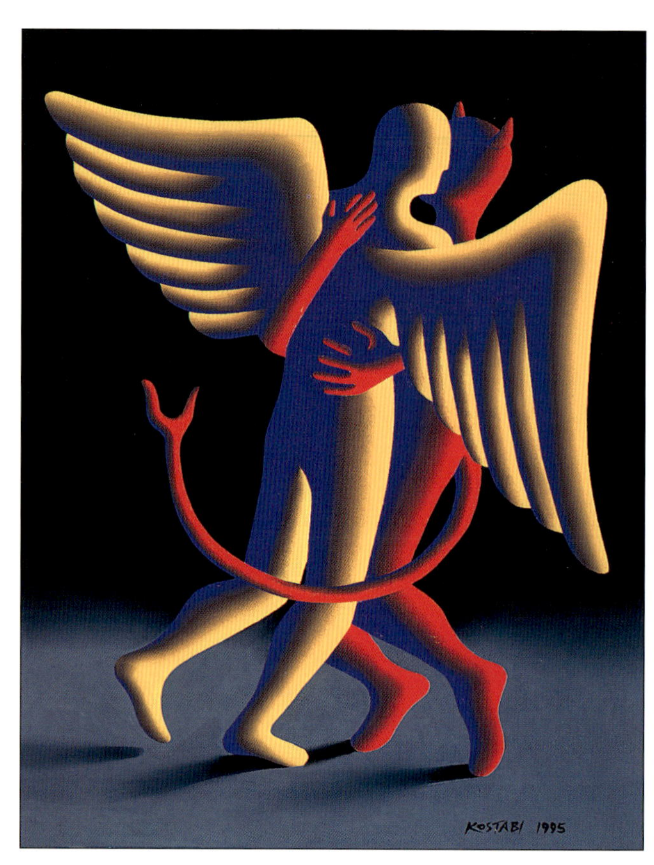
KOSTABI 1995

Conversations

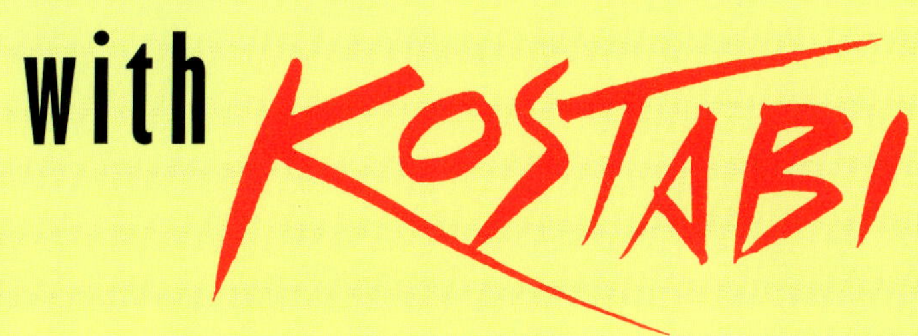

BY MARK KOSTABI

Foreword by Thomas McEvilley

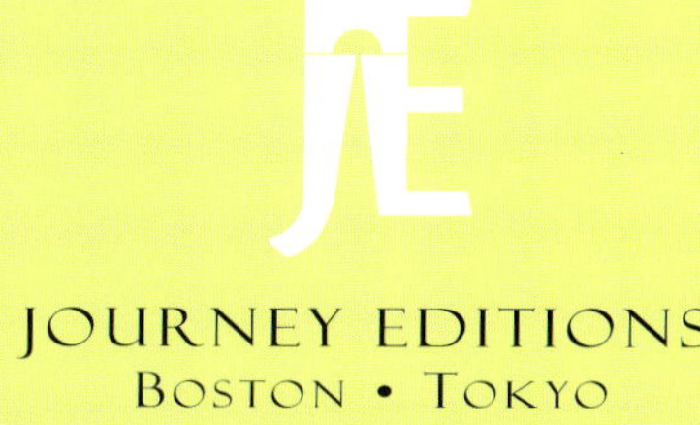

First published in 1996 by Journey Editions, an imprint of Charles E. Tuttle Co., Inc., of Rutland, Vermont, and Tokyo, Japan, with editorial offices at 153 Milk Street, Boston, Massachusetts 02109.

Photo credits appear on page 210

Library of Congress Cataloging-in-Publication Data

Kostabi, Mark, 1960–
Conversations with Kostabi : by Mark Kostabi.
p. cm.
ISBN 1-885203-25-X
1. Kostabi, Mark, 1960– —Interviews. 2. Painters—United States—Interviews. I. Title.
ND237.K65A35 1996
759.13—dc20 96-18774
CIP

frontispiece: *The Last Dance*, 1995
Oil on canvas
24 x 18 inches
Collection of Tim Bock

page vi: *88 + 1*, 1995
Oil on canvas
34 x 34 inches
Europa Art Gallery,
West Bloomfield, Michigan

First edition
1 3 5 7 9 10 8 6 4 2

Book design by Jill Winitzer
Edited by Judith Estrine

Printed in Hong Kong

Dedicated to all the art lovers in the world,
without whom I'd be nothing.

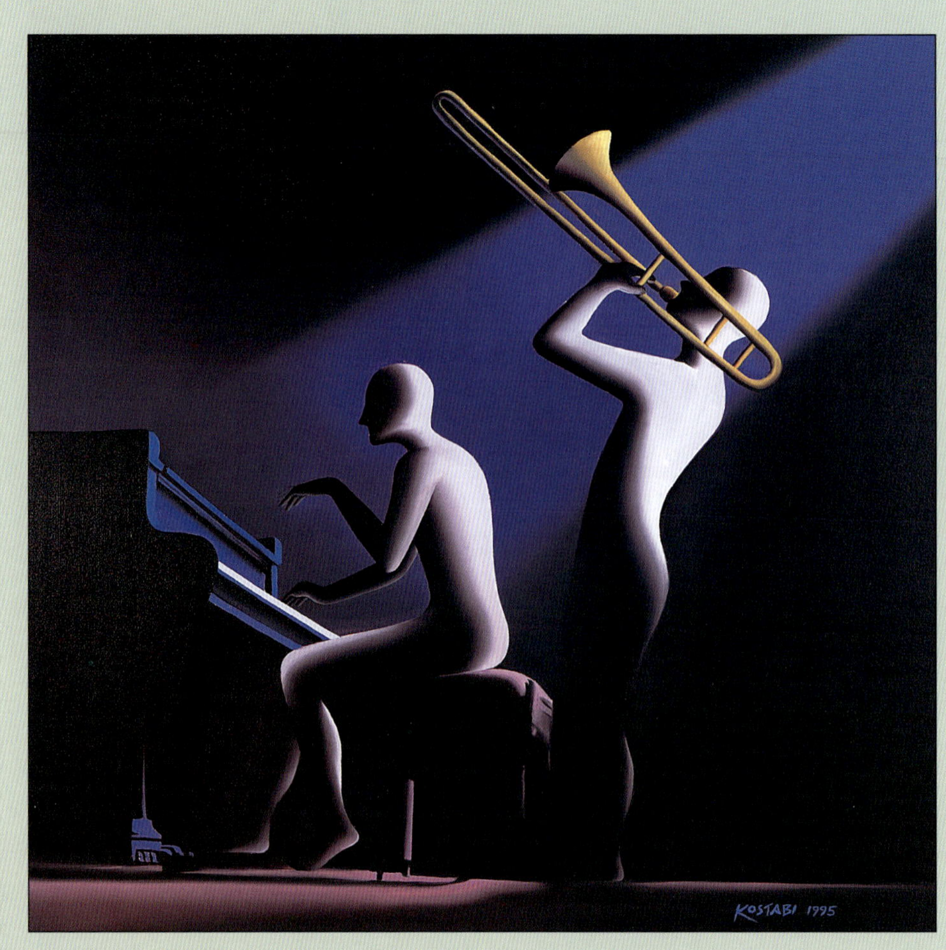
KOSTABI 1995

CONTENTS

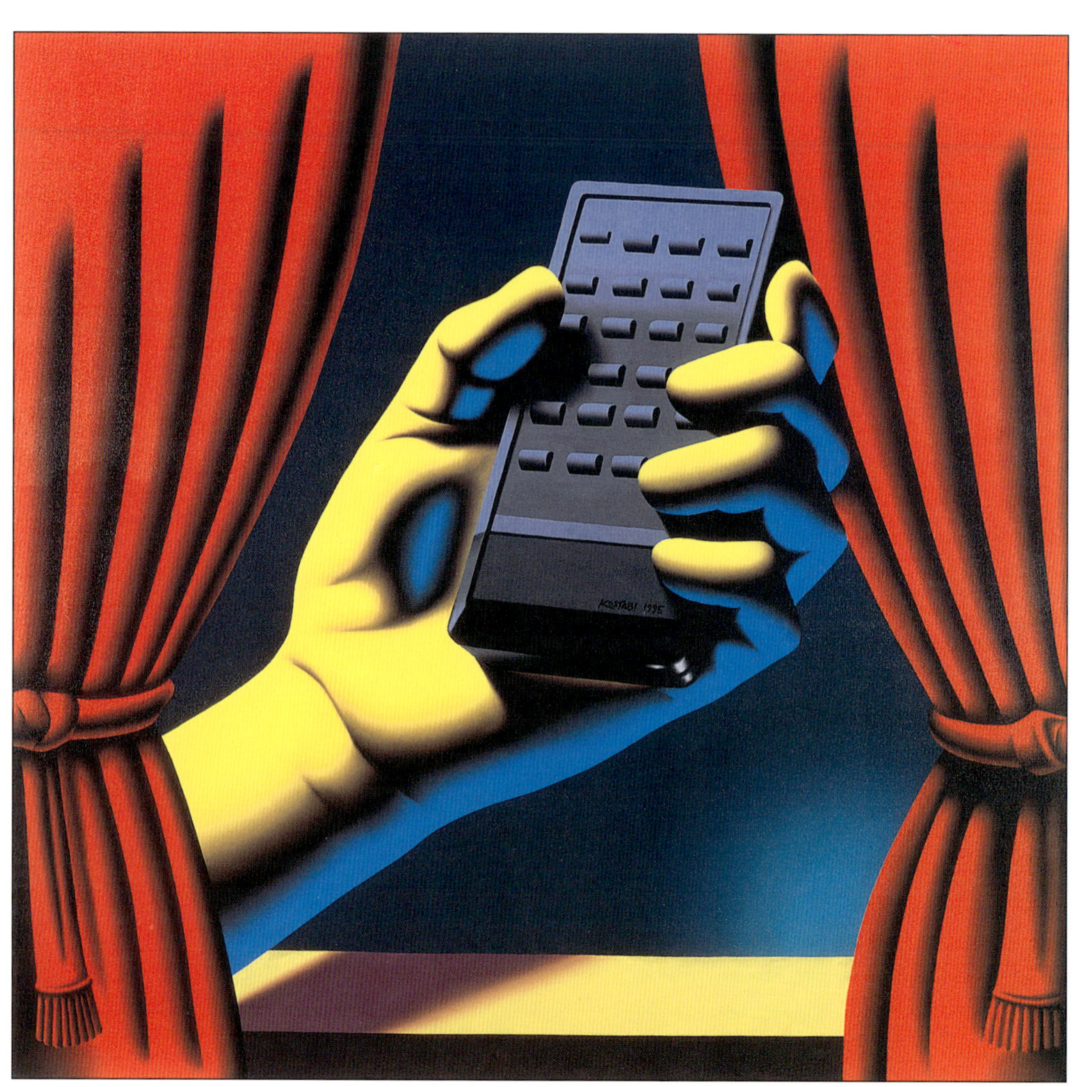
KOSTABI 1995

INTRODUCTION

***Conversations** with Kostabi* is my first serious self-interview, unlike the many tongue-in-cheek interviews I've written over the years.

I started writing my own interviews in 1984. Until then I hadn't really learned how to talk about my work, and hoped that it would speak for itself. I was reticent around people who wanted to discuss my paintings, and consequently, interviews with me were boring non-events. It was probably a combination of fear, arrogance, and naïveté, but whatever the reason, I wasn't getting any press attention, and my exposure as an artist remained limited to a closed circle within the art community. Then in 1984 I had a breakthrough. Frustrated by my self-imposed media blackout and anxious to reach a wider audience, I made a list of questions that people most frequently asked me, and prepared interesting and provocative answers. When the interviewer arrived, I handed him the script. He loved it! It was all the material he needed to write the piece. I was delighted, because I had broken through and discovered the secret of getting the media attention I wanted.

From that day on, I did everything I could to polish my irreverent, funny, and provocative persona. I massaged my mystique and became an artist who makes news. At the same time that I was building a career as a serious painter, I was also building my reputation as a

✧ page viii:
The Final Icon
1995
Oil on canvas
54 x 54 inches
Kostabi World

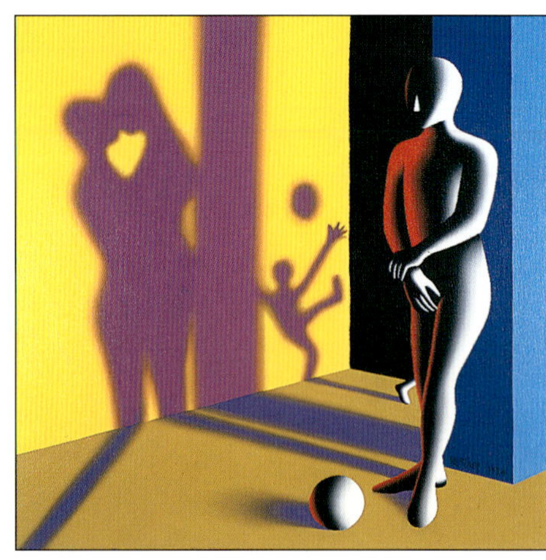

✧ Singled Out
1995
Oil on canvas
48 x 48 inches
Collection of Donald and Helena Resnick

controversial public figure. My aim was to continually surprise and have people talk about me. This worked so well that I took it to the next level and began publishing mock interviews in my art books. It was all in jest, and most people recognized it as a parody of the art establishment.

This self-interview is different, because I think it's time to level with you about what it's like to be a professional artist. I've heard people say it's nearly impossible. They say you've got a one-in-a-million chance of making it. But that's just not true.

If I were starting out today, I would want to talk to an expert. Someone who knows the ropes (and the strings to pull). Someone who knows what rules to break and the ones that are inviolate. Someone who started at the bottom (and managed to get even lower). I would want to talk to me. *Conversations with Kostabi* is that discussion.

FOREWORD

Mark Kostabi's paintings are well known, and most people will have made up their minds, by now, about their qualities simply as pictures. But there is more to them than the simplicity of pictures. Here are two other ways to encapsulate what Kostabi has accomplished.

First, he has posed a conundrum, through a kind of shape-shifting trickster persona, about the location of the artwork. Is the painting the artwork? Is the mode of production of the painting the artwork, with its elements of both conceptualism and performance art? Or is the constructed persona of the artist who controls that mode of production the artwork? Where does object art give way to conceptual and performance art?

These conundra have been posed to us before—by Andy Warhol, for example, and earlier by Yves Klein—and there is a pattern. As an additional performative element, for example, one that harks back to both Warhol and Klein, Kostabi has presented himself as a scapegoat or ritual sacrifice, a would-be sanctified clown who is making a point: as his reputation gets progressively trashed, the parable he is acting out gets clearer and clearer.

Second, as his texts in this book make clear, Kostabi has investigated the assistant-based mode of artistic production intensively for years, and has presented an unusually detailed and honest account of this method that goes back, in the European tradition, at least to Giotto. This account is located mostly in chapter three,

"Kostabi World," where his method of producing paintings through committees (made up of idea people, painters, and occasional random visitors) is spelled out. In this account, Kostabi subjects the power dynamics involved in the working relationship between artist and assistants to a grueling interrogation that echoes, at moments, Hegel's exposition of the master-slave relationship in the *Phenomenology of Spirit.* The economic bottom lines are also made explicit, as this tradition is recast in the 1980s and 1990s mood of *Late* Late Capitalism. The survival of humanistic impulses in a hierarchy of power is always a subtext.

On the one hand, Kostabi seems anxious to fend off accusations of exploitation. He stresses the claim that certain of his assistants have gone on to higher things—as if Kostabi World were a kind of art school in which they were trained. But, on the other hand, he also lays the economic reality of the relationship on the line explicitly, because the conceptual nature of the idea that underlies it may require an appearance of exploitation, as one performative brush stroke, so to speak, among others. It is primarily through his unrelenting stress on the artist-assistant relationship—the artist's perverse yet triumphant claim, "I don't make my own artworks!"—that Kostabi has kept alive the provocation that gets him written about on the *New York Post's* "Page Six" more often than in the art magazines.

To me, Kostabi's oeuvre seems to consist in this entire system. With its implicit references to Warhol's Factory, the enterprise as a whole seems to have a performative nature. There is in this relationship something of Marx's famous dictum, in the *18th Brumaire,* that everything in history happens twice, first as tragedy, then again as farce. Kostabi has accepted the fact that history has assigned him the second role in this formulation; he takes it on seriously and professionally, as if thinking: Whatever articulation the shadows of the times happen to throw across the details of a moment must be worked with—that *is* the material.

Any artifact carries with it, invisibly, the memory of the process that produced it, but ordinarily this memory is neglected or even repressed. Whereas paintings are usually intended to declare their presence simply as themselves, a Kostabi picture openly asserts the complex memory of the process of its production. The structure of Kostabi World, its hierarchies of relationships, and the performative project of working these relationships out in the hard, high-contrast lighting of capitalism—all this hangs invisibly suspended around each picture. In addition, many of the paintings of the 1990s feature a quotational aspect, with overt references ranging from Michelangelo to Duchamp to Magritte. This adds another layer to what the paintings actually *do*—which is to occupy cultural space-time with an appearance of simplicity that masks a genuine complexity.

THOMAS MCEVILLEY

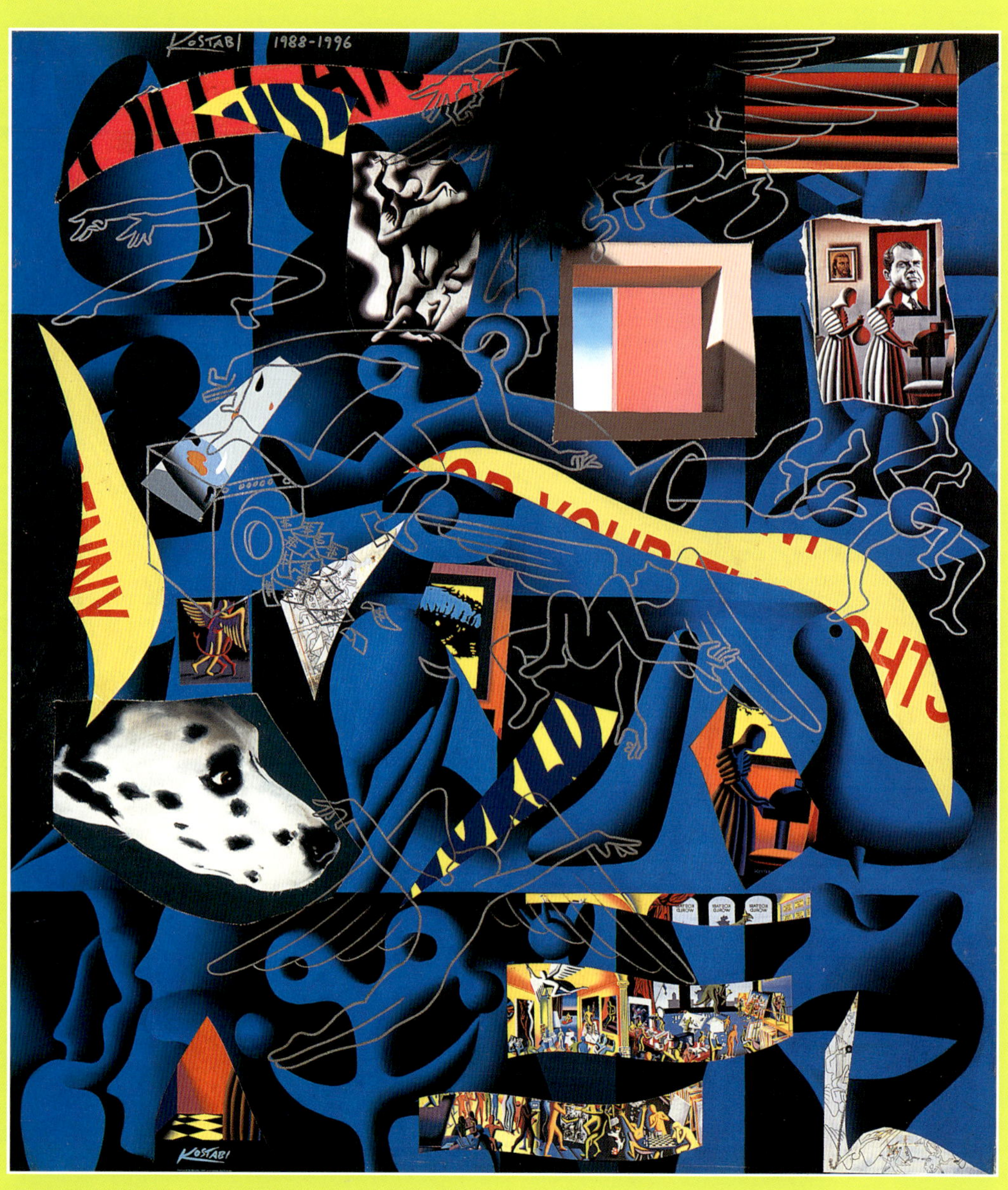
KOSTABI 1988-1996
KOSTABI

CHAPTER ✧ ONE

BEGINNINGS

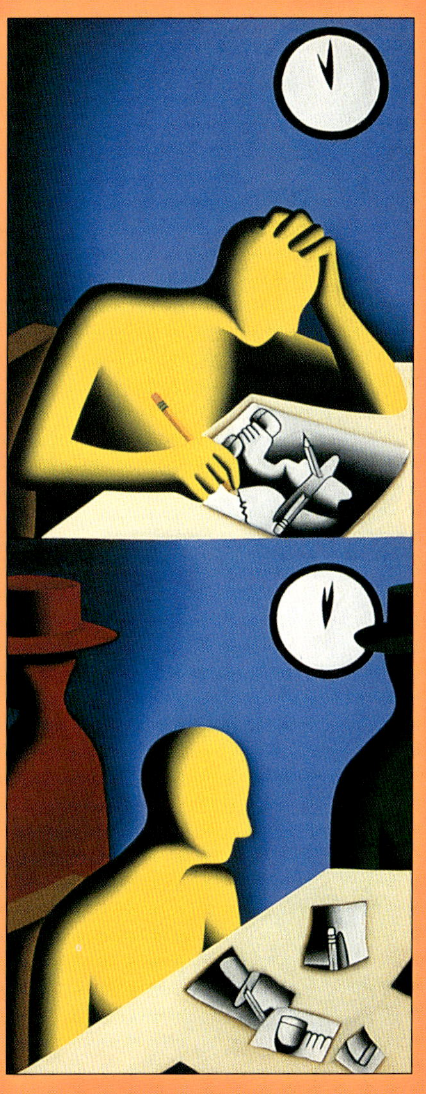

pick up those techniques from comics and science fiction illustrations?

✧ **Picking up a technique is like learning a new word. Sure, you learn lots of words in childhood that you continue to use in later life. But the statements you make don't necessarily have anything to do with your childhood, although it's true that as a teenager I had a huge collection of comic books and aspired to draw for Marvel Comics. My figures actually evolved from thousands of calligraphic marks that I made on rolls of receipt paper when I was in college.**

✦ Aside from a fascination with comics, is there anything about your paintings that reflect your formative years in Whittier, California?

✧ **Some of my paintings refer to events from my childhood. For**

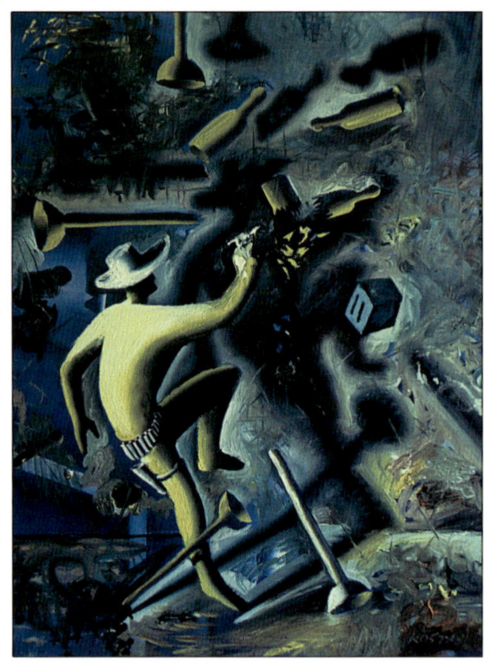

✧ **Wild West #1**
1983
Oil on canvas
48 x 36 inches
Private collection

✧ page 5:
Gravity Fuels the Rocket to Inner Space
1985
Oil on canvas
96 x 72 inches
Marrs Gallery, Tokyo

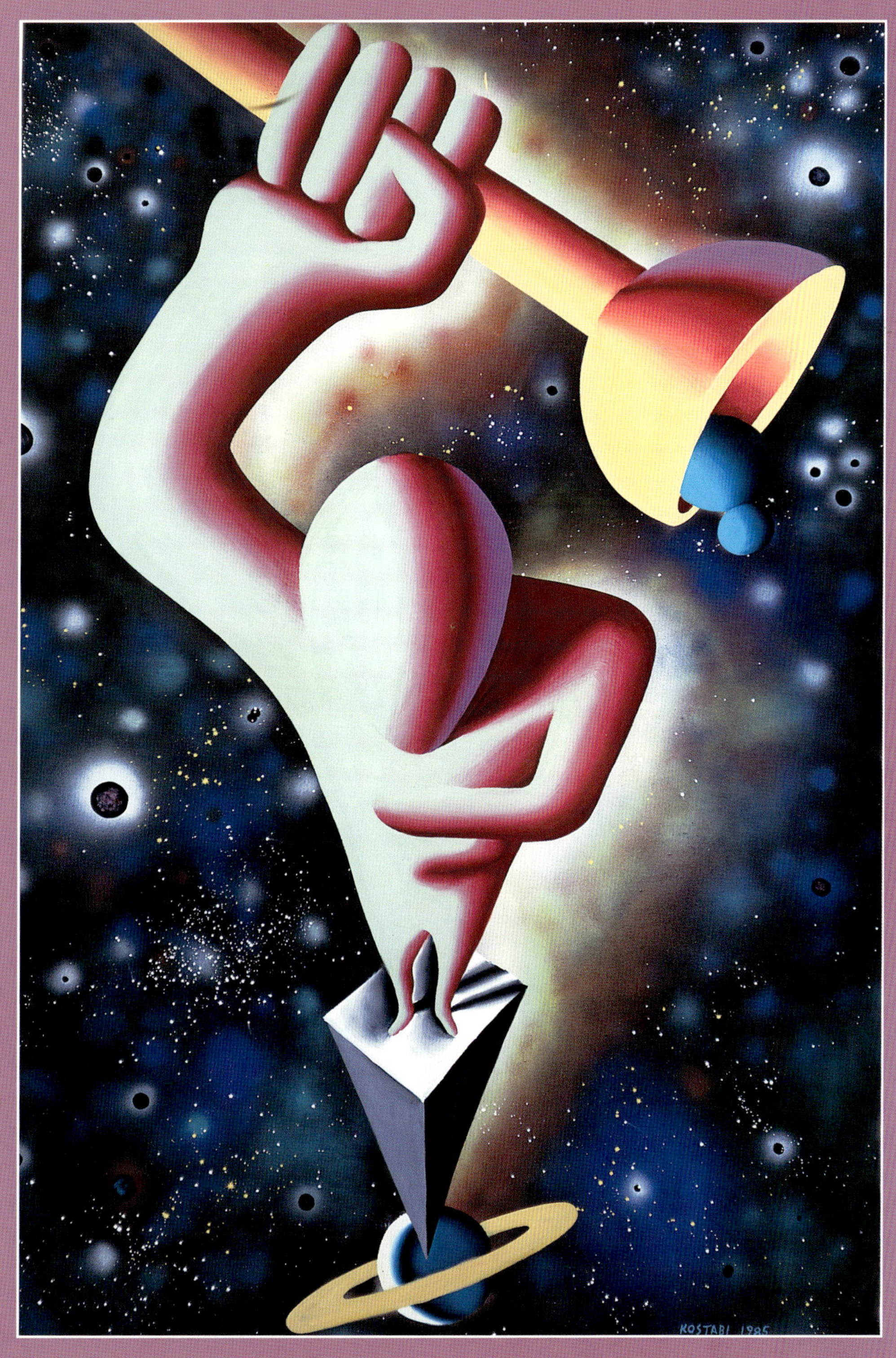
KOSTABI 1985

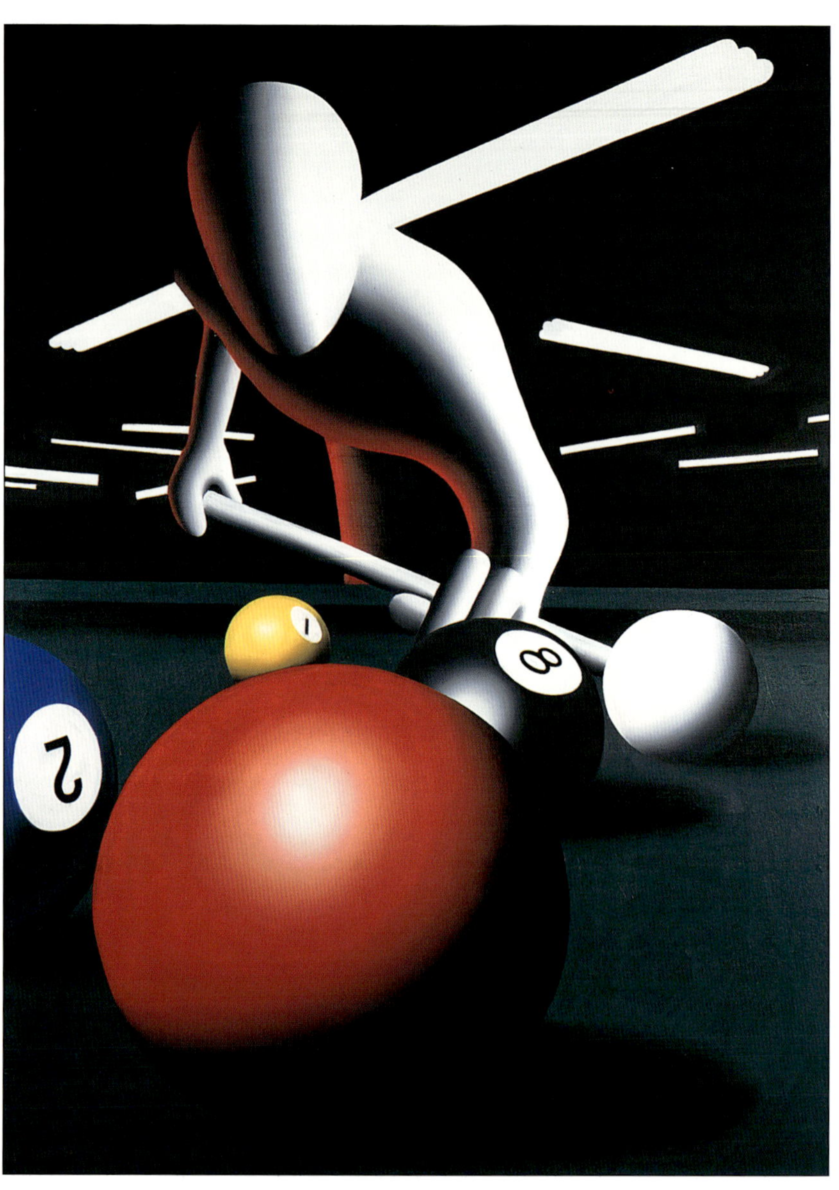

✧ **The Combination**
1989
Oil on canvas
84 x 60 inches
Collection of
The Billiard Club

instance, *The Combination* relates to the fact that I played pool at the Boy's Club across from La Habra High. And one of my most successful paintings from 1994 is called *Useless Knowledge,* which was inspired by my experiences in high school. In 1995 I made a new version, with the same faceless figure studying a chess game, called *Alekhine's Defense (Alburt Variation),* which alludes to my membership in the high school chess club.

✦ Was your childhood important in your development as an artist?

✧ The great works of Rembrandt, Picasso, and Warhol had little, if anything, to do with their childhood. Their table manners, maybe . . . I'm formed more by what happened yesterday in New York than by what happened twenty years ago in Whittier.

It's not that my childhood is unimportant. It's very important, especially since I'm still in it, and probably always will be.

✧ **Useless Knowledge**
1994
Oil on canvas
48 x 36 inches
whereabouts unknown

✧ page 9:
Alekhine's Defense (Alburt Variation)
1995
Oil on canvas
48 x 48 inches
Collection of Mr. and Mrs. Mitchell Dancik

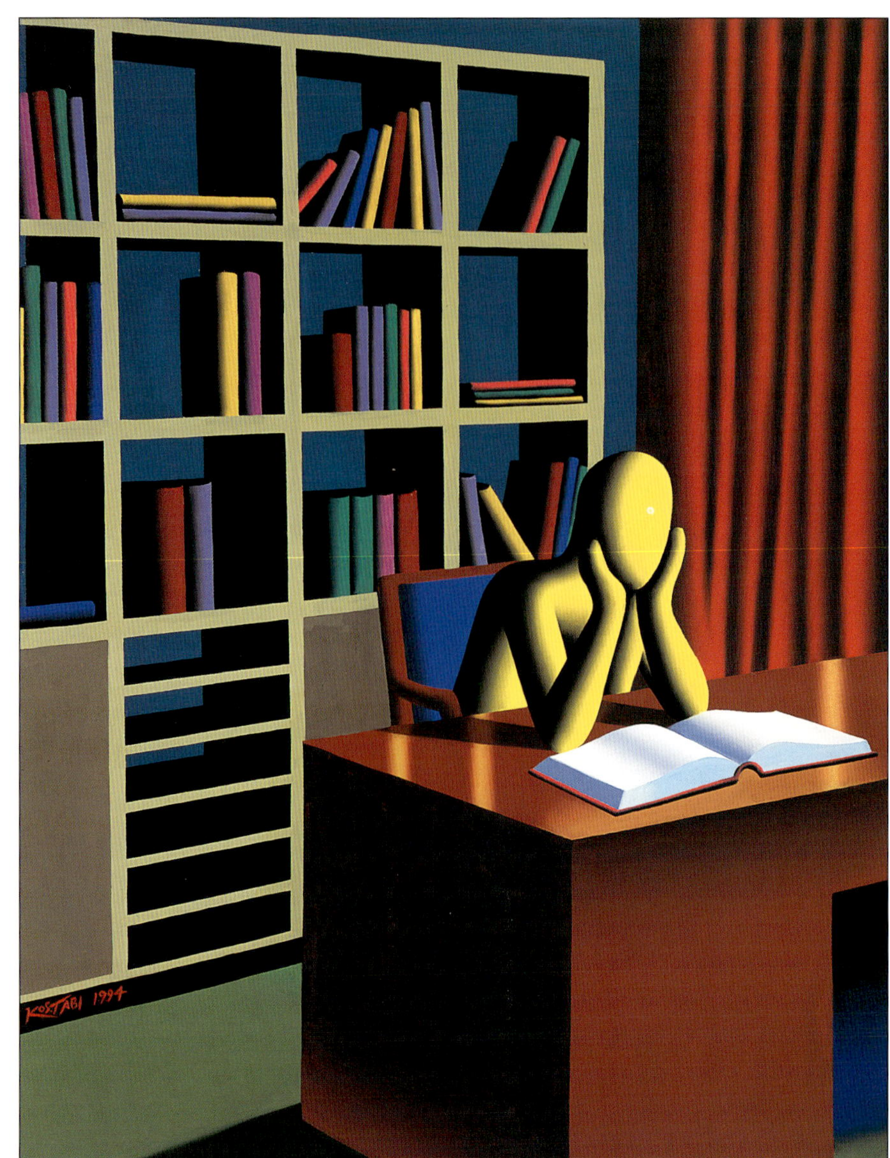

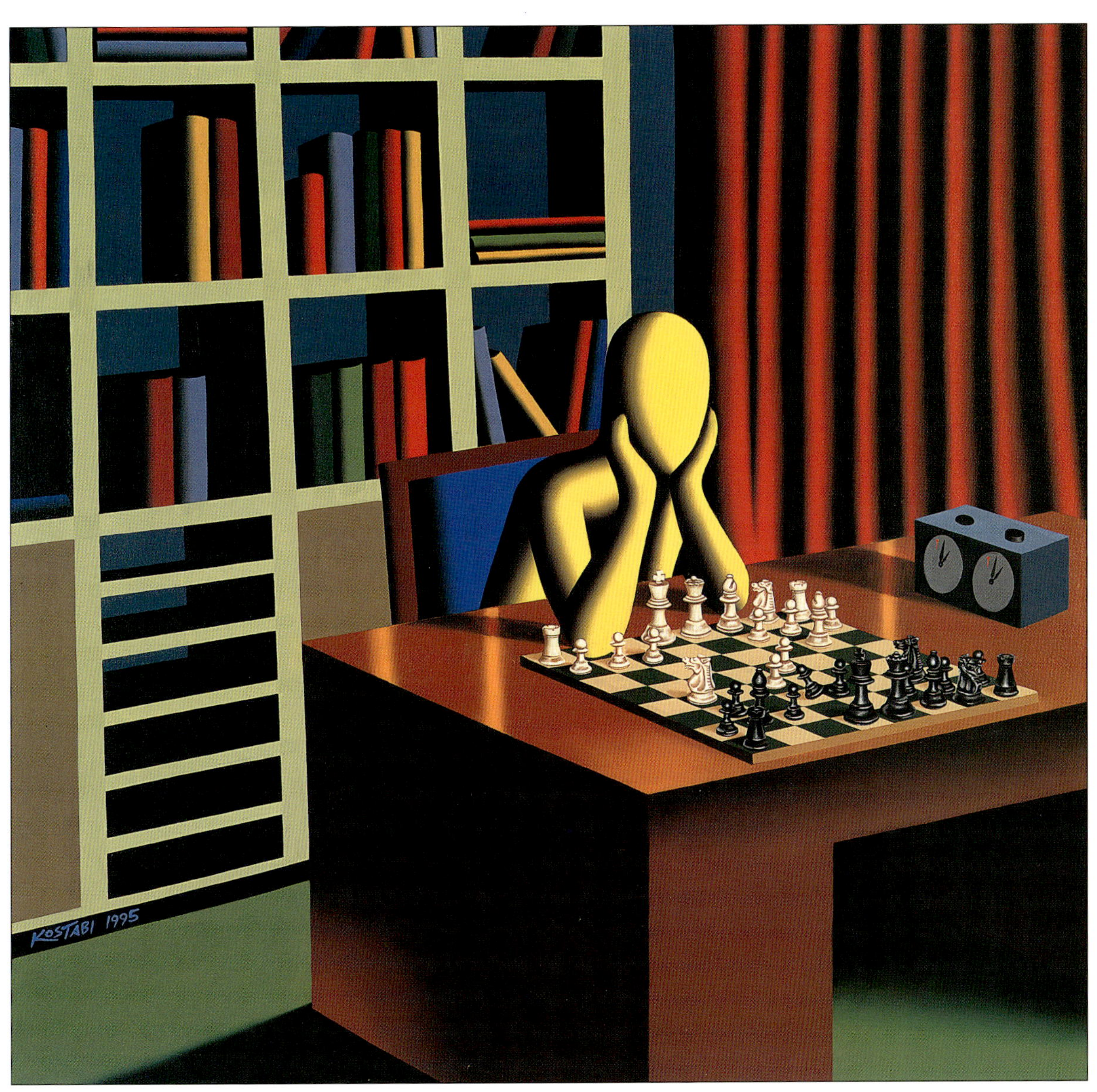
KOSTABI 1995

✧ A PICTURE

✦ Can you tell me about your Estonian roots and their influence on your life?

✧ **My parents are Estonian, and I've visited many times. My mother fled Estonia over fifty years ago, and I recently accompanied her back there. It was very moving. I've also had an art exhibit and a concert performance in Estonia, both of which were very well received. I'm very patriotic, and I include the Estonian flag in some of my paintings, like *The Rhythm of Inspiration*. I'm told that my work has some echoes of Estonian illustrators throughout history.**

✦ Do you believe in an ethnic creative unconscious?

✧ **Not really. But I do feel at home when I'm in Estonia.**

✦ Why do you make outrageous comments like: modern art is a con and I'm the world's greatest con artist?

✧ **I'm just shining a light on some of the pretensions and hypocrisy in the art world. I'm saying that the art business is a game and I'm a hustler, like everyone else. We're all trying to win and what's wrong with that? We can afford to expose**

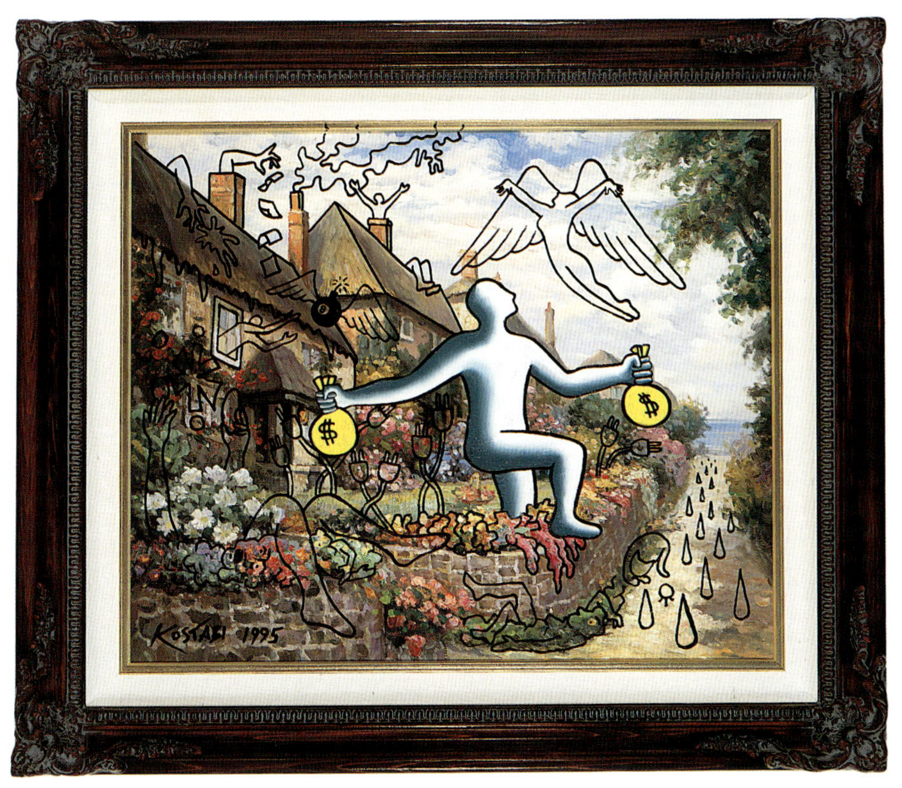

✧ **Pin Money**
1995
Oil on canvas
20 x 24 inches
Martin Lawrence Galleries

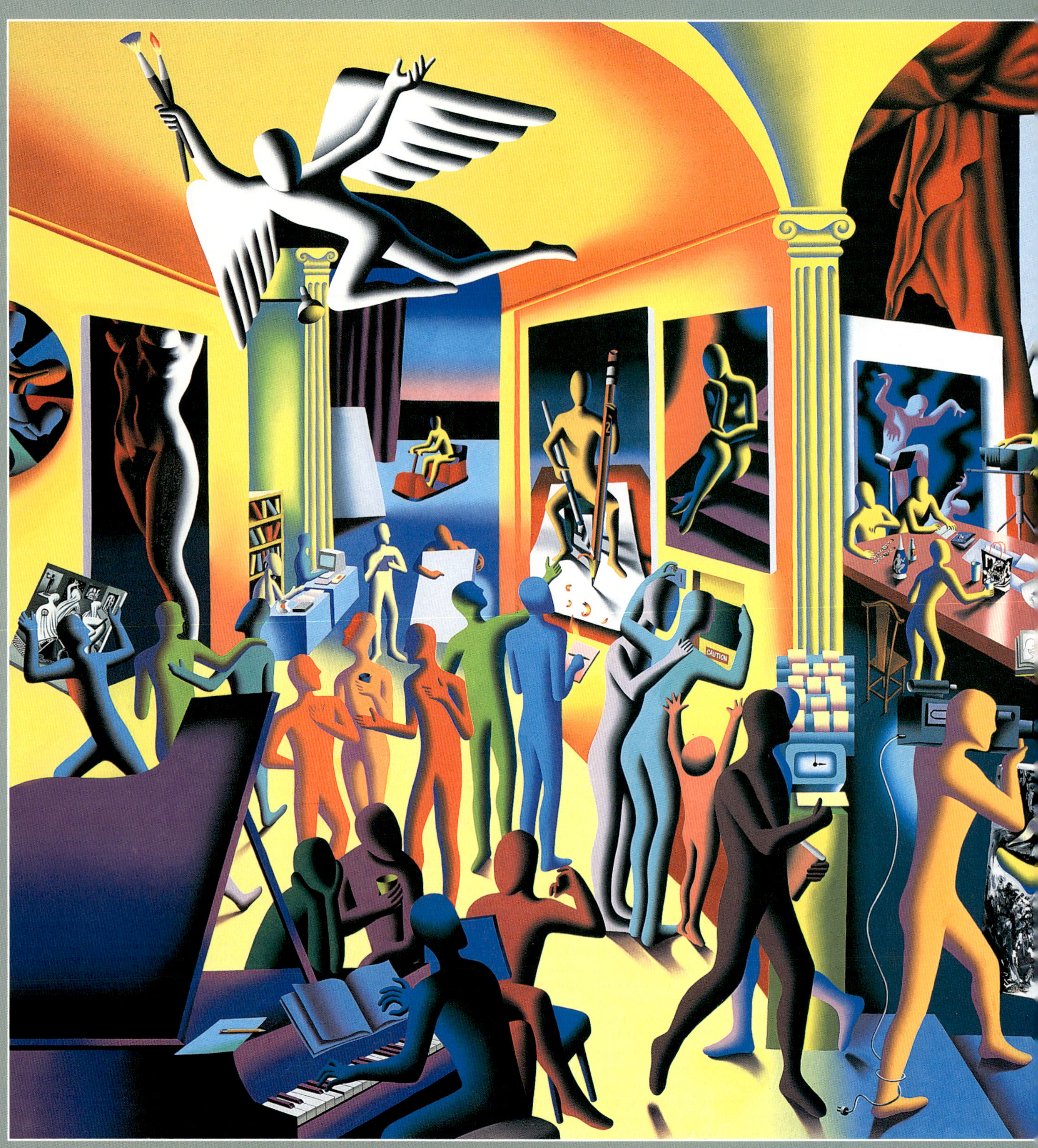
CAUTION

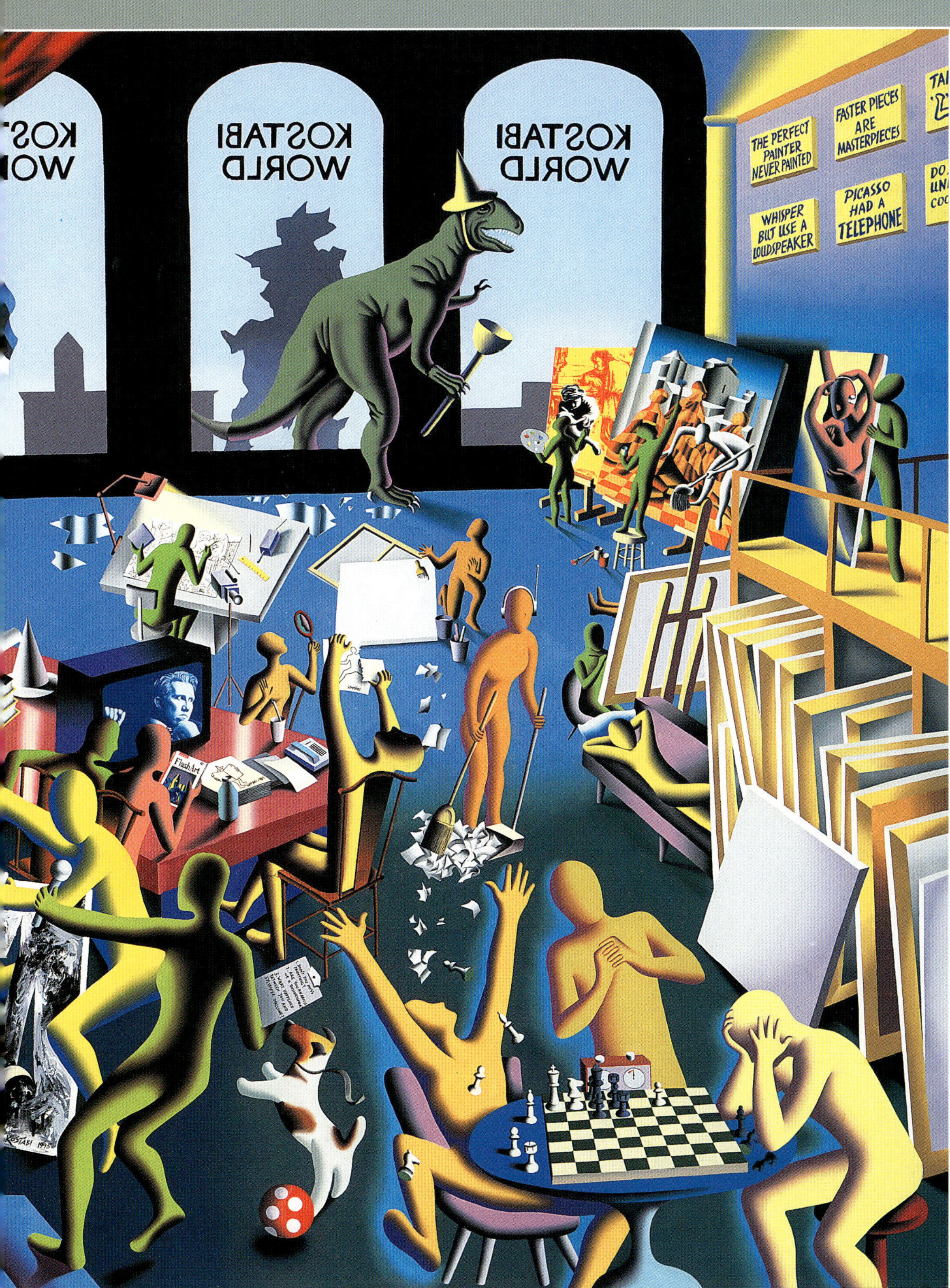

✧ **The Rhythm of Inspiration**
1995
Oil on canvas
7 x 12 feet
Kostabi World

some of our "secrets," and the more we do, the more interesting we become.

✦ What kind of "secrets" are you talking about?

✧ **Prices, for example. Most major artists would never dare to publicly reveal the real discounts that dealers get. The public believes that artists and galleries split the retail price and share the profits fifty/fifty. But that's not true. Sometimes we sell paintings to dealers for as low as 25 percent of retail.**

✦ Do your dealers expect to get a 75 percent discount?

✧ **The truth is, I only give big discounts to special dealers who do special things, like buy in huge quantities, publish catalogs, sell to prestigious museums, or generate loads of publicity. For many years I never gave a dealer more than a 50 percent discount. And many of my artist colleagues felt that 50 percent was way too generous. But when I finally swallowed my pride and became more flexible, I suddenly became much more successful. You asked about my childhood? See, I'm really just a product of suburban pop culture.**

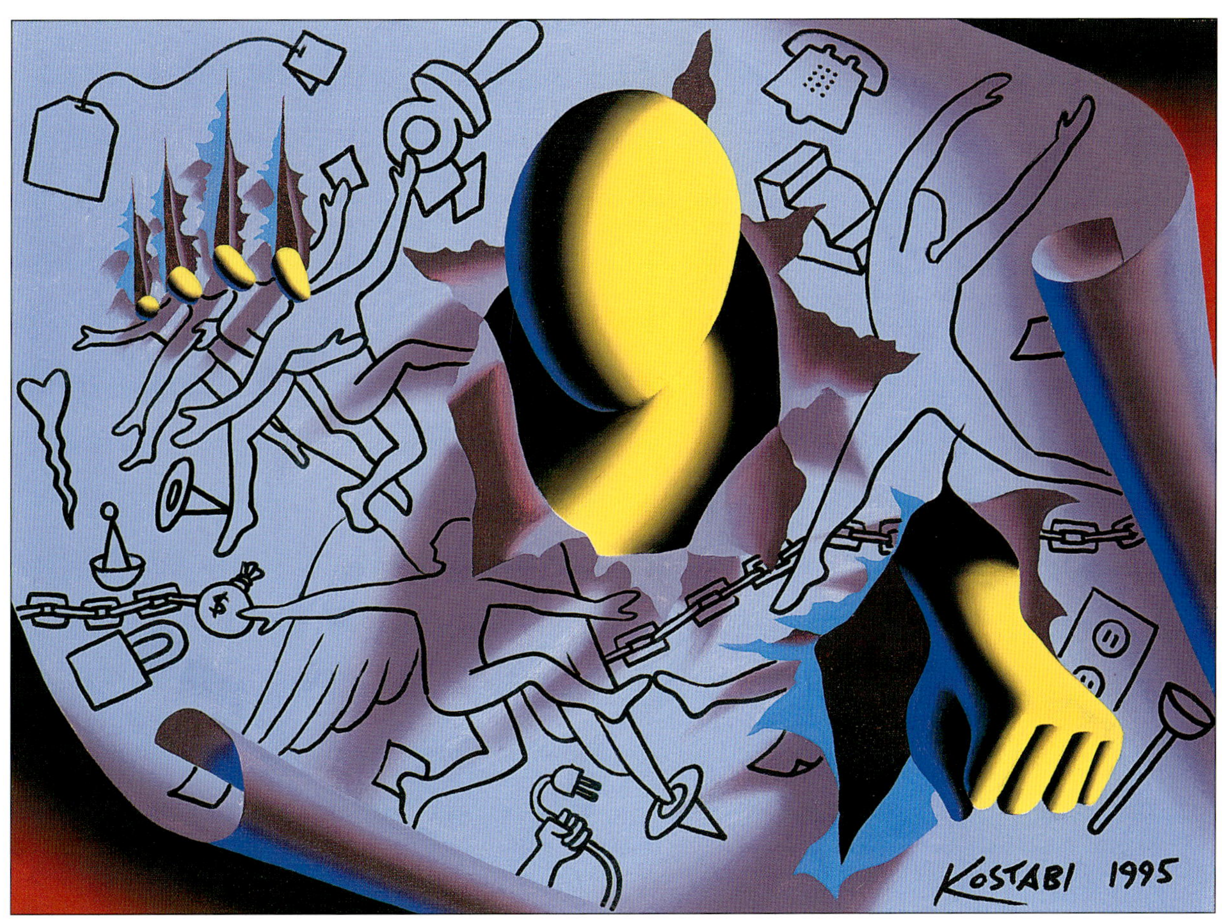

✧ **Breakthrough**
1995
Oil on canvas
18 x 24 inches
Collection of the artist

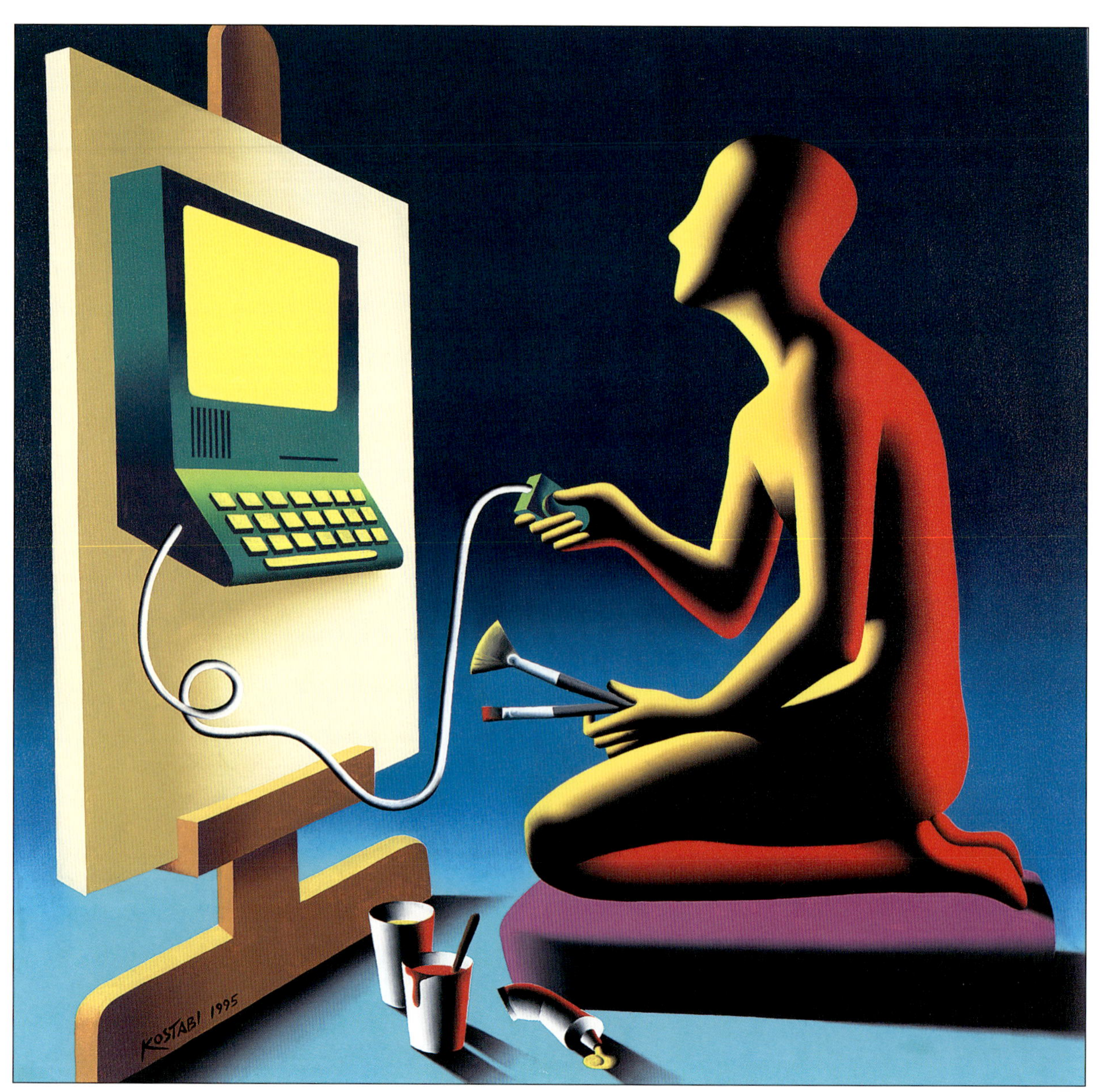
KOSTABI 1995

✦ How's that?

✧ **It's similar to marketing compact disks. A CD costs only pennies to manufacture. But the public pays sixteen dollars. The artist gets about two bucks and the rest goes into promotion and record company overhead. Now my work sells in such large quantities in shopping malls that I have become Suburban Pop Culture.**

✧ page 16:
Pygmalion and Galatea
1995
Oil on canvas
40 x 40 inches
Kostabi World

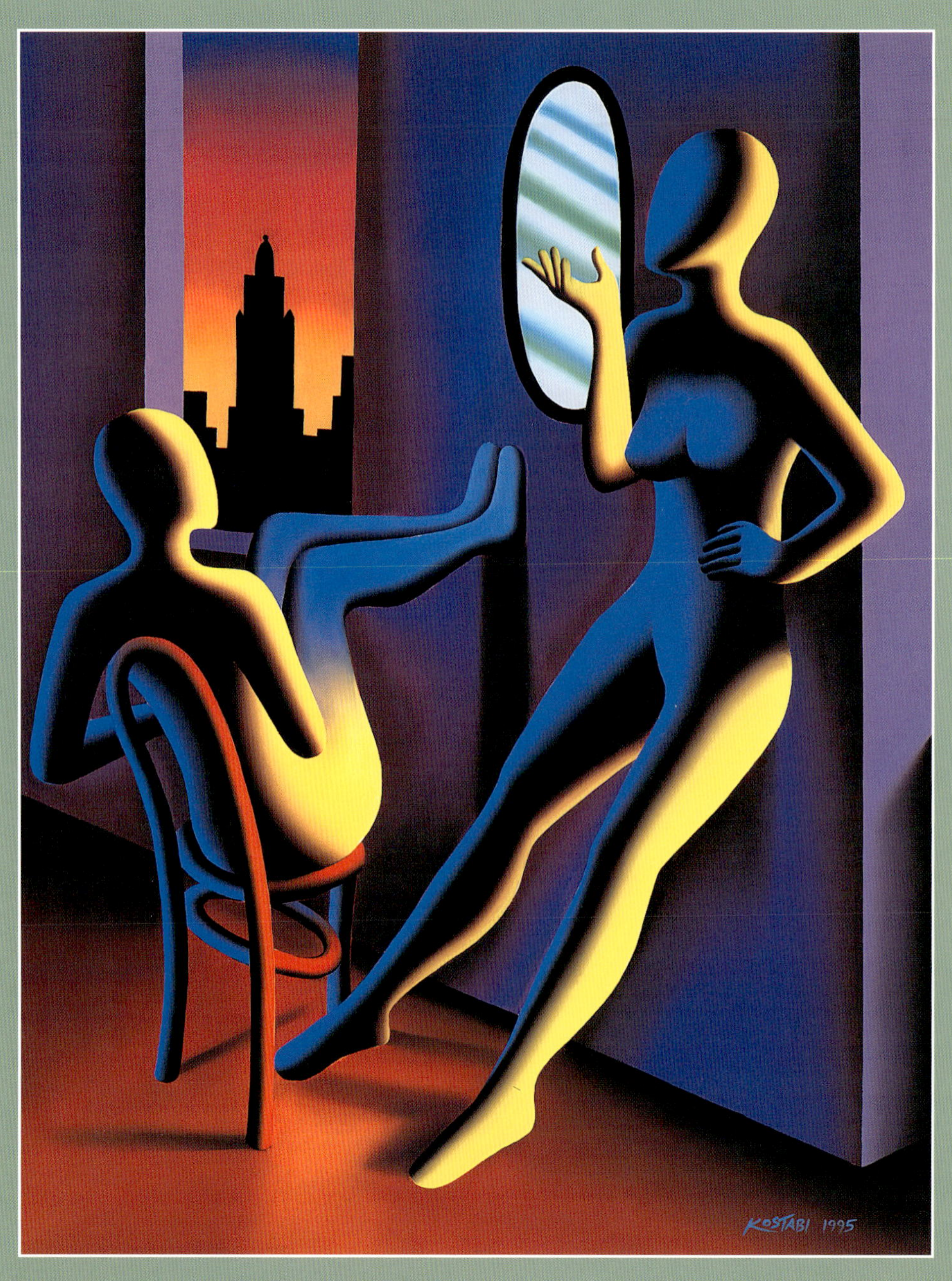
KOSTABI 1995

CHAPTER ✧ TWO

NEW YORK IN THE EXPLOSIVE EIGHTIES

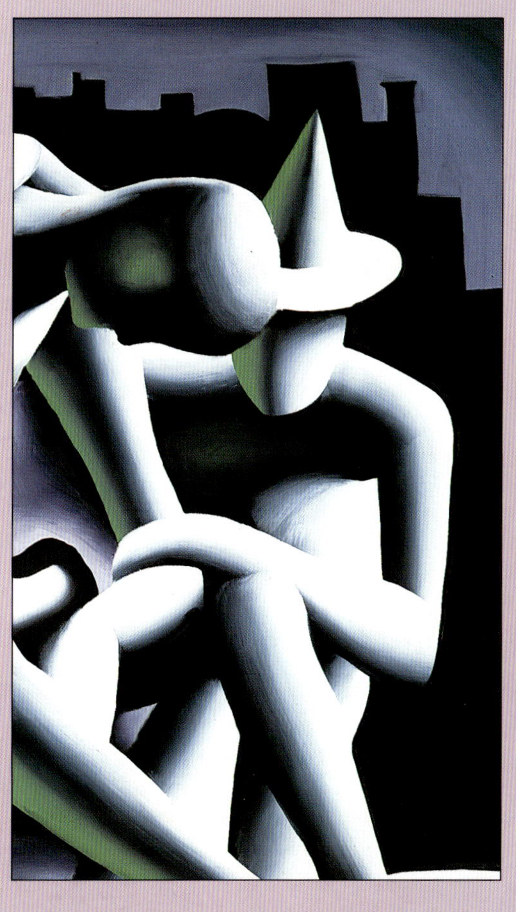

✦ What was it like breaking into the art scene in the explosive eighties?

✧ It was like a turbulent whirlpool. Everybody was twirling in it, screaming for attention. It felt good, even though we were being sucked under.

✦ How did you avoid drowning?

✧ I didn't drink or take drugs. I stayed focused on my goals.

And I built my own ship called Kostabi World. You'd need more than a whirlpool to sink it.

✦ How did you break in?

✧ After seemingly endless rejections from galleries, I finally started networking in the art scene and got recommended to dealers by other artists.

✦ Where did you network?

✧ Mostly in the East Village. When I arrived on the

✧ page 18:
Metropolitan
1995
Oil on canvas
48 x 36 inches
Collection of Rob P. Andrews

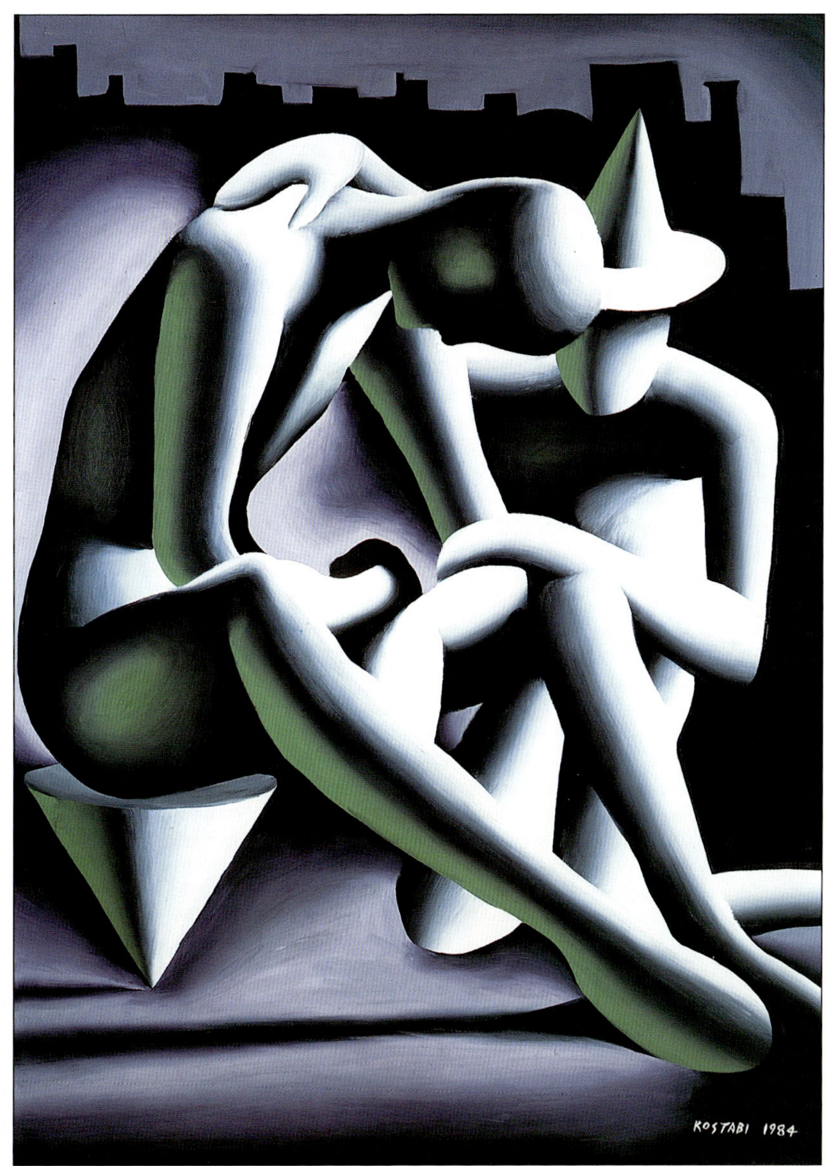

✧ **Solace Near a Street Light**
1984
Oil on canvas
68 x 48 inches
Collection of Simon Cloquet

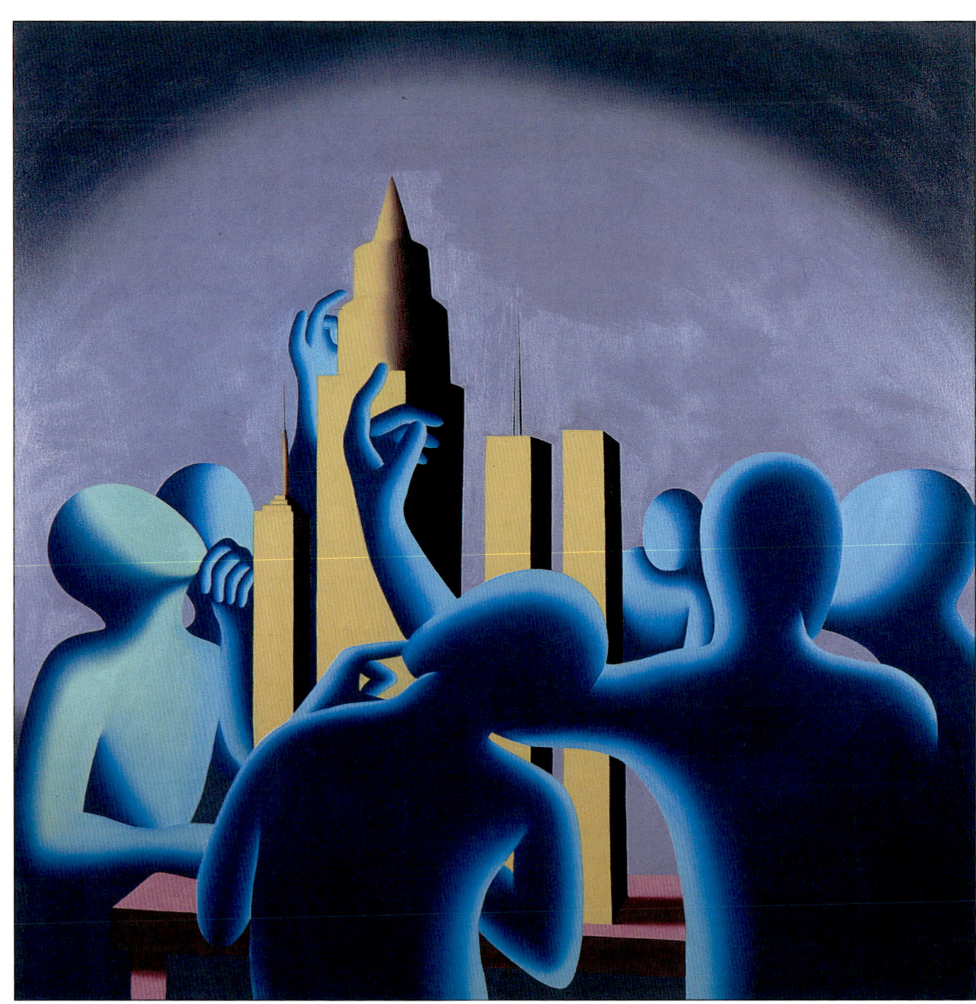

Aspire
1990
Oil on canvas
60 x 60 inches
Flash Art Museum, Trevi, Italy

scene in 1983, the system had just finished chewing up and spitting out neo-expressionism and graffiti art, and it needed a new meal. I sensed its hunger to devour all the little art hustlers and mini-galleries that were popping up and buzzing around the East Village. So I very opportunistically labeled myself an East Village artist, even though I lived in Hell's Kitchen. I hung out in the East Village every night and squeezed myself into every possible group show. I won the Proliferation Prize from the *East Village Eye* for being in more group shows than any other artist. My name was always preceded by the word "ubiquitous."

✦ The critic Eleanor Heartney called you "the ultimate art whore."

✧ **I don't understand the point of that criticism. There's nothing wrong with seizing every opportunity that comes your way.**

✦ Did the East Village art scene influence the look of your work?

✧ **The East Village art of the 1980s was pluralistic and eclectic. There was a predominant East Village stereotype: funky expressionism, angry dogs,**

WIN AND

syringes, crumbling apartment buildings, and intentional kitsch, characterized by artists like Rick Prol, David Wojnarowics, Rodney Greenblat, and Rhonda Zwillinger. But my work didn't fit that image at all. That's probably one reason the work stood out. I was never hip, but I was at the center of hipness.

✦ How did you make the shift from the funky "rough and ready" East Village art scene to the tony, big-ticket, SoHo art world?

✧ **My first group show and first one-person show were actually in SoHo. I invaded both fronts simultaneously. I never felt an allegiance to the alleged East Village ideology. The media portrayed it as a vital, grassroots rebellion against the slick commercialism of SoHo and Fifty-seventh Street. But like the rest of my colleagues, I had one eye on the media opportunity of being labeled an East Village artist and the other eye on the real prize.**

✦ The real prize?

✧ **Being sanctioned by a "legitimate" big-league gallery.**

✧ page 25:
Collaboration with L.A. II
Mischief and Majesty
1990–95
Paint marker and oil on canvas
60 x 84 inches
Collection of Thomas Schonnebeck

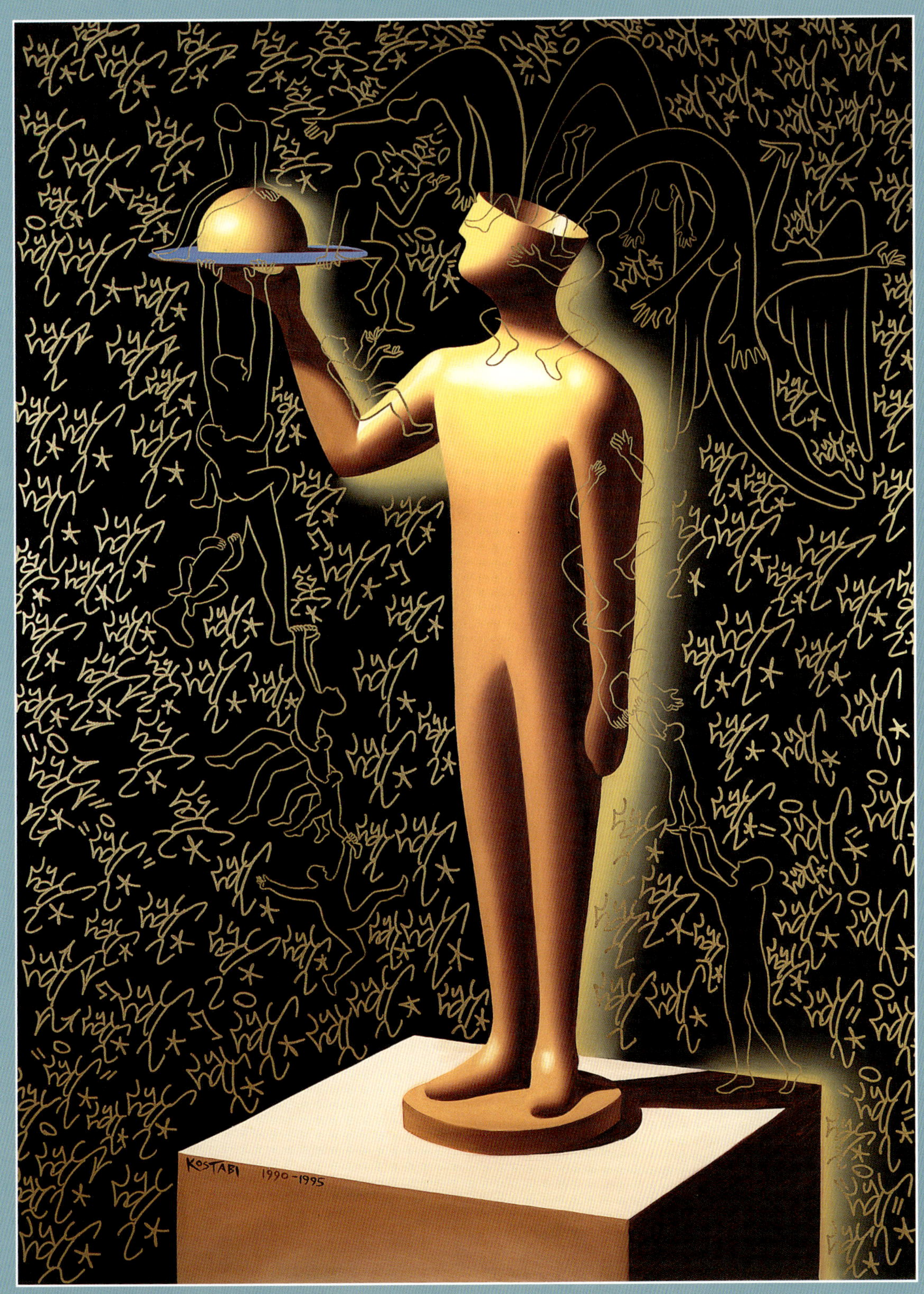
KOSTABI 1990-1995

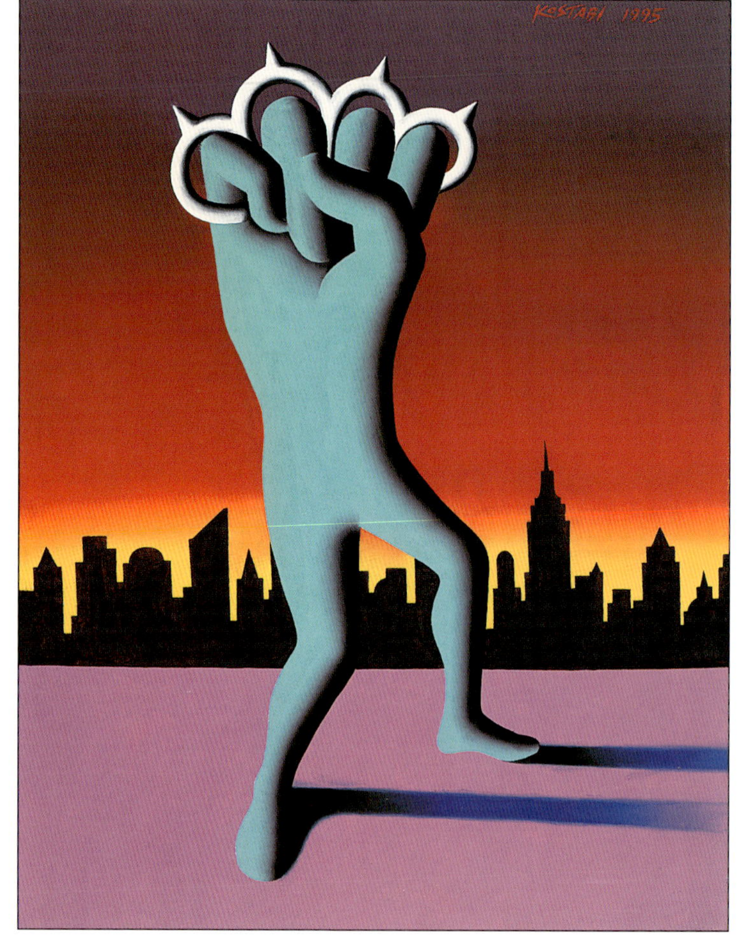

✧ **Self Defense (Jersey Boy)**
1995
Oil on canvas
24 x 18 inches
Collection of Margot Travis and Peter Sugleris

✦ When did you go "legitimate"?

✧ **Before I started showing anywhere in New York, I was already showing at a major Los Angeles**

G WITH THAT?

TO: KOSTABI WORLD FAX #(212)268-7119
10·15·1990

ATTN. IDEA PEOPLE

PLEASE RE-INTRODUCE THE ANGEL INTO THE KOSTABI VOCABULARY.
ANGEL PLAYING GOLF.
ANGEL CRYING.
ANGEL PETTING A CAT.
ANGEL PLANTING A TREE.
ANGEL VISITS A BOARD MEETING.
ANGEL RECEIVING A FAX.
ANGEL BLESSING A KOSTABI PAINTER.
ANGEL GETTING INTO A TAXI.
ETC.

THANK YOU
MARK KOSTABI

JESSICA: PLEASE RE-FAX
THIS TO CLIFF.
THANK YOU

✧ **Palimpsest/Lines**
1985
Oil on canvas
60 x 44 inches
Collection of the artist

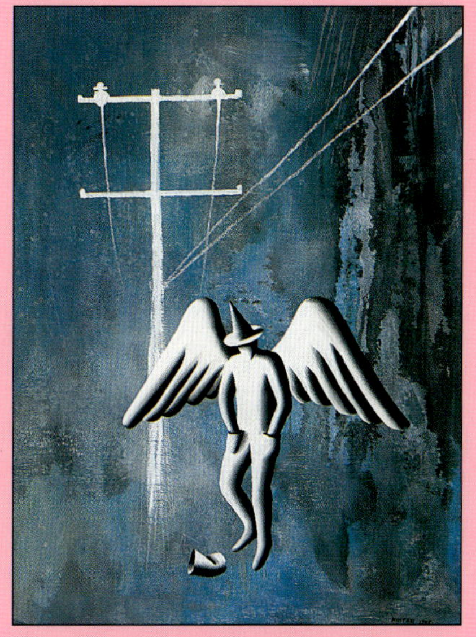

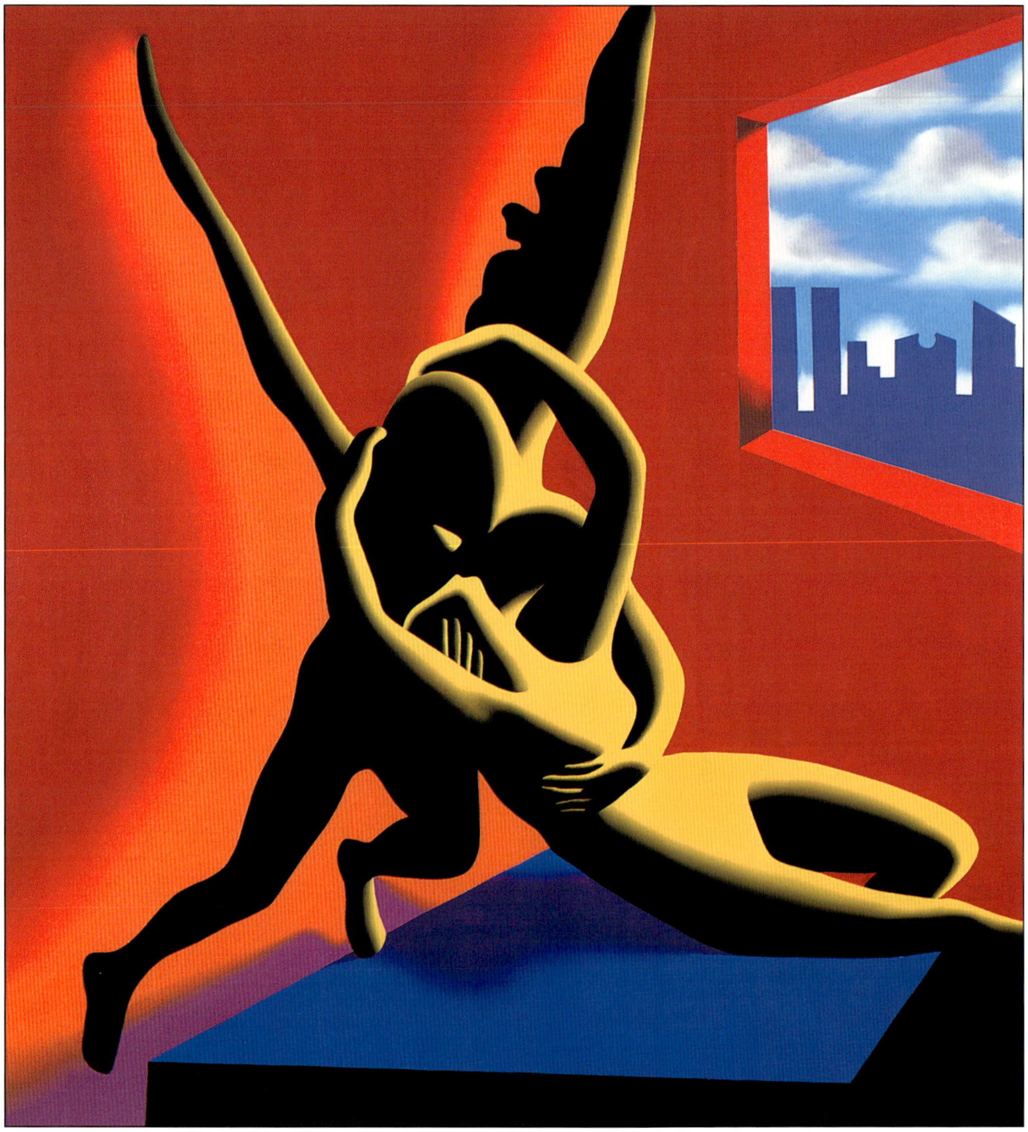

The Last Kiss (In New York)
1993
Oil on canvas
60 x 54 inches
Galerei Baraz, Istanbul

gallery, the Molly Barnes Gallery, getting good reviews in the *L.A. Times* and selling to top TV and movie producers. So I already had a taste of the big league before moving to New York.

✦ Were you identified with any group within the East Village scene?

✧ **I was never a member of a clique. I always felt I had my own scene going. To make it in the art world, you must create your own art world.**

✦ How did you make the jump from showing at the A&P Gallery and Chronicide Gallery to the Ronald Feldman Gallery in SoHo?

✧ **Perception is a learned phenomenon. And I've learned that the A&P Gallery is just as important as any chic SoHo gallery.**

✦ The A&P Gallery doesn't exist anymore.

✧ **Neither will the SoHo salons, eventually. By going out of business first, perhaps the A&P was ahead of its time.**

✦ How did you get into the Feldman Gallery?

✧ **I had a one-thousand-square-foot storefront studio on Broome Street in SoHo. I put a six-by-four-foot painting in the window and changed it once a week. Sean Elwood, head salesperson at Ron**

Feldman's gallery, passed my window every day on his way to work. Some days I kept my door open and welcomed anyone who felt like visiting. One day Sean walked in, told me he loved my work and wanted Ron to come by. A few days later he did, and told me he wanted me to participate in a group show. At our next meeting Ron told me he wanted to represent me. It wasn't just the store-front window; I had already been in over fifty group shows and several one-person shows. I was perceived as a hot property on the rise.

✦ Did you agree to an exclusive deal?

✧ Yes, because I was impressed by the stature of the gallery.

Up until then I had turned down many offers of exclusivity, and consequently, I'd infuriated dealers. Eventually, I switched back to being independent because stature alone doesn't always pay the rent. My productivity was increasing. My artistic need to realize all my ideas led me to hire more painters and rent a bigger studio, and I went back to having a stable of dealers.

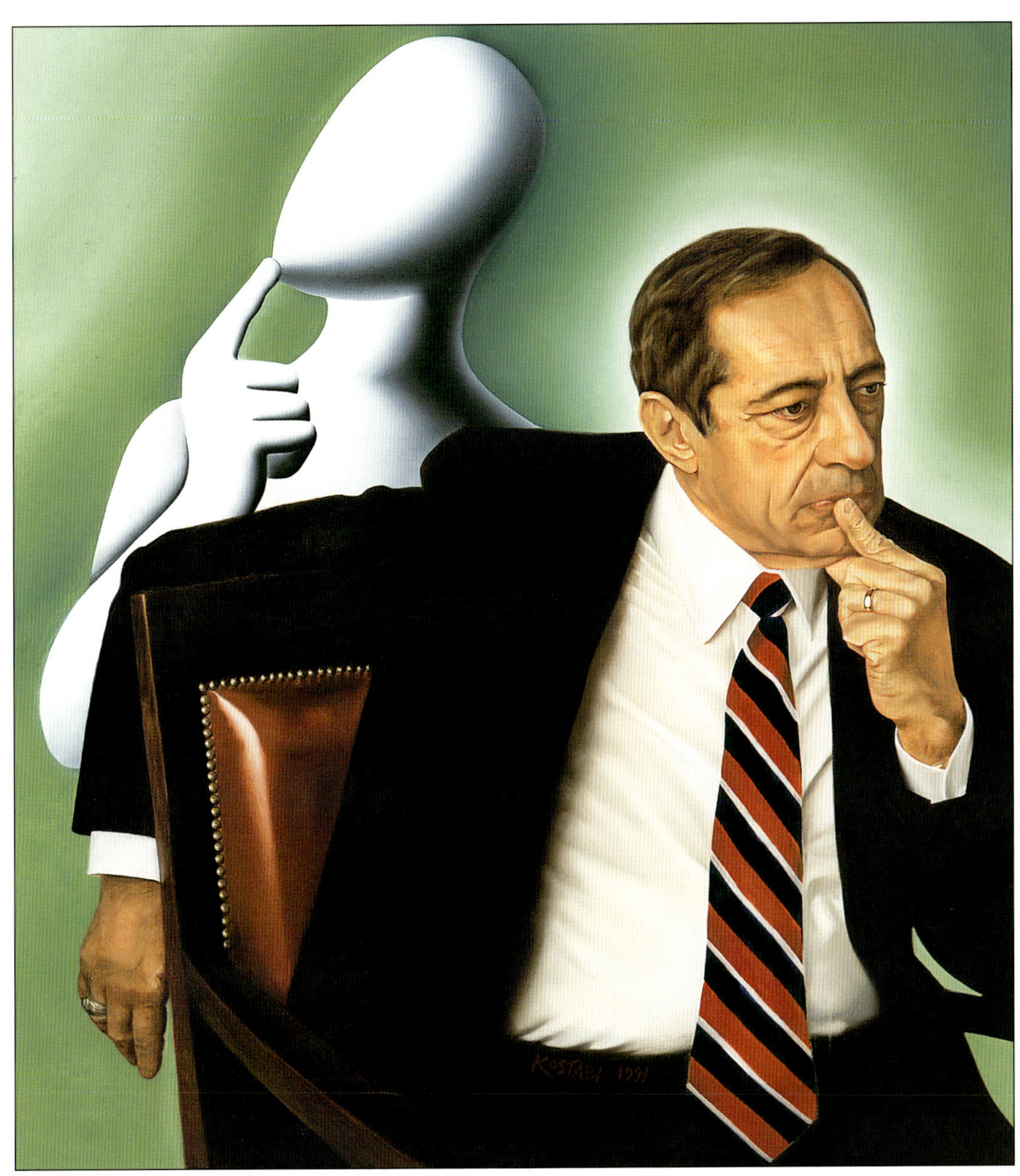

✧ **Mario and His Muse**
1991
Oil on canvas
46 x 40 inches
Collection of Mario Cuomo

Summer Night
1986
Oil on canvas
68 x 90 inches
Memphis Brooks Museum of Art, Memphis, Tennessee

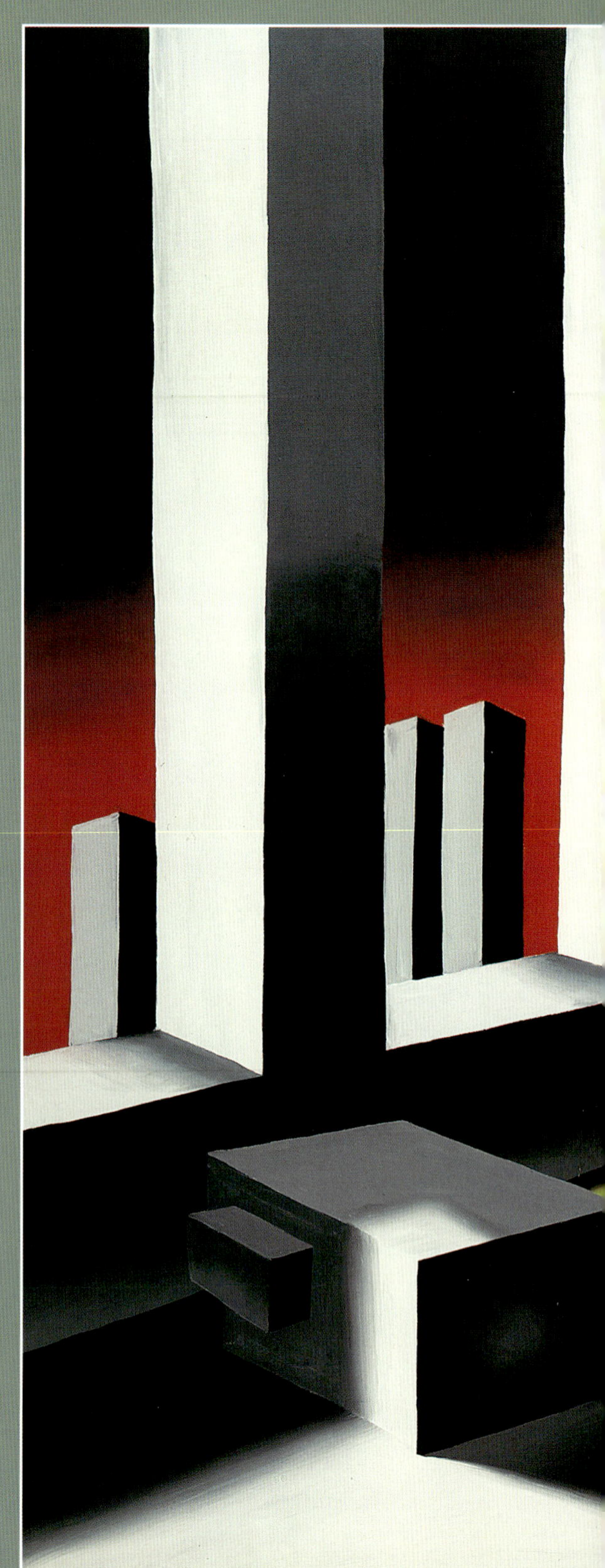

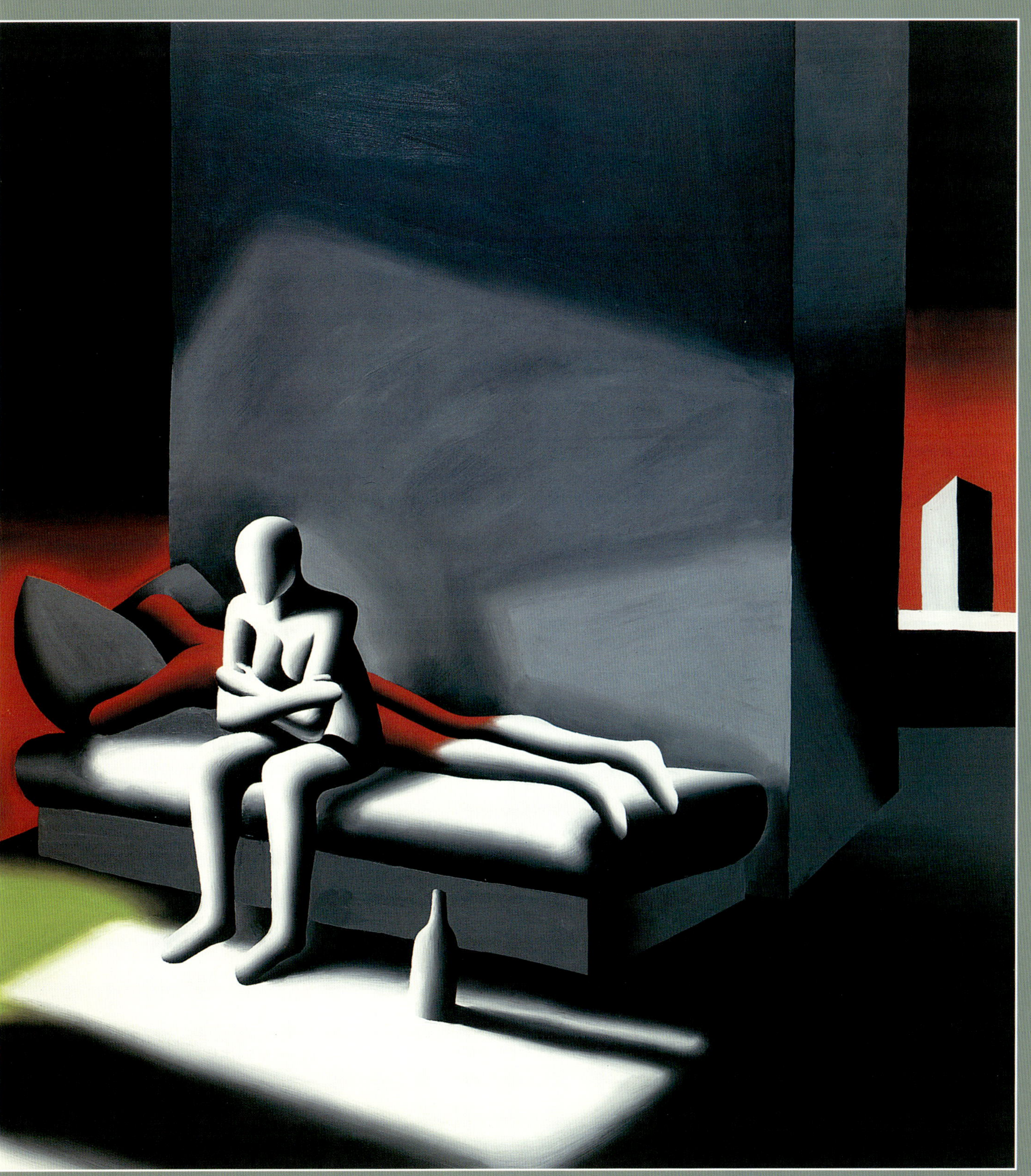

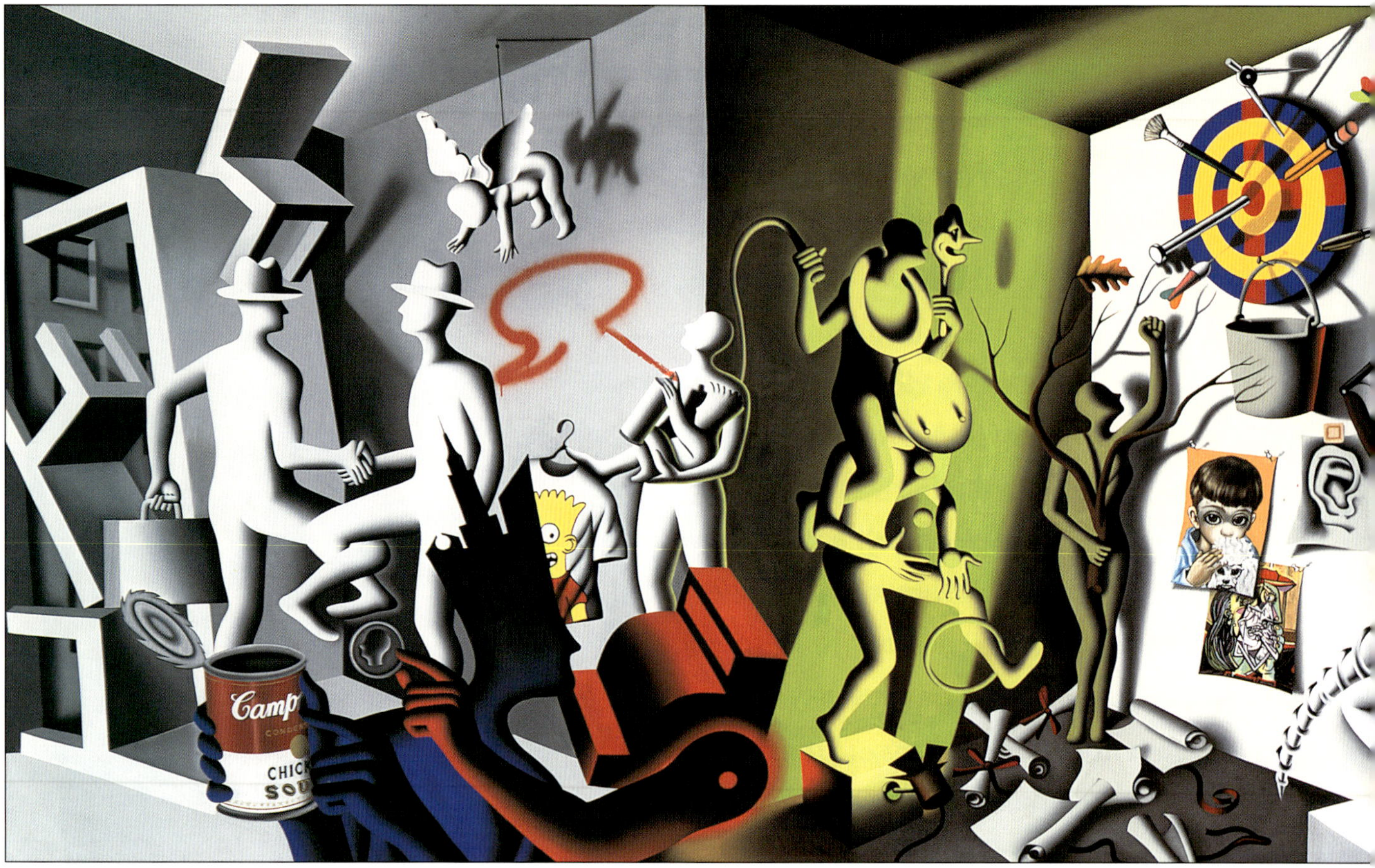

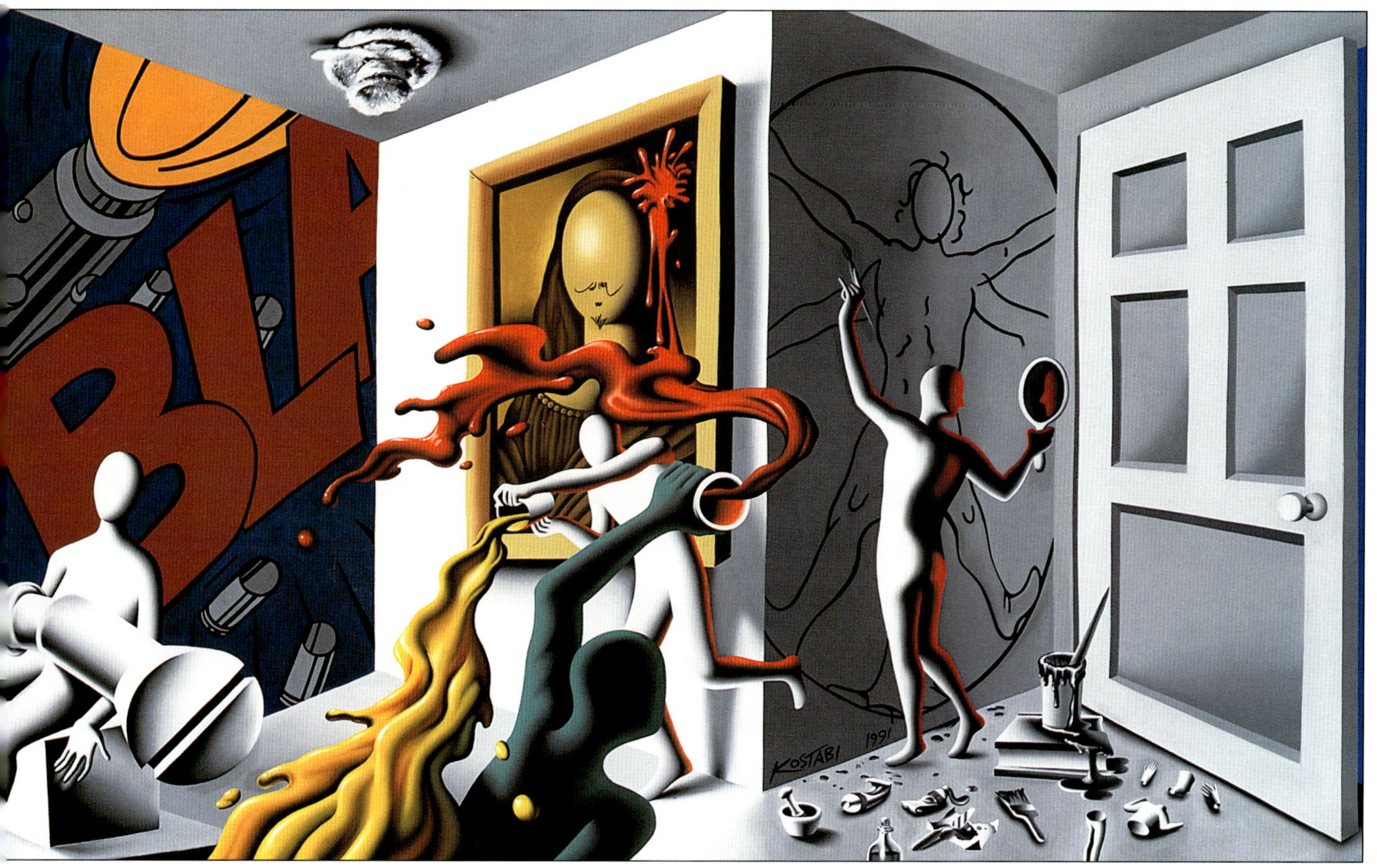

✧ **The History of Inspiration**
1991
Oil on canvas
6 x 20 feet
Kostabi World

FOR COMME

60 Minutes, *Lifestyles of the Rich and Famous* . . . The art world got a little annoyed with you, didn't they?

✧ **Not the whole art world. Some people within the art world got jealous, and that's about as deep as it went.**

✦ You broke into the art world and then broke out of it. How did you get there?

✧ **How did I start getting so much publicity? It's important to understand that I got it because I was open to it. Some artists actually say no to journalists who want to interview them for *People* magazine. They think it might jeopardize their chances of being written up in *Artforum.* So they say yes only to the *Artforum* journalist. *Artforum* is a small magazine that's read mostly by other artists. It's nice, but it's like preaching to the converted.**

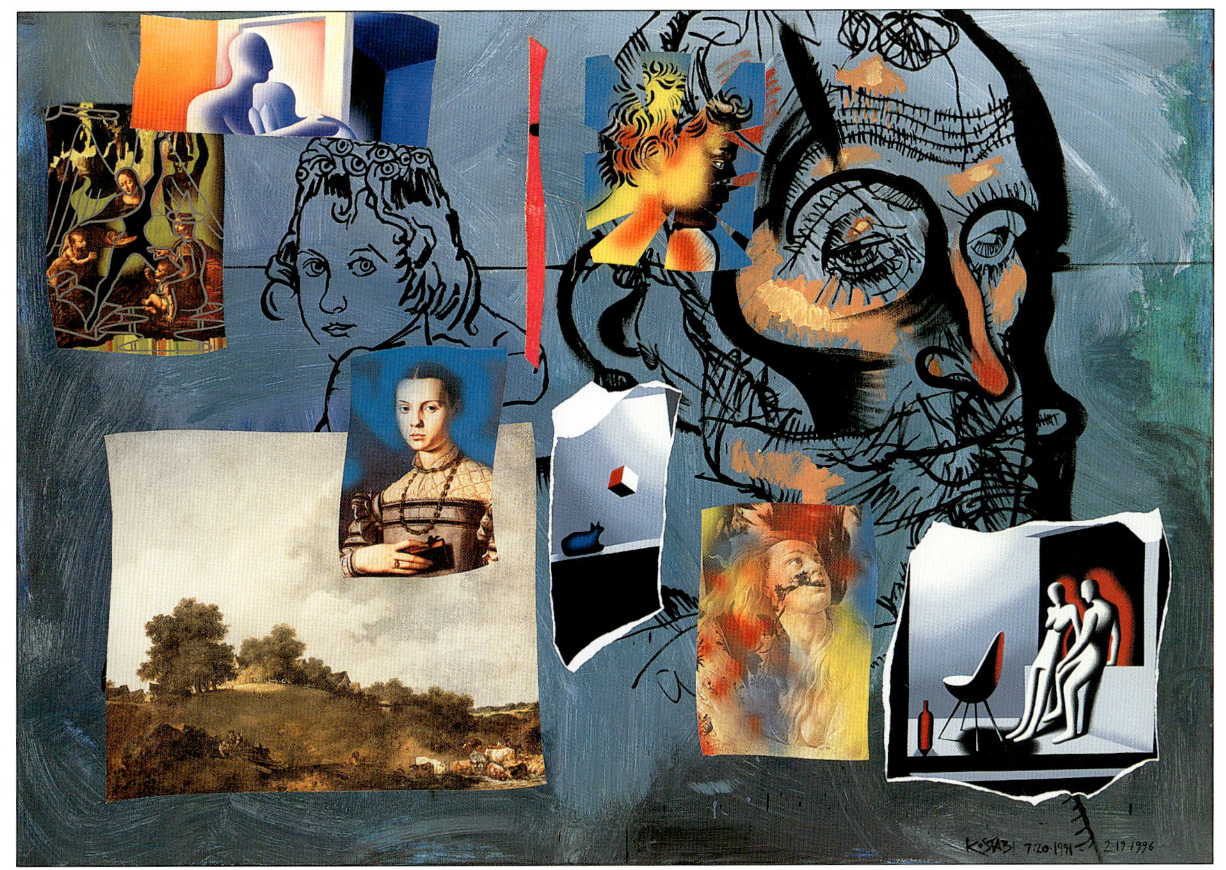

✧ **I've Got a Feline You're Foolin'**
1991–96
Collage & oil on canvas
60 x 84 inches
Kostabi World

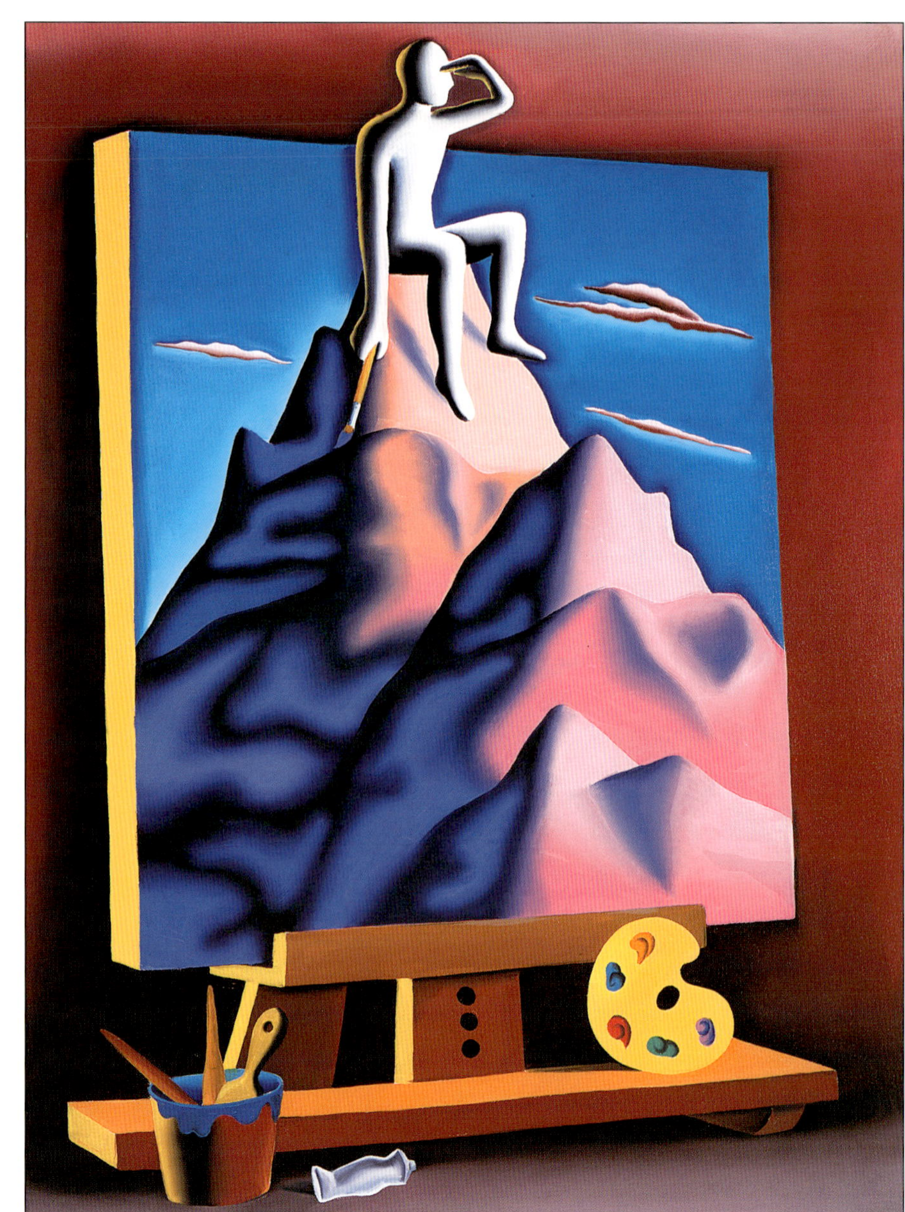

✧ **Look Out**
1992
Oil on canvas
50 x 36 inches
Galleria d'Arte Modena, Il Castello, Milan

✦ But aside from being willing, how did you actually do it?

✧ **I did it by being my own publicist. I kept calling Michael Small, the art writer for *People*. I tried to convince him that my story was "very *People*." Finally, after a year, he agreed to visit my studio. The minute he entered, I had him in my clutches. I fed him sound bite after sound bite, showed him my painters, my idea person, my Kostabisms. I looked wild: spiky hair, outrageous designer clothes, sunglasses. The story was there. I made his job easy for him. I believe in the Kostabism, "Say less and say yes," unless you're talking to the press. Then you have to give them as much interesting information as possible. Turn that three-thousand-word article into a five-thousand-word piece. And photos. Let them take outrageous** photos. *People* had the idea of shooting me in a money suit. But they wouldn't use their own money. They provided the armed guard, but I had to withdraw seventeen thousand dollars of my own cash and have my assistants tape it all over my body for the four-hour photo shoot. I'm convinced that the reason *New York* magazine put me on their cover in 1994 instead of the original plan of just making me an inside story was that I agreed to pose nude. They didn't use the nude photo on the cover. They used it on the spread inside. But the point is they had it, and they really wanted to use it. But they had so many other great "standard" photos that they upgraded it to a cover story. Another example is Abbeville Press. An editor there told me that the reason they reproduced so many of my paintings in their book, *New Used and Improved, Art for the Eighties*, was simply because I provided them with so many more photos of paintings than any other artist in the book did.

✦ What about your public fights with other media figures? Was that part of the publicity?

✧ **Conflict sells. I got into fights with people like talk show host Morton Downey Jr. and Sylvester Stallone. In retrospect, I have to admit that it was rather childish, but I can't deny that it got me a lot of press.**

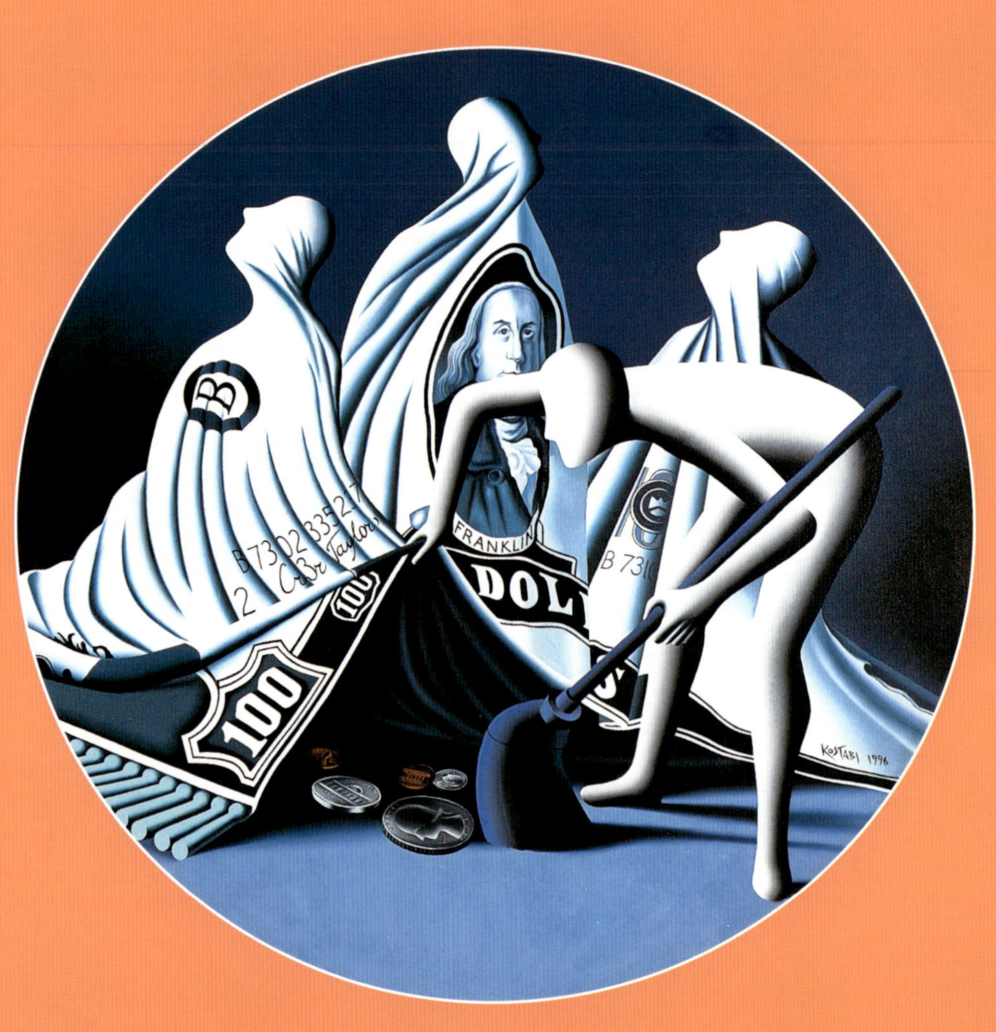

FRANKLIN
DOL
100
100
KOSTABI 1996

CHAPTER ✧ THREE

KOSTABI WORLD

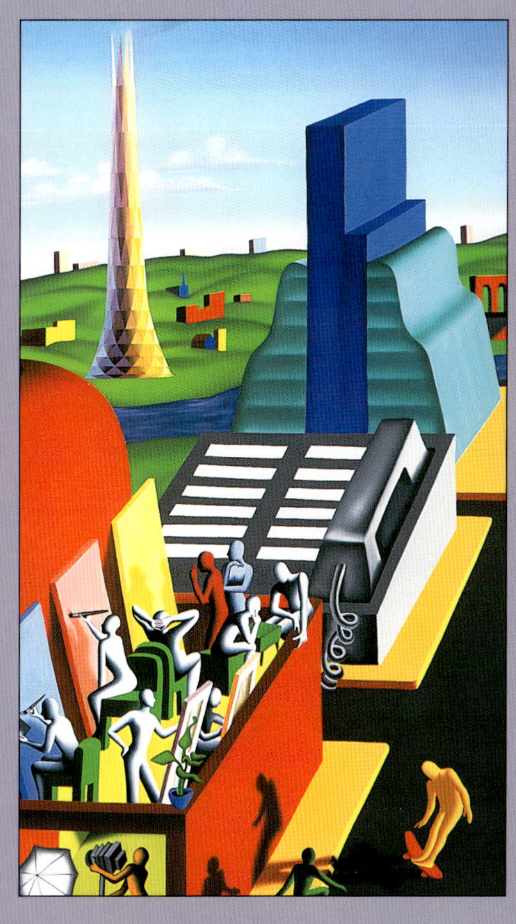

AMATEURS

✦ What's the philosophy behind Kostabi World? Is it a factory? A conceptual art project? A group effort? Some people wonder why your publicity focuses predominantly on you, if it's a group effort.

✧ **It's no more a group effort in my studio than it is in the studio of any other artist who has a lot of assistants. I just speak more openly about it. I also have a more intricate division of labor, with unusual job descriptions like "idea person," "color theorist," "rhetorician," and "creative consultant," in addition to the conventional jobs you might find in a big art studio, like "painter" and "canvas stretcher." But my goal is identical to that of most artists. I want to make interesting, good work. My work.**

✦ But you frequently call attention to Kostabi World's factory-like aspect. Like your ad in *Flash Art*, where you reproduced four

✧ page 44:
Secrets of the Psyche (Circular Currency)
1996
Oil on canvas
48 x 48 inches
Kostabi World

✧ page 47:
The World According to Mark
1992
Oil on canvas
84 x 84 inches
The Groninger Museum, Holland

IMITATE,

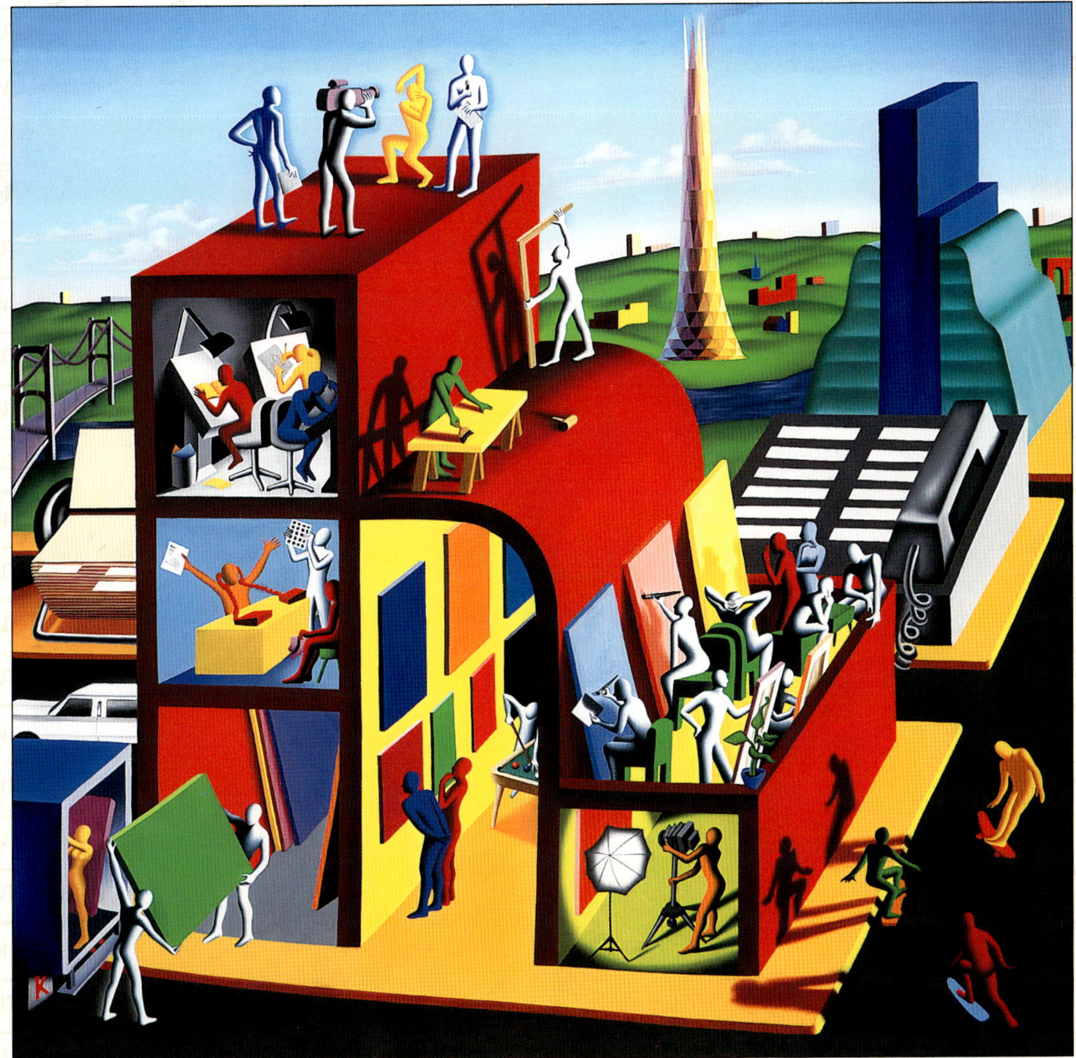

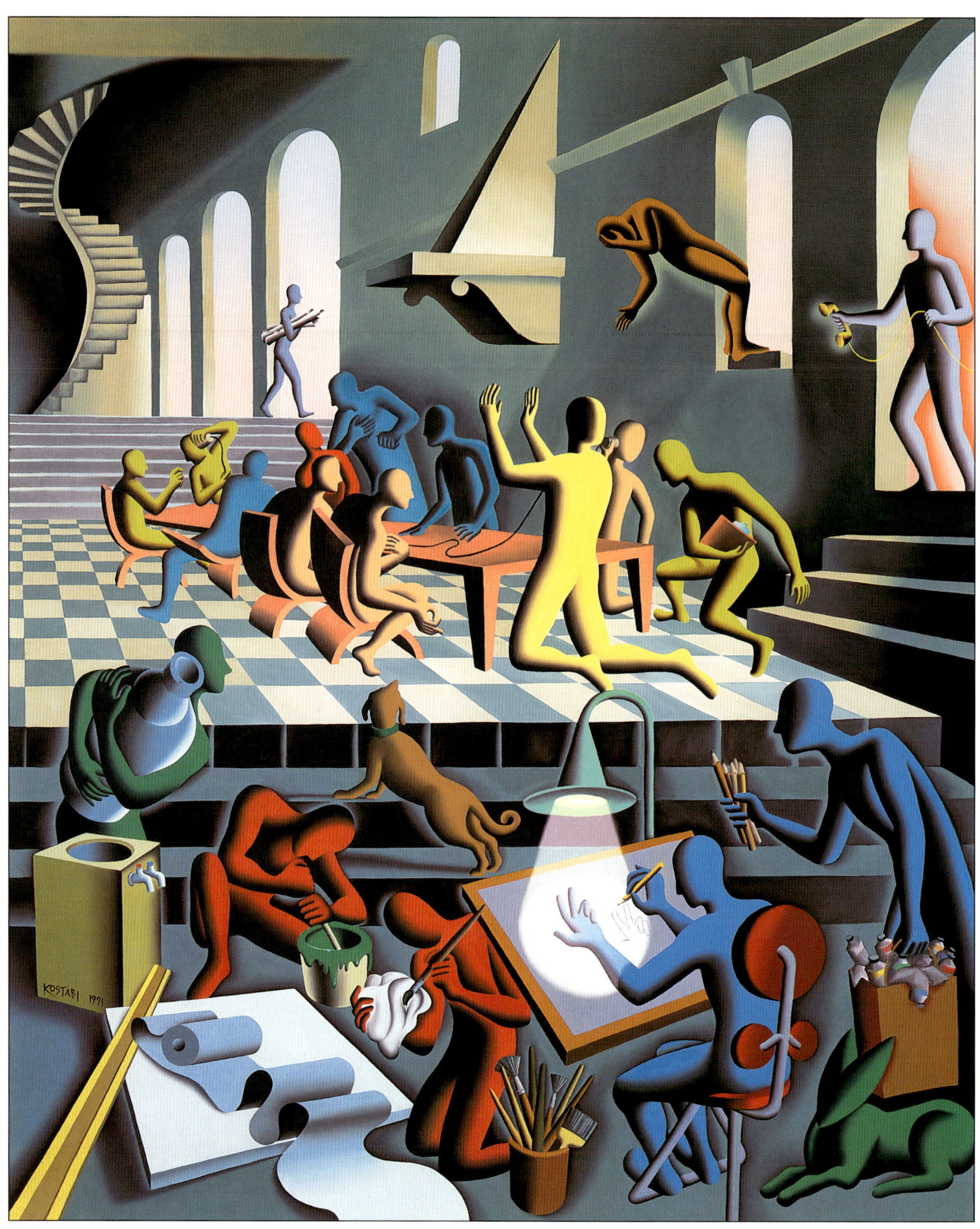
KOSTABI 1991

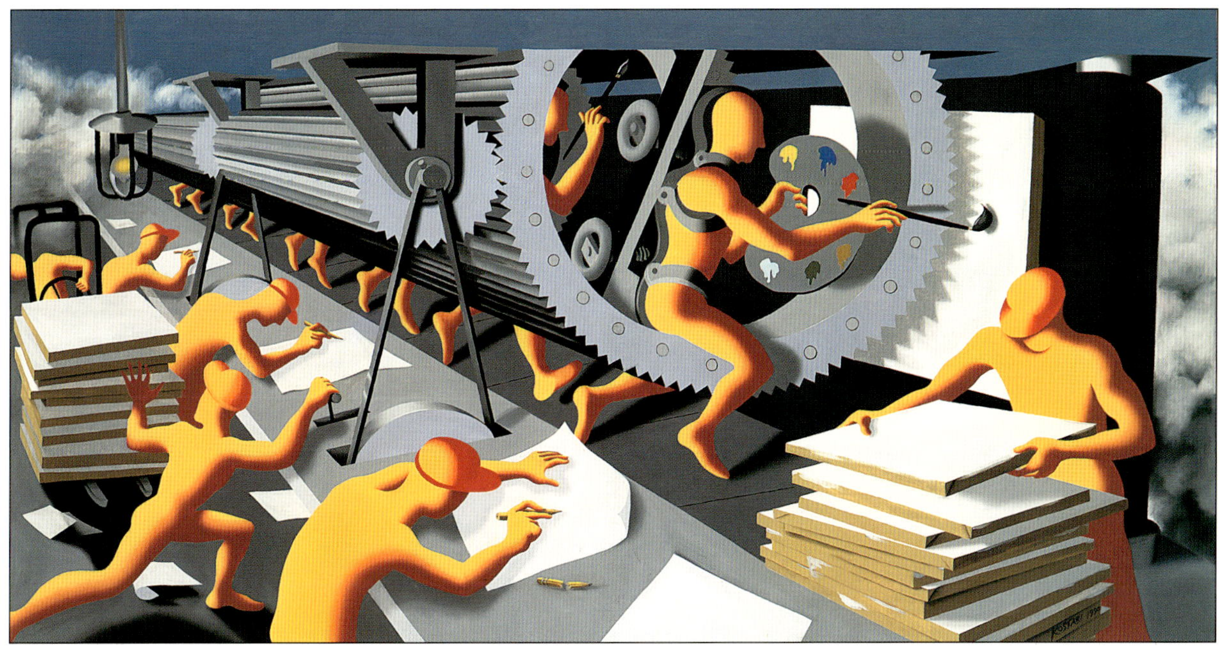

✧ **Modern Times**
1990
Oil on canvas
46 x 84 inches
Kostabi World

✧ page 48:
Studio System
1991
Oil on canvas
10 x 8 feet
Kostabi World

PROFESSION

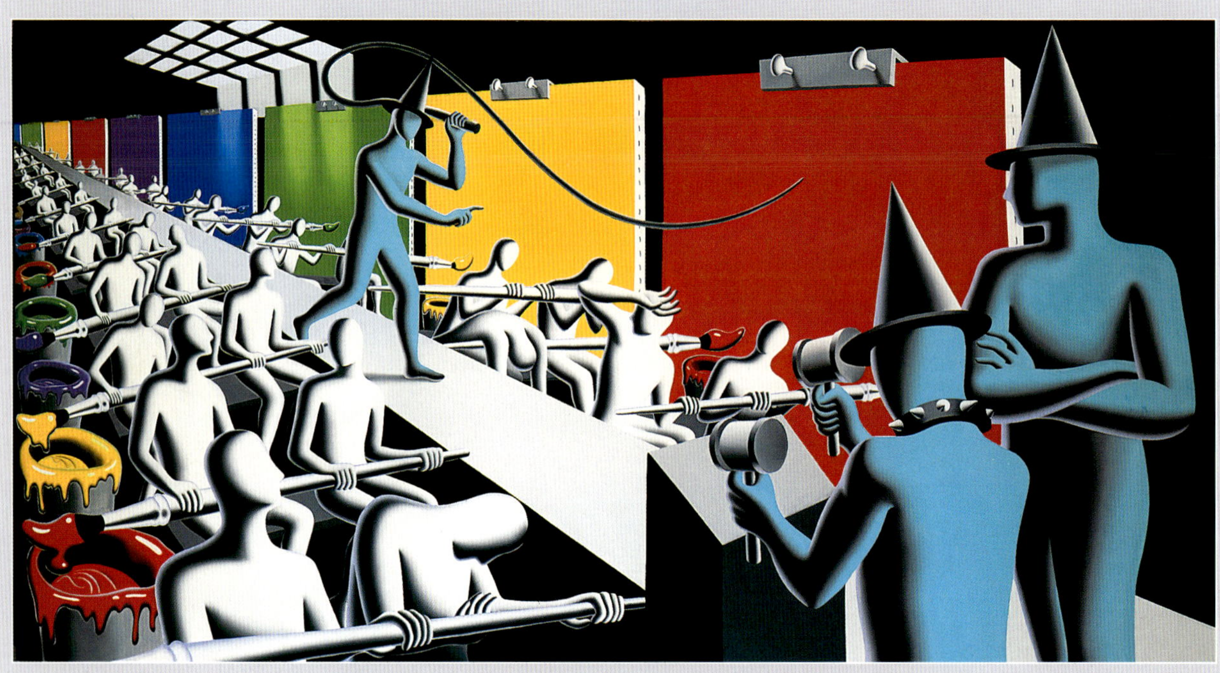

✧ **Backlash**
1991
Oil on canvas
48 x 90 inches
Kostabi World

of your painters' time cards in full color on a two-page spread. And there are paintings like *The World According to Mark*, *Studio System*, *Modern Times*, *Backlash*, *Automatic Painting*, and *Mass Production*.

✧ **They're my ongoing artistic dialogue with the public's misperception of me. Some of my critics say that I exploit down-on-their-luck artists, so I painted *Backlash*, which shows an art boss brandishing a whip on a slave ship of minimalist painters. I'm just having fun with my image. If I'm exploiting anything, it's my own bum rap.**

✦ Some critics praise you for orchestrating Kostabi World as an innovative collective effort.

✧ **They're praising me for the wrong reasons. I've never tried to make it a collective effort. Even though I rarely exercise my veto power, the fact remains that I have it. There is no profit-sharing, and I've always made it clear that I'm the employer and they are employees. It's part of their job description to be creative. When I collaborate with other artists, like Howard Finster, Enrico Baj, Tadanori Yokoo, or my brother, Paul Kostabi, then it's a**

collective effort. We both sign the canvas and split the profits fifty/fifty. It's a collaboration. When my assistants paint for me, it's work for hire, even if they pour their hearts and souls into it. More accurate social praise for Kostabi World is that it's a pleasant, interesting place to work, almost like an art school where students get paid to attend. They get to make their own hours, they can paint at night or on weekends, often while a classical orchestra rehearses in another part of the studio. There's a well-stocked art library; interesting people visit frequently and interact with the employees. The idea-approval meetings are filled with lively art dialogue. Many of my former assistants have gone on to enjoy successful art careers after leaving Kostabi World: Roman Scott, Cliff Leigh, Ron English, Thom Merrick, Claude Saccaro, and Cliff Land, to name a few.

✦ How do you find your painters?

✧ **My first full-time painter was Claude Saccaro. He was the last person to respond to an ad I placed in the *Village Voice* in 1986 that read, "Help wanted.**

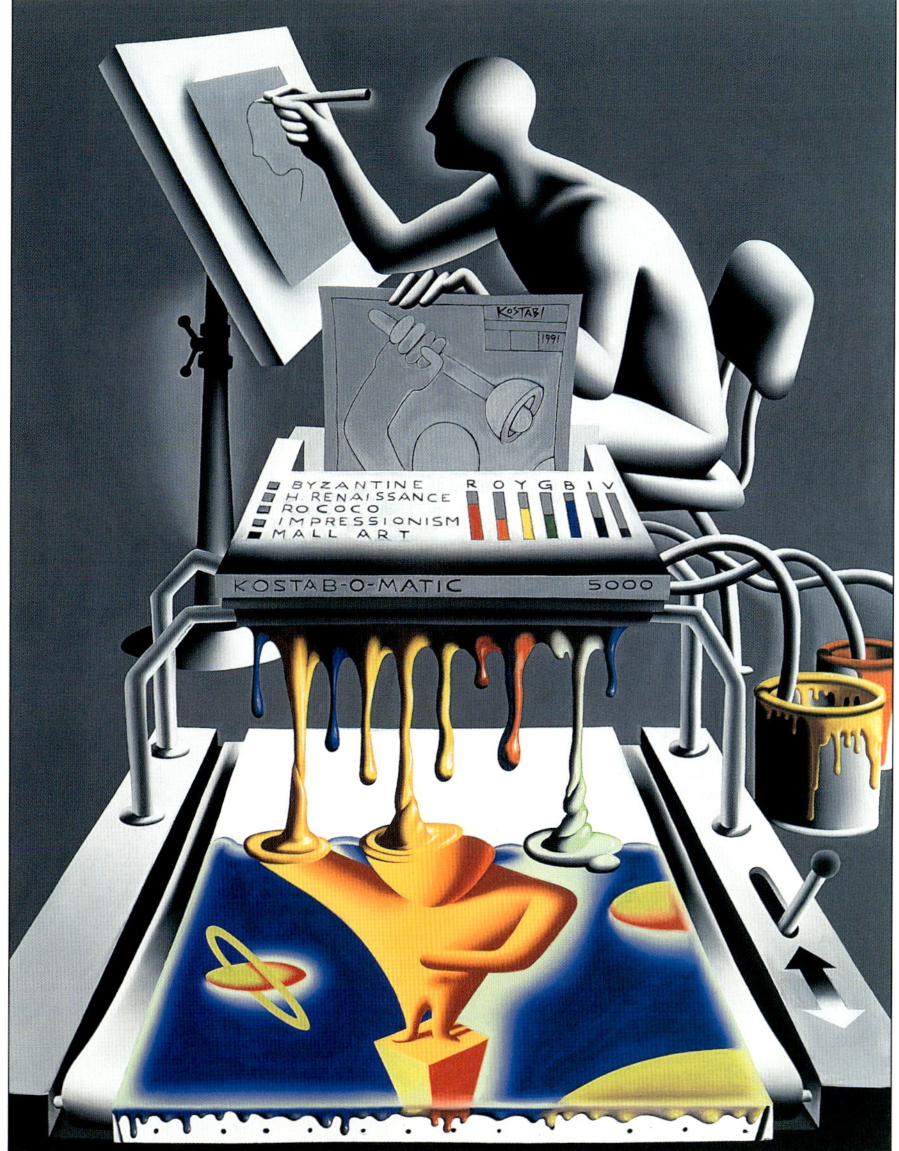

✧ **Automatic Painting**
1991
Oil on canvas
48 x 36 inches
Collection of the artist

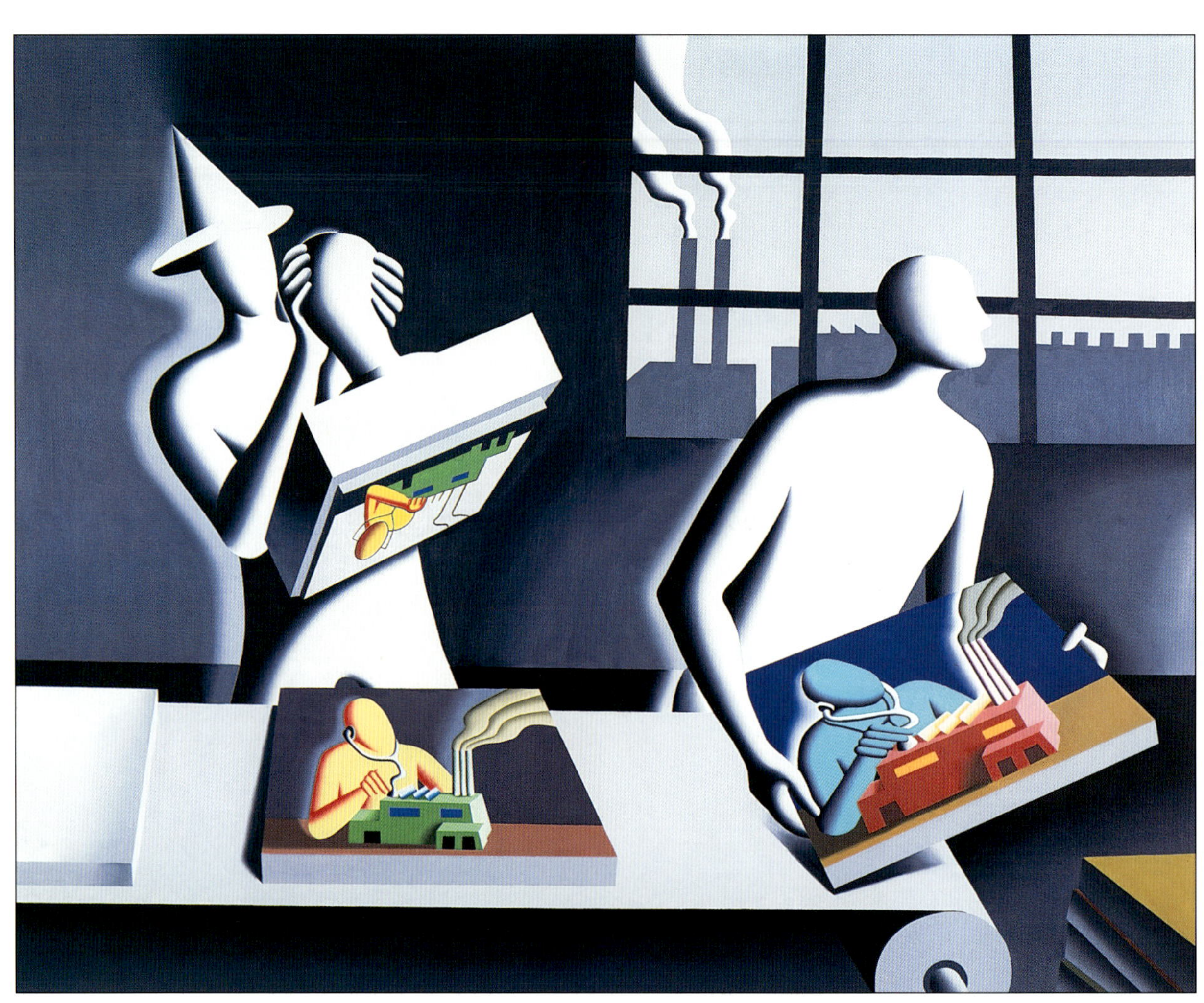

✧ **Mass Production**
1990
Oil on canvas
54 x 66 inches
Collection of Nathan Berman

Artist's assistants. Skilled academic, realist painters wanted to execute large, wet-into-wet oil canvases after drawings by Mark Kostabi. Bring slides or originals to interview. Absolutely no expressionists. $5.00/hour." The fact that I put my name in the ad shocked my dealers and led to a media blitz about how I don't paint my own paintings.

✦ Was it another effort on your part to get publicity?

✧ **Not at all. It took me by surprise, because it honestly never occurred to me to conceal my identity. I didn't realize it was taboo to be honest about using painting assistants. I assumed it was common knowledge. In fact, I thought one measure of success was having lots of assistants. I remember one day, prior to the posting of my ad, the painter Ross Bleckner asked me, "How many assistants do you have?" as if they were notches in my belt. Another successful artist, Gary Stephan, actually gave me the idea of hiring assistants to execute my**

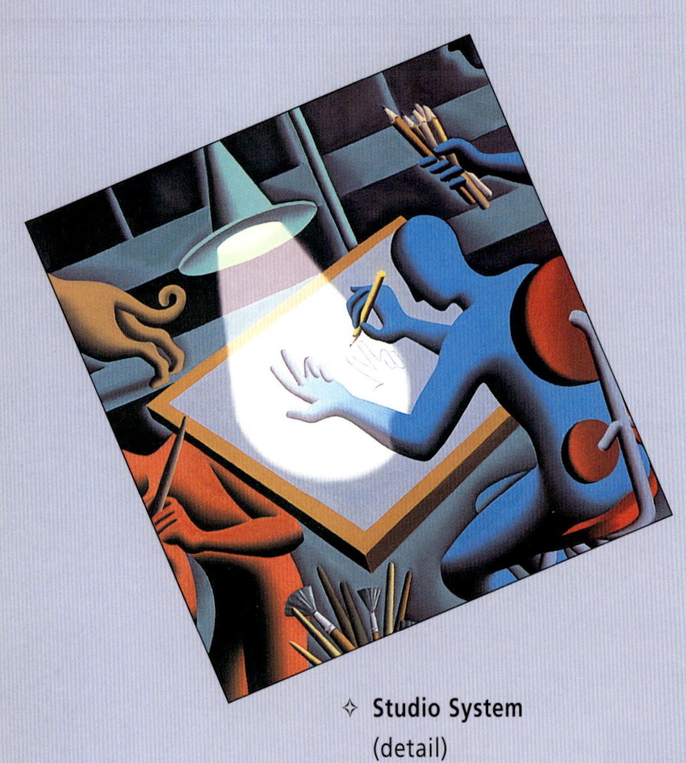

✧ Studio System
(detail)

paintings. He referred one of his ex-assistants to me. She made beautiful watercolors but couldn't paint in oils. I tried her out anyway because I was excited to be hiring one of Gary Stephan's ex-assistants. I felt like I was joining the successful artists club. Plus, she was very attractive. (Later, I learned that it's not a good idea to hire people based on their looks.) So I invented a job for her even though I wasn't making watercolors at the time. She did beautiful work but charged too much and didn't make them fast enough to justify my investment, so I ran the ad in the *Village Voice* instead. Many of the applicants had master's degrees in fine arts. They were willing to work for five dollars an hour, but their technique didn't meet my standards, which makes me very concerned about America's art schools. Claude was from Canada and had brilliant technique. He brought in a copy of an old master painting that he had done in a museum as one of those "permit to copy" artists. I hired him on the spot.

✦ What did you pay?

✧ **At first I paid five dollars an hour. Later, I gave him a raise to six dollars an hour. Every so often I gave him a fifty-dollar bonus to show my appreciation for the work he did.**

✦ Did you ever feel that you were exploiting him?

✧ **At first I felt timid about signing the work in his presence, even though he understood that I would be getting all the credit. But I was genuinely appreciative, because not only was Claude doing great work but he was a nice guy who enthusiastically shared his knowledge of old master paintings with me. Claude worked for me for over six years. When he finally left to go out on his own, he was getting sixteen dollars an hour. I recommended him to a New York gallery, where he had two successful shows.**

✦ What do you look for in a painter?

Technical virtuosity with oil paint, and a good attitude.

✦ Have you had problems with employee attitudes in the past?

✧ **Yes, and now I won't tolerate it. When the recession of the early 1990s hit, I was forced to lay off**

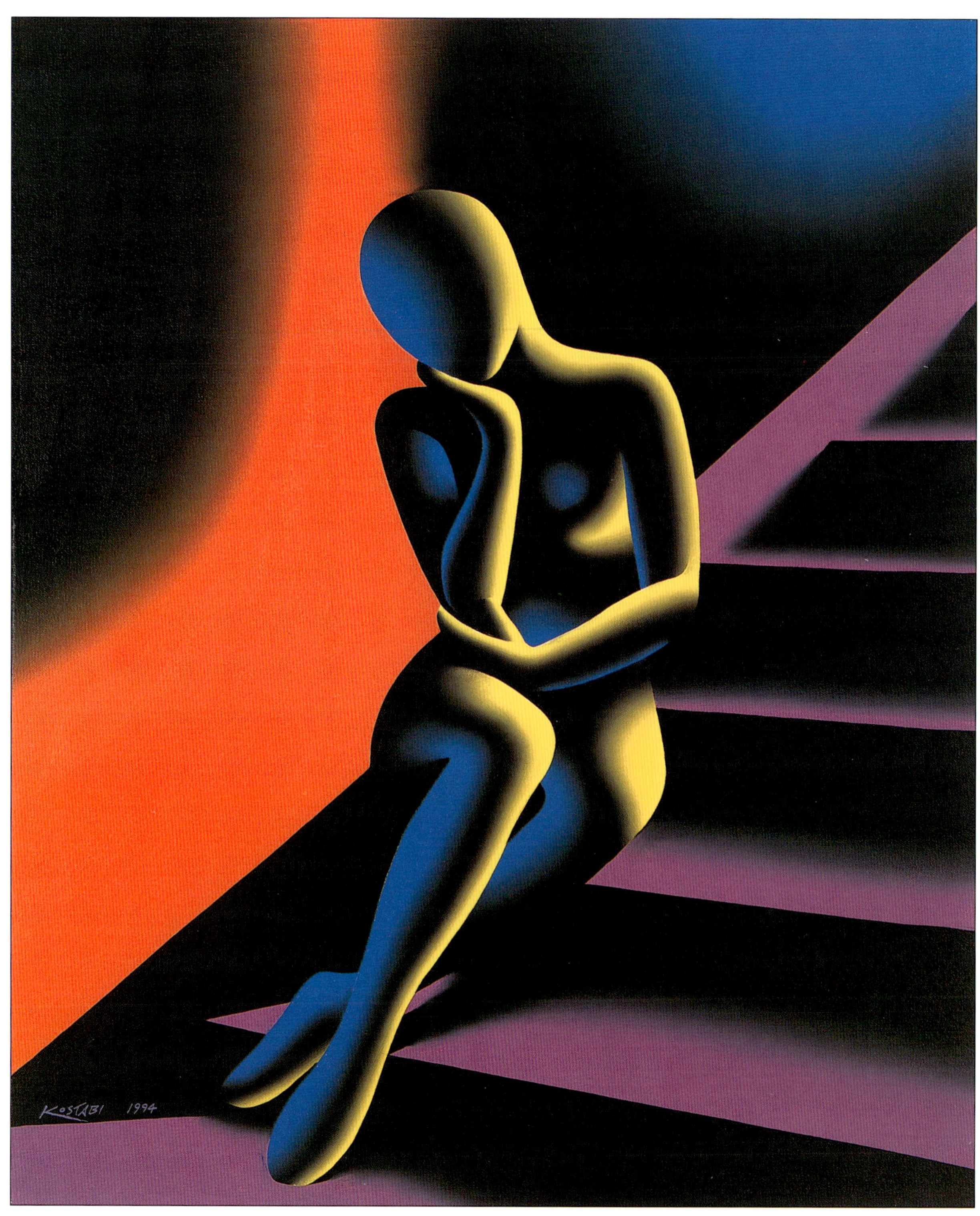
KOSTABI 1994

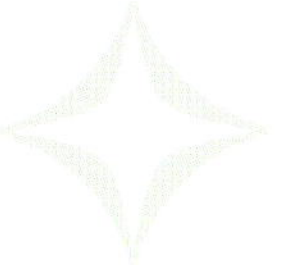

half my workforce. It was a blessing in disguise because the first to go were the complainers, the slough-offs, and the suspected thieves. Suddenly, morale went up and even productivity increased, despite the smaller staff. Michelangelo never fired anyone, even though some of his employees were unreliable and deceitful scoundrels, liars, and thieves. He said, "One must have patience." Two of my assistants once conspired to make forgeries of my paintings that they sold in Japan. One of them went to prison. The other one is still on the loose. I wonder if Michelangelo would have tolerated that!

✦ That incident generated a lot of news coverage. People said it was an oxymoron to have a forged Kostabi.

✧ **Implying that they're all forgeries anyway. A twelve-member jury in Federal Court didn't agree.**

✦ How do you interact with your painters?

✧ **Sometimes when they finish a painting, they come to me and say, "What's next?" I inspect their completed work, sometimes with the help of a committee, and if no changes are necessary, I give them a new idea in the form of a pencil drawing.**

✧ page 58:
Upwardly Mobile (Folia)
1994
Oil on canvas
30 x 24 inches
Collection of the artist

Sometimes I let them choose from several new drawings. We briefly discuss color and size and then they're on their own. Unless I have something very specific in mind, they usually make their own color choices but they rely on basic Kostabi color principles like "Think in terms of value. Imagine how the painting would look if reproduced in black and white."

Frequently, I call spontaneous five-minute meetings with all the painters to discuss a color choice or perhaps an anatomical or perspective decision.

✦ Do your painters ever get bored with the subject matter?

✧ **Yes, and they have the freedom to tell me without fear of offending the boss. I've created an atmosphere where honest constructive criticism is expected. But usually they just get tired of working in a certain size for too long. If they've just painted fifty intricate eight-by-ten-inch canvases, they're probably ready for a nice four-by-three-foot painting with bold, simple imagery. One of my painters, Tom Kolenski, said he wouldn't mind painting my**

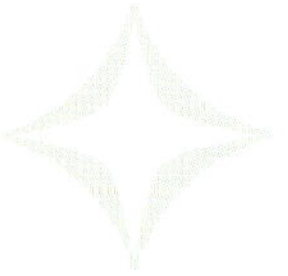

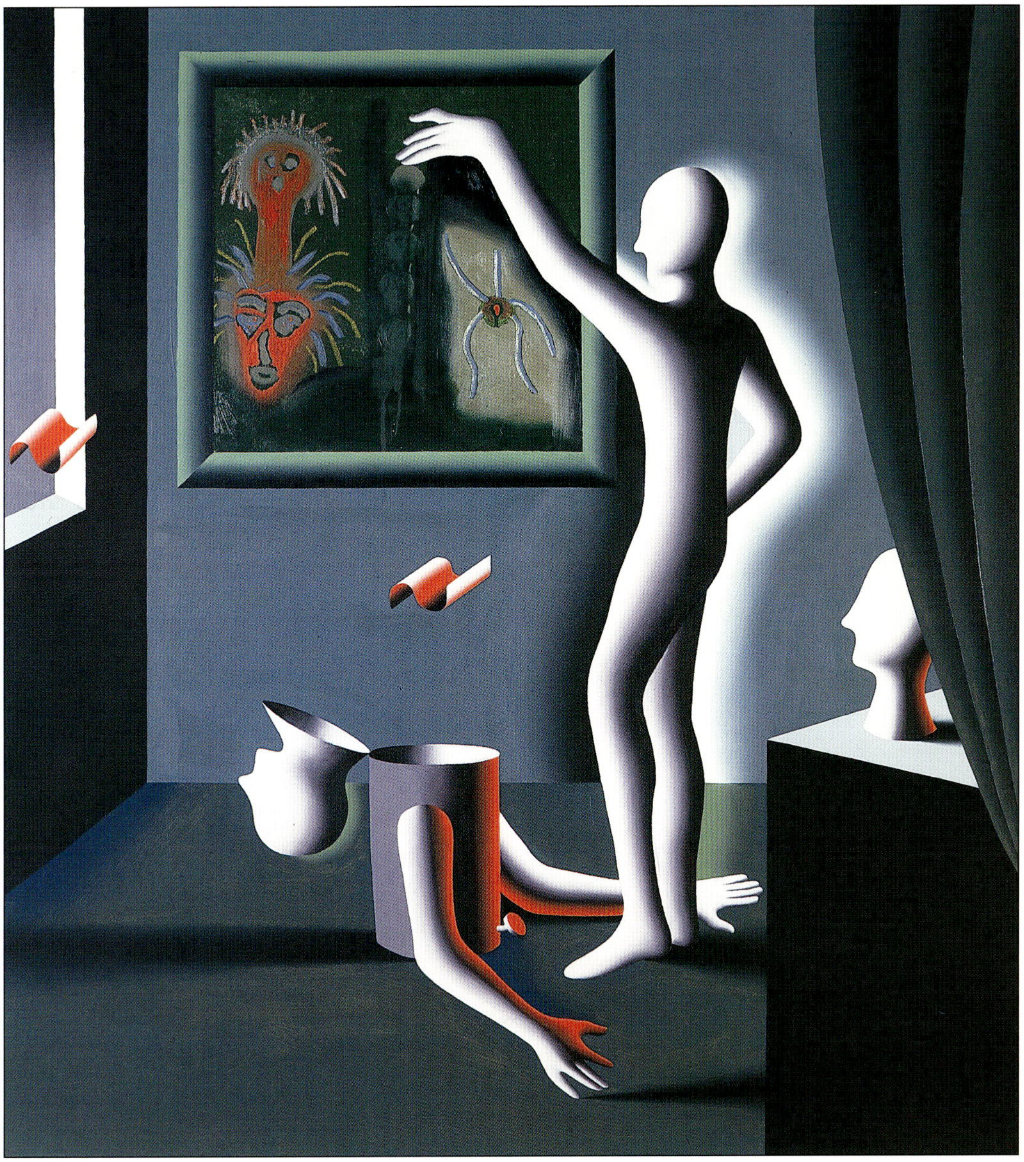

✧ *Collaboration with Paul Kostabi*
Litmus Test
1987
Oil on canvas
68 x 60 inches
Solomon R. Guggenheim Museum, New York

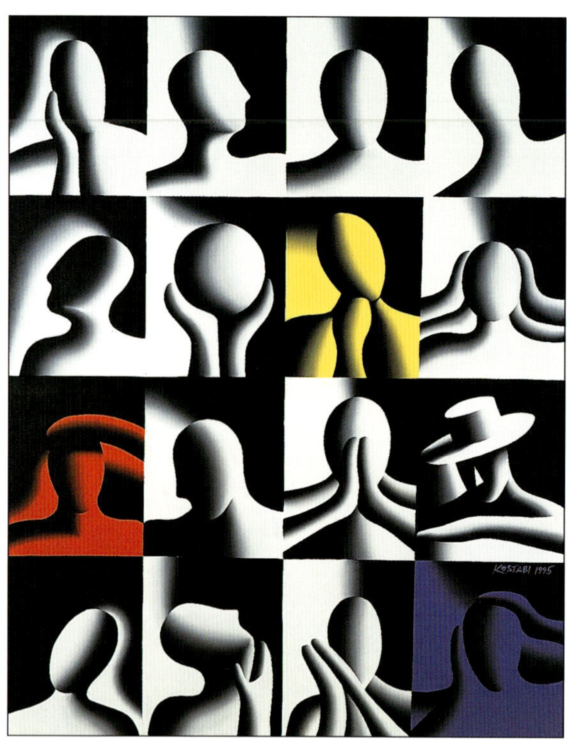

✧ Conversation Pieces
1995
Oil on canvas
60 x 46 inches
Kostabi World

image *Upwardly Mobile* over and over again. He said that for him it's a "universal message of love, solitude, and sadness." It inspires him to devise fresh color solutions each time.

✦ You commented earlier that the graduates of American art schools disappoint you. Could you elaborate?

✧ **European art schools still stress the fundamentals of technique, which American art schools lack. I've had much better luck with Eastern European and Japanese painters than I've had with painters who were born in America. Immigrants have more respect for job opportunities and have a better work ethic. Some of my**

American painters seem more interested in their tattoos than their jobs.

✦ You have so many ideas of your own, why did you start hiring idea people?

At first it was just for fun, a publicity stunt inspired by the growing outrage about my allegedly not doing any of my own work. I placed an ad in the *Village Voice* that said, "Help wanted. Inventive artists wanted to provide ideas for Mark Kostabi paintings. Submit sketchbook, notebooks or miscellaneous artifacts displaying ingenuity. $7.00/hour." I got over seventy-five applicants and hired Diana Gentleman not only because her whimsical drawings vaguely resemble my own but because she was a beautiful ex-model and I knew she would look good in photos and on TV. Some of her ideas were very successful. One was the basis of a collaboration I did with my brother,

✧ Heads of State
1993
Oil on canvas
36 x 36 inches
Collection of Don J. Christal

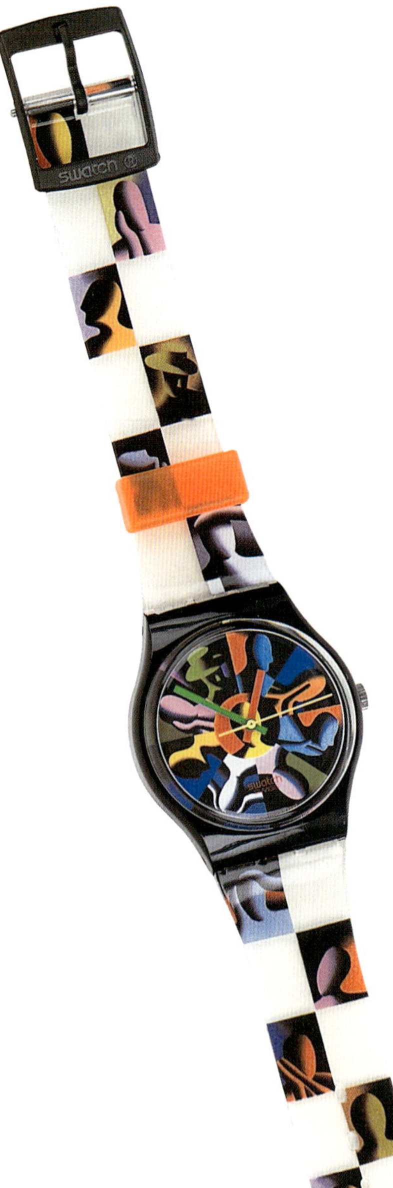

Paul, *Litmus Test*, which ended up in the permanent collection of the Guggenheim Museum. Another was *Gentlemen*, named after Diana. Years later, another idea person, Roman Scott, designed a round version of *Gentlemen*, called *Heads of State*, which became the Kostabi Swatch watch called *The Twelve Apostles*. Actually, Roman's version had more heads but the Swatch company simplified it. So you see how many hands and minds can go into the creation of a simple image. Diana Gentleman's initial idea was inspired by a famous photo by Man Ray of the Surrealists in a grid. True authorship is difficult to attribute.

✦ Yet you have full legal ownership.

✧ **I'm surrounded by a whirlwind of creativity and every once in a while I see this illuminated green button about the size of a silver dollar that says "signature" on it. And they tell me I'm supposed to press it. So I do.**

✦ Diana was part of your publicity?

✧ **She was perfect. I told her to tell the press that I was exploiting her, to complain about the**

seven dollars an hour she was making while I made millions. Eventually, she started to believe her own script and quit after I refused to give her a second raise. She went on to pursue her own art career, thanked me for the opportunity I gave her, and we're still friends.

✦ Did you really need an idea person?

✧ **I wanted to need one. I liked the idea of an idea person. So I kept hiring painters and by the time I got up to twenty-seven painters, they caught up with me. I couldn't come up with that many different good ideas a day. So I promoted two of my painters to idea people: Cliff Leigh and Lis Fields.**

✦ Does anyone stand out in your mind as having been an exceptional idea person?

✧ **Roman Scott was one. He came up with ideas that were brilliant. One after another. His imagination is bizarre and wonderful. He no longer works at Kostabi World, but is enjoying a very successful career showing in a good New York gallery and as an illustrator for the *New York Times* and the *Wall Street Journal*. He recently told me that his years in**

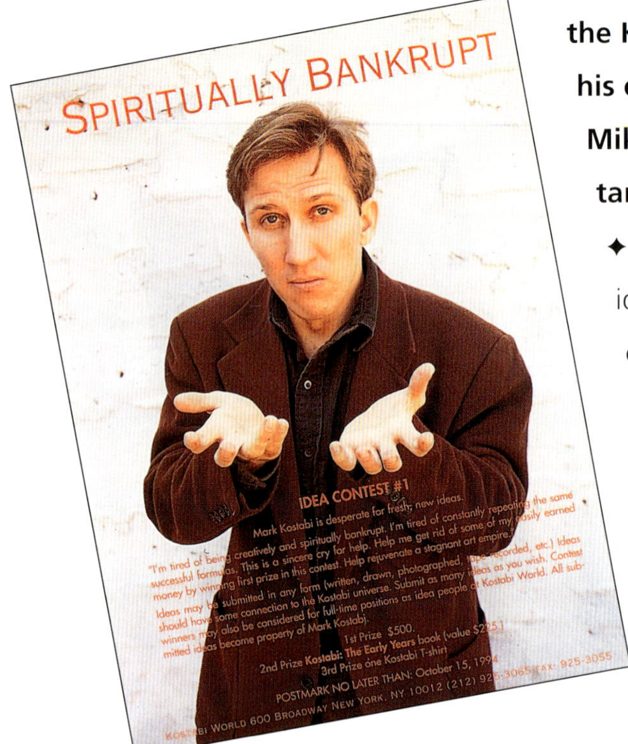

the Kostabi World think-tank helped him develop his career as an illustrator. Also, Cliff Leigh and Mike Cockrill were stars in the Kostabi think-tank.

✦ Do the idea people ever think that their ideas have been butchered by the painters or the committee?

✧ **Yes, and sometimes they're right and sometimes they're wrong. But they are not the artist. They're an important part of the equation, however. If an idea needs to be changed, it'll be changed. Once, the idea people collectively complained to me about how frustrating it was to have their ideas so frequently rejected by the committee. I said, "Use that frustration as fuel for your next idea. Fight back." And Cliff came back with a great drawing, which became the painting *Minutemen*.**

✦ You ran an idea contest in *Flash Art* called *Spiritually Bankrupt*. How did that turn out?

✧ **I'm still processing the submissions. Actually, my "in-house" contests have yielded the best results so**

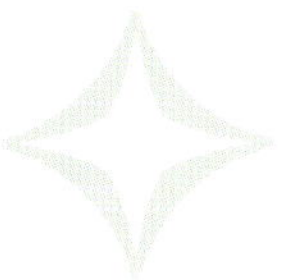

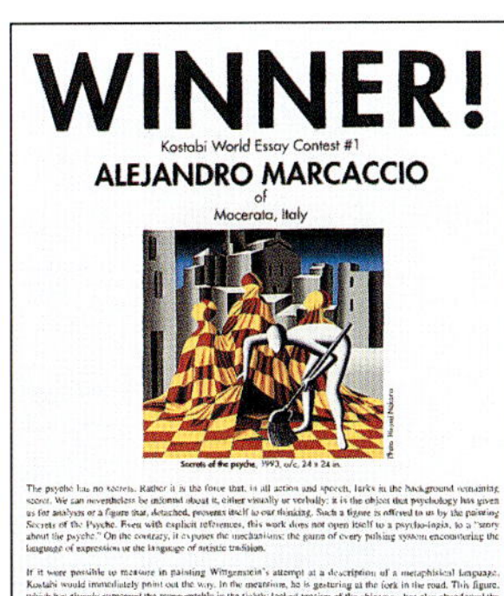

WINNER!

Kostabi World Essay Contest #1

ALEJANDRO MARCACCIO

of

Macerata, Italy

Secrets of the psyche, 1993, o/c, 24 x 24 in.

The psyche has no secrets. Rather it is the force that, in all action and speech, lurks in the background remaining secret. We can nevertheless be informed about it, either visually or verbally: it is the object that psychology has given us for analysis or a figure that, detached, presents itself to our thinking. Such a figure is offered to us by the painting Secrets of the Psyche. Even with explicit references, this work does not open itself to a psycho-logia, to a "story about the psyche." On the contrary, it exposes the mechanisms: the game of every pulsing system encountering the language of expression or the language of artistic tradition.

If it were possible to measure in painting Wittgenstein's attempt at a description of a metaphysical language, Kostabi would immediately point out the way. In the meantime, he is gesturing at the fork in the road. This figure, which has already surpassed the representable in the tightly locked tension of the chiasmus, has also abandoned the sayable for the infinite game of paradoxes, and the artist is left with no choice other than to become a sophist or a magician. Kostabi, who incarnates both of these manifestations, is the salesman-artist who conceals, like Psyche in her cloak, his act of self-concealment in the unfolding of his artifice, not just to bedazzle us but also to show, beyond the easy secret, the rapport between revelation and mystery. It is almost as if to say: "Now you can see with the eyes of your mind."

Alejandro Marcaccio

KOSTABI WORLD 600 BROADWAY NEW YORK, NY 10012 (212) 925-3065 FAX: 925-3055

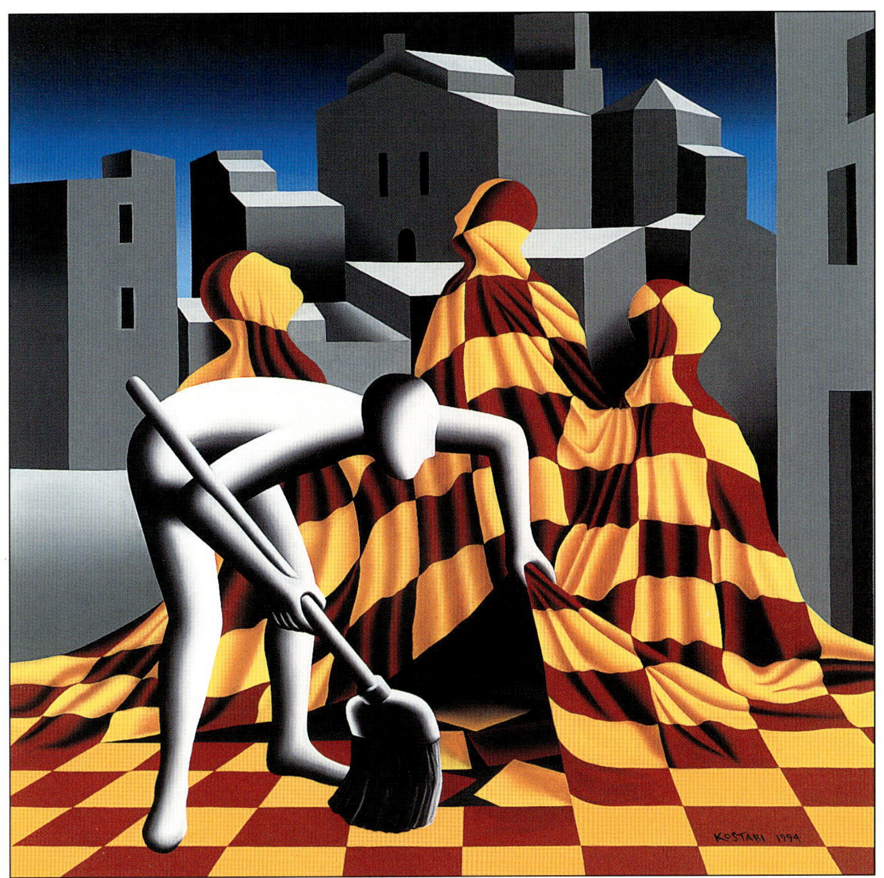

✧ **Secrets of the Psyche**

1994

Oil on canvas

48 x 48 inches

Private collection

far. Once, I took the best drawing from a Kostabi World Drawing Survey and used it as a schematic for a painting contest. I asked all my painters to execute their own versions, loosely staying within the Kostabi style. They all tried to outdo each other, motivated by a cash award. The winning painting was so good that I couldn't even explain it myself, so I ran an essay contest in *Flash Art* to analyze the picture. Then I had Jennifer Tull, another painter, execute a larger mirror-image version

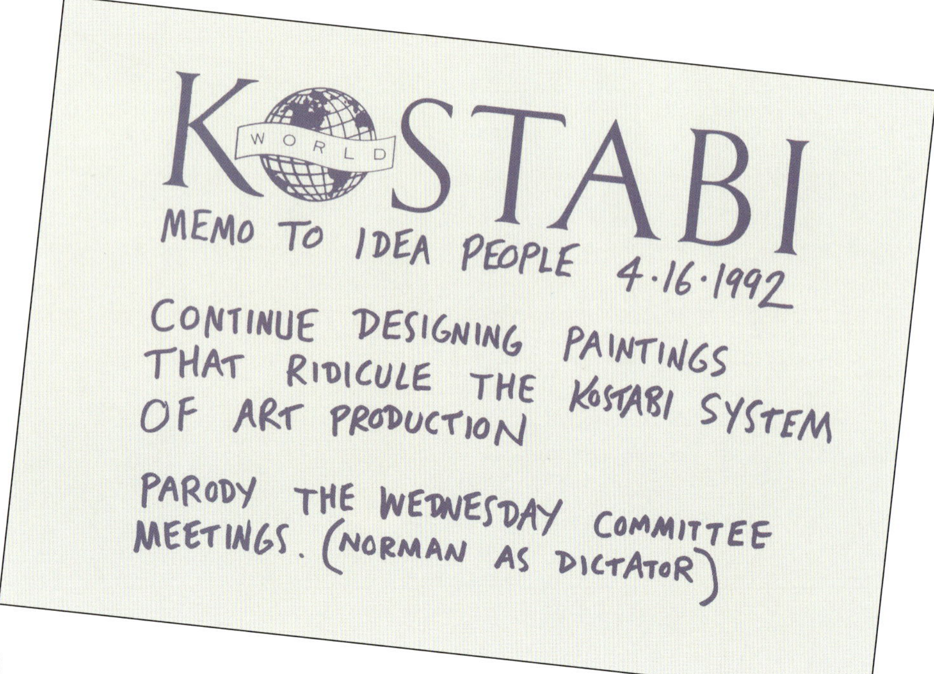

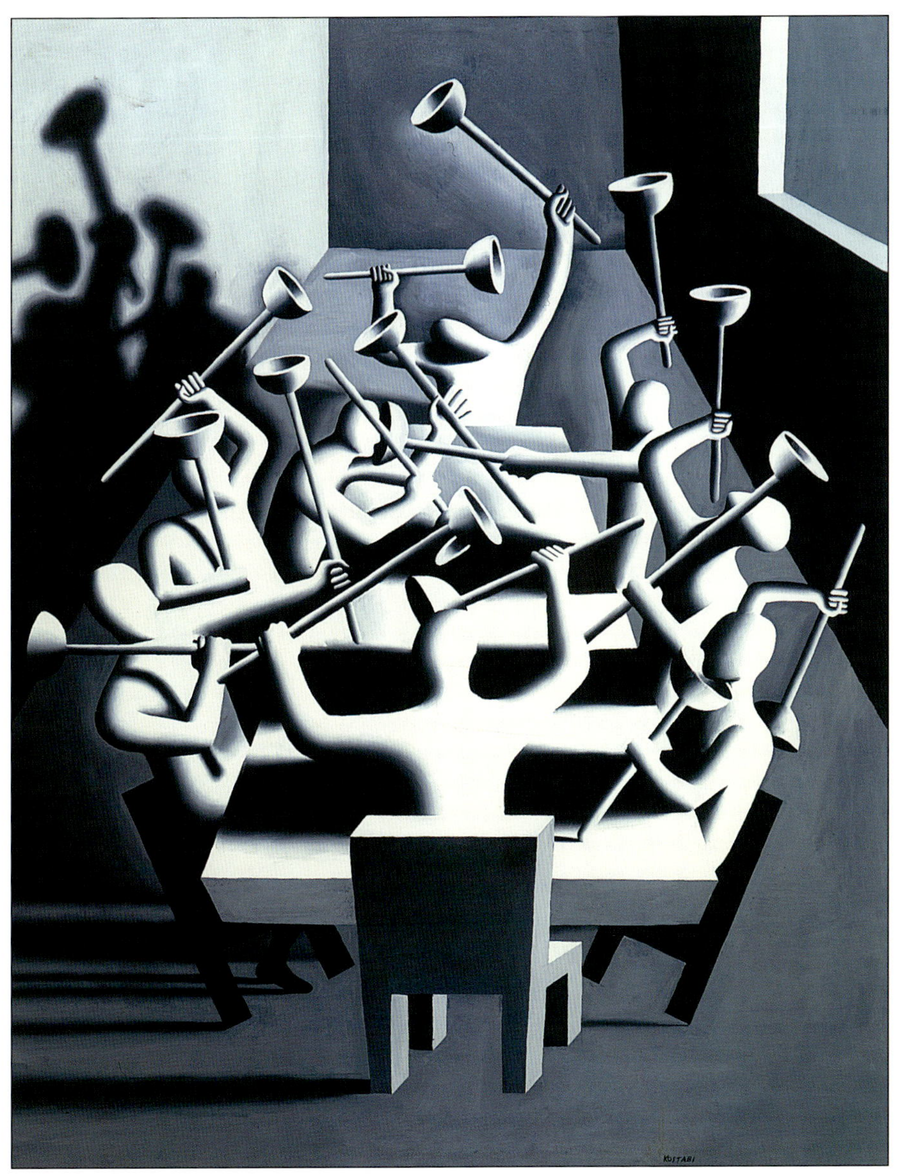

✧ **Upheaval**
1984
Oil on canvas
96 x 72 inches
Collection of Herbert and Leonore Shorr

of the painting, with some improvements in the background tonality. The result was *Secrets of the Psyche*.

✦ Do the idea people feel more exploited than the painters because they're actually "inventing" rather than just "filling in"?

✧ They never complain. In fact, they don't like going back to the easel, even for the same money. Perhaps they prefer not having to change into painting clothes and not getting paint on their hands. I guess it's the appeal of a white-collar job.

✦ Where does the committee come in?

✧ I've been using committees in various forms all my life. We all use them. Anytime you ask someone for advice, you've formed a committee between yourself and that person. Committees run the world and I like that. Museums show committee-approved art. Sometimes the public is the committee. They eventually decide whether or not your painting is a dud.

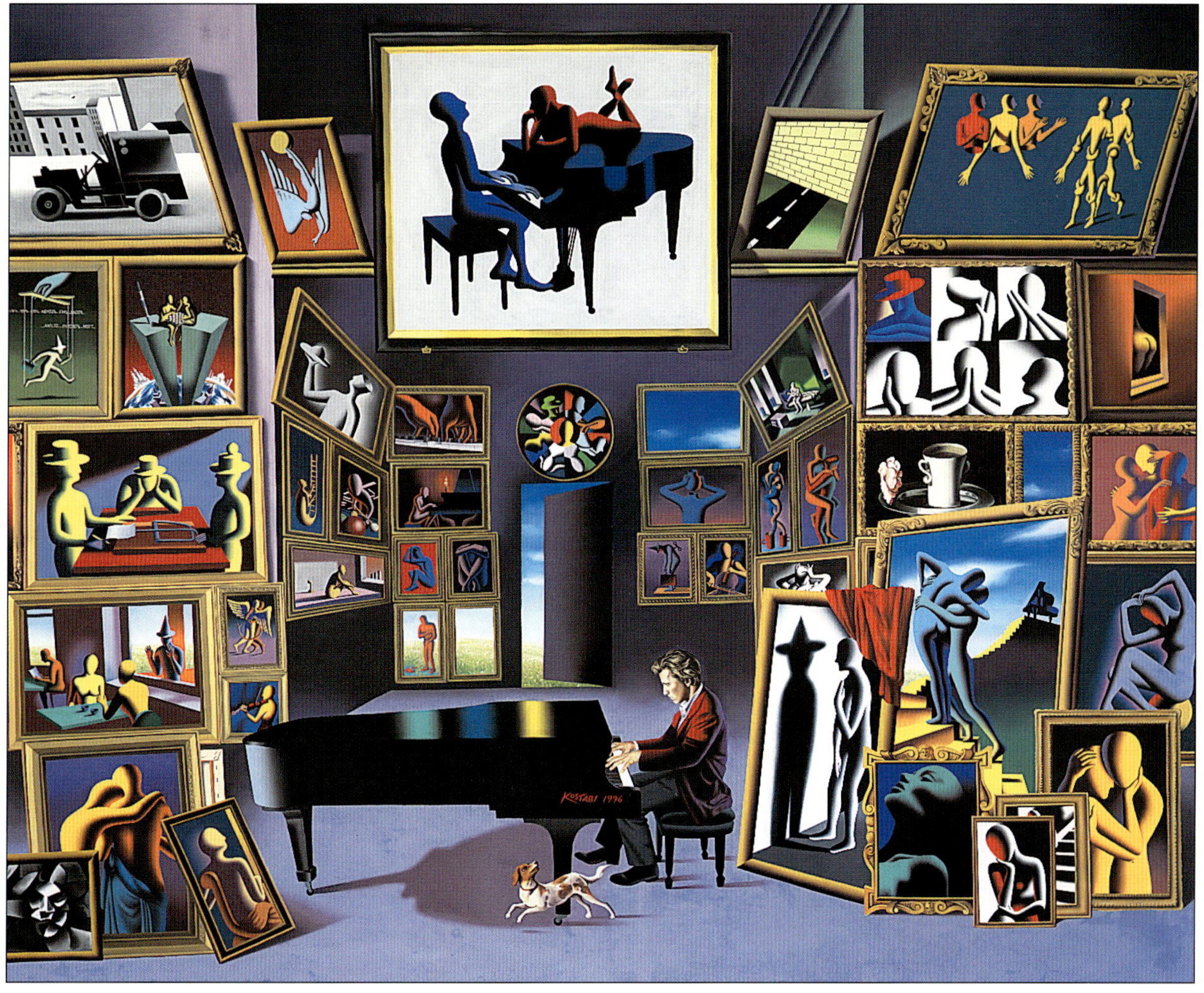

✧ **The Keys of the Kingdom**
1996
Oil on canvas
10 x 12 feet
Kostabi World

✦ Who is on your committee?

✧ **It changes, based on my intuition and on who is available at the moment. Sometimes it's an informal gathering of a few painters, or my whole staff. Sometimes I turn a visiting tour group into a committee and ask them to rate a group of paintings on a scale of zero to ten. Sometimes I hold specific idea-approval meetings where I invite friends to be guest creative consultants; people as diverse as cartoonist Art Spiegelman, art historian Gail Levin, and art dealer Molly Barnes. In the early 1990s art collector Norman Dubrow was a regular creative consultant. For two years he came every Wednesday, bursting with energy and good advice.**

✦ What is your role at committee meetings?

✧ **I ask questions, people vote, and I process the answers.**

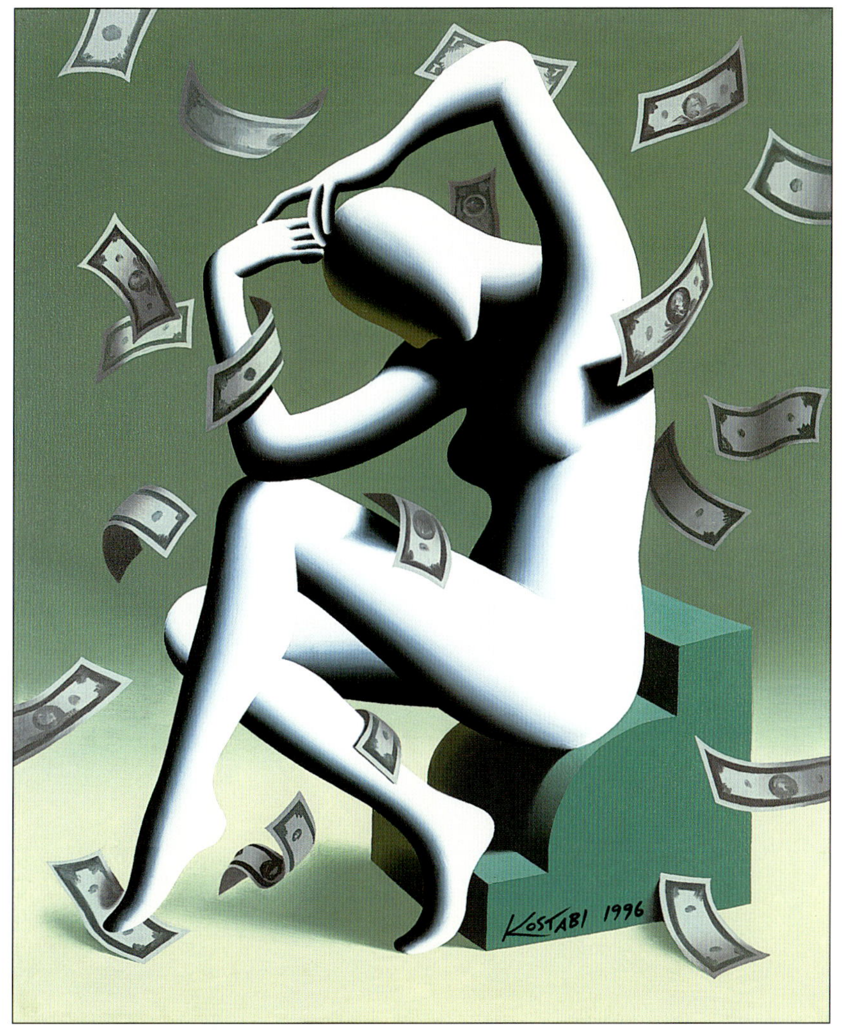

✧ **Cash Euphoria**
1996
Oil on canvas
30 x 24 inches
Private collection

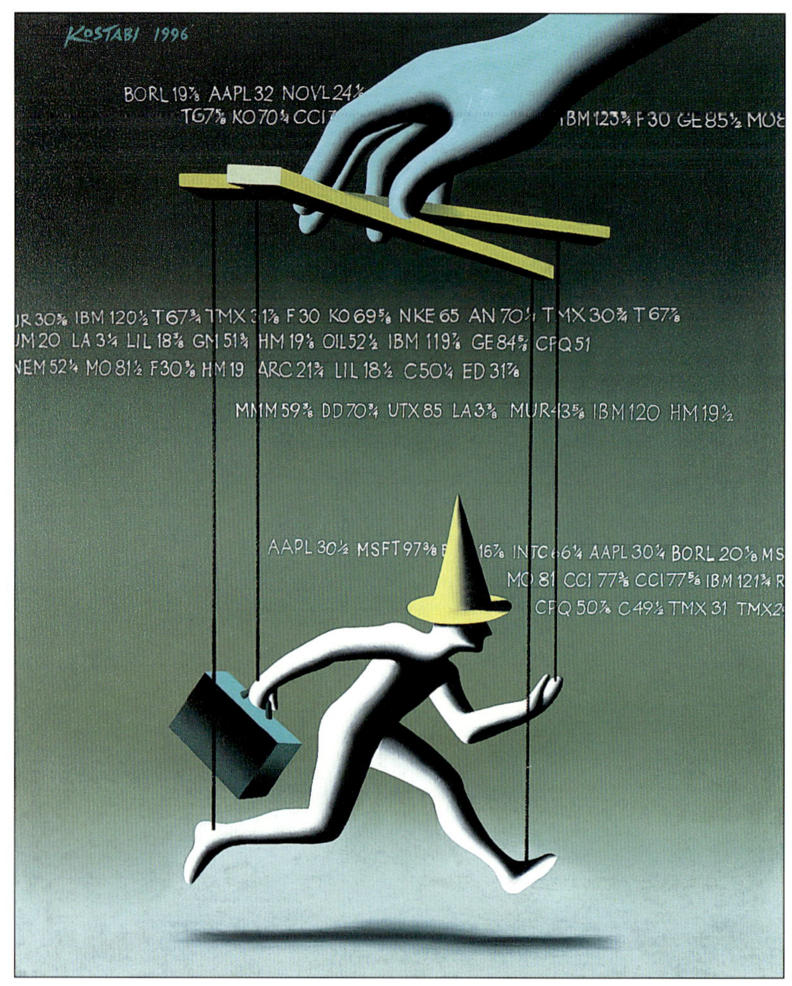

✧ **Green Day Job**
1996
Oil on canvas
30 x 24 inches
Private collection

SELLS ✧

✦ Do you vote yourself?

✧ **No. I want to remove my ego from the creative process.**

✦ Why is that?

✧ **Because it gets in the way of art.**

✦ Is there a danger that the committee might sap the spirit from your work?

✧ **On the contrary. The committee is the soul of Kostabi World.**

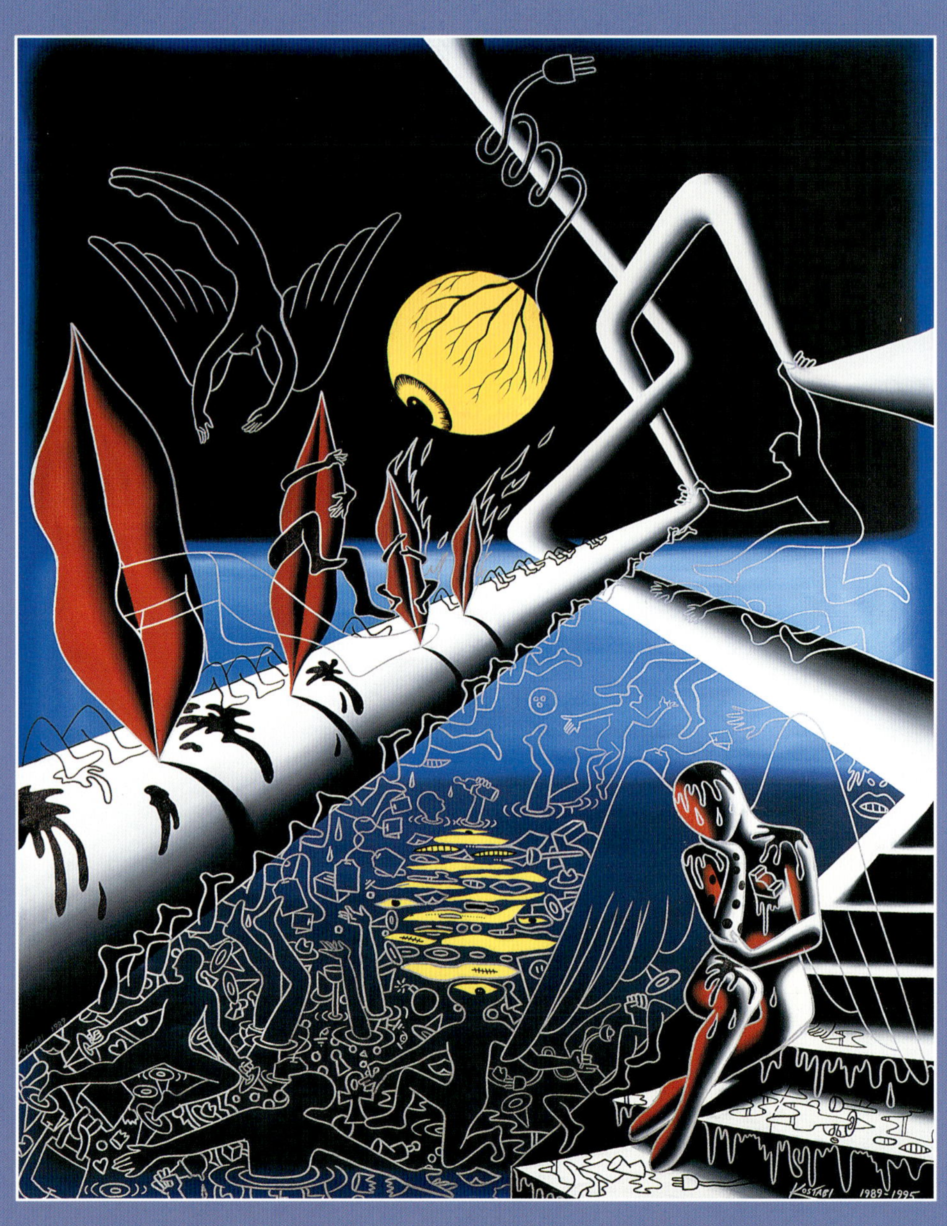
KOSTABI 1989-1995

CHAPTER ✧ FOUR

WHAT MAKES A KOSTABI PAINTING TICK

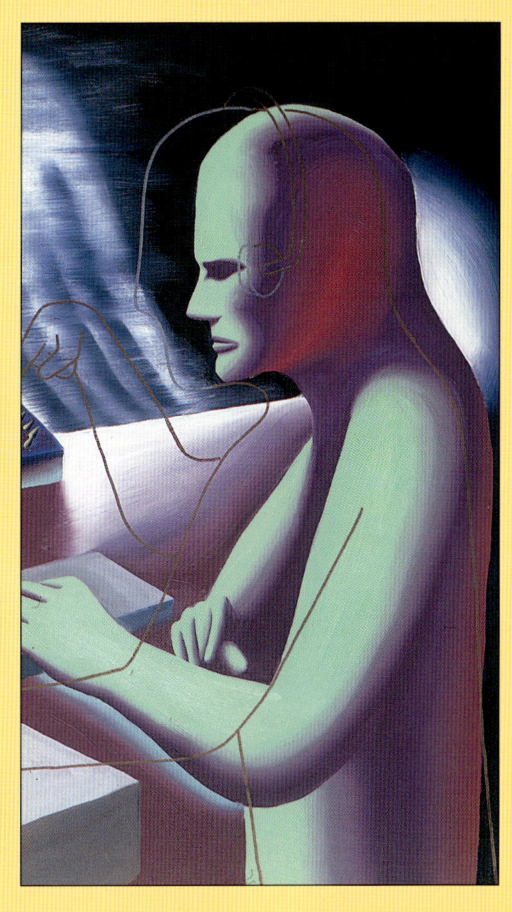

✦ What makes a Kostabi painting tick?

✧ **Years of experimenting. Processing feedback and reacting in an interesting, universally understood visual language.**

✦ Are there constant elements that make up a Kostabi painting?

✧ **The figure, the color, the lighting, the idea, the composition, the title, the irony, and the signature.**

✦ Okay, let's start with the figure. Why do most of your paintings have figures?

✧ **Because people perceive themselves as figures and it's easier to identify with the illusion of the familiar. Actually, we're all just localized bundles of consciousness in an ocean of consciousness, but every time I try to paint that, it just ends up in the curiosity archives.**

✧ page 76:
Electric Eye
1989–95
Oil & paint marker on canvas
90 x 70 inches
Kostabi World

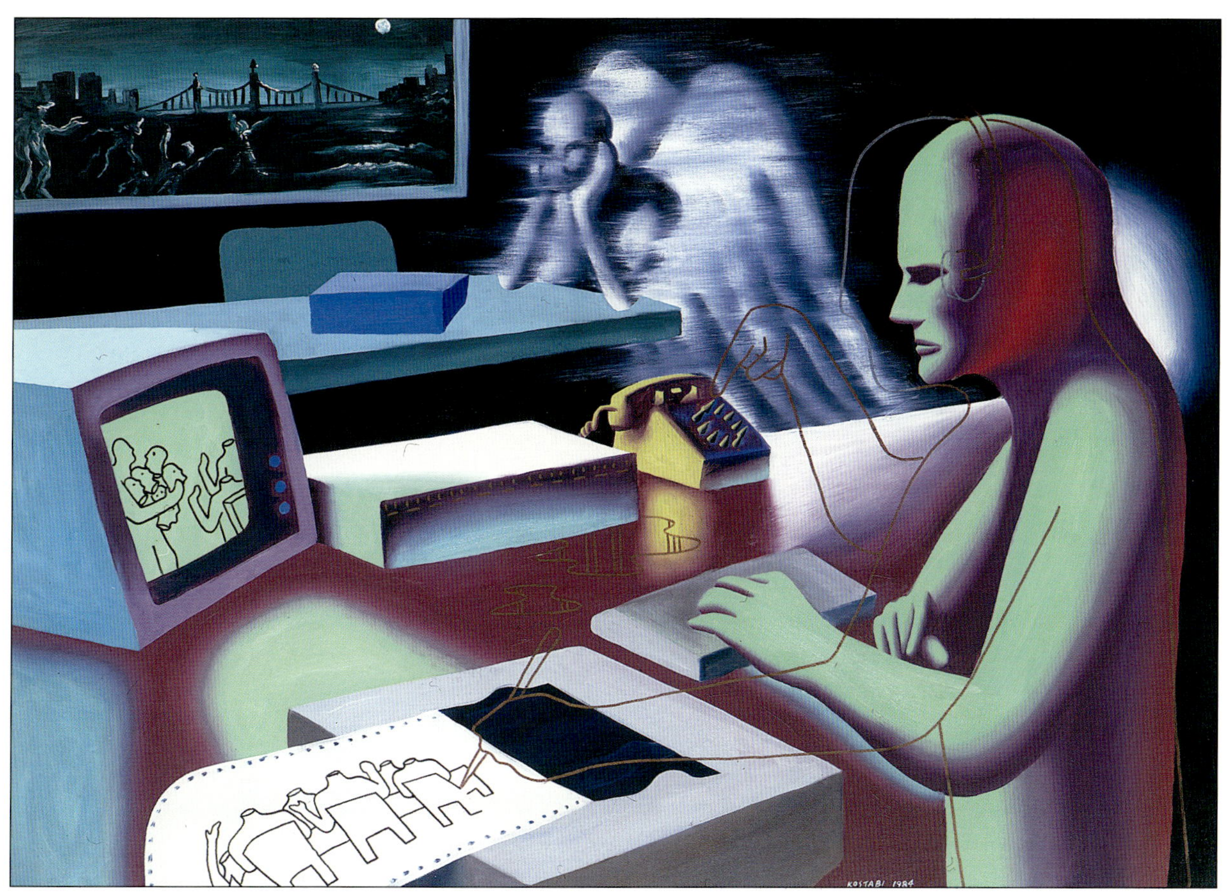

✧ **Control**
1984
Oil on canvas
50 x 70 inches
Collection of Martin Sklar

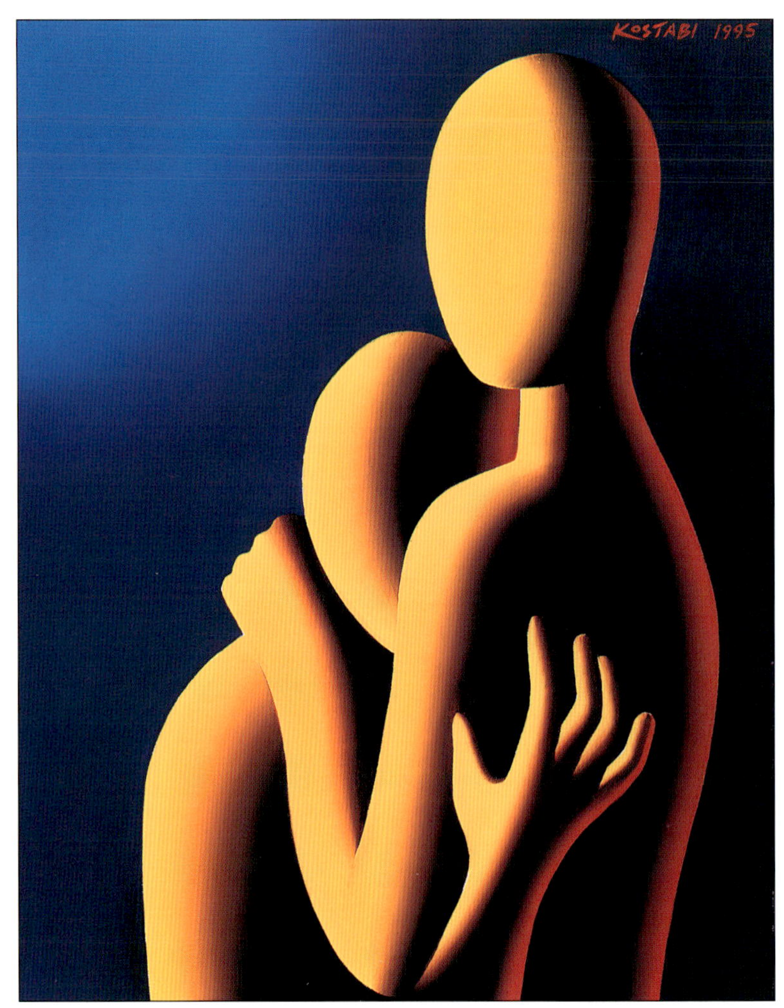

✧ **Comfort Zone (Draco)**
1995
Oil on canvas
24 x 18 inches
Collection of Hong J. Lee

✦ What are the curiosity archives?

✧ **I have boxes and drawers filled with miscellaneous things that I can't figure out how to use but don't have the heart or courage to throw out. I hope in the future to mine the archives and uncover hidden treasure.**

✦ Why are the figures faceless?

✧ **To express the truth that we're all the same being in different disguises. It's a universal language free of racial limitations, and a reflection of society's fear of individuality.**

✦ It's also faster to paint?

✧ **Time is money.**

✦ How did you end up with the Kostabi figure?

✧ **I was in art school at Cal State, Fullerton, and I was experimenting with different types of art: academic portrait painting, conceptual art, expressionism, impressionism, minimalism, performance art, assemblage. I also composed music for piano. But one of my main activities was making marks in a sketchbook, on flip books, on rolls of receipt paper, in the margins of my art history notes, and on**

✧ **Restaurant**
1982
Oil on canvas
36 x 48 inches
Collection of Joseph Stabolito

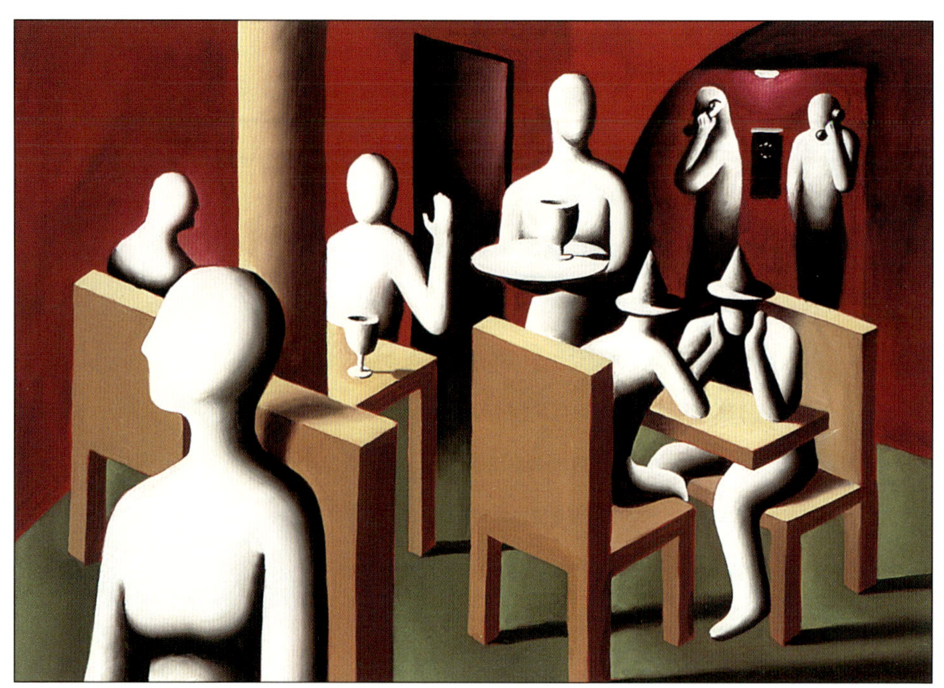

whom I showed my drawings as soon as I got to New York. He said, "Where are the works on canvas?" Implying that I couldn't make it in the art world without works on canvas.

✦ Why is that so?

✧ Because works on canvas command much higher prices than drawings that can't possibly pay the monthly gallery overhead.

✦ How did you make the transition from drawings to paintings?

✧ I approached my first paintings by imagining what the images in my line drawings would look like if they were sculptures, with subtle halation around them. I actually tried sculpture first and they looked good. But they fell apart because I lacked knowledge of sculpture techniques. People told me my drawings would make great sculptures. It took me until 1986 to figure out how to make successful Kostabi sculptures.

✦ How?

✧ Hire a trained sculptor.

✦ Can you tell me more about your transition to painting?

✧ No one ever told me the drawings would make

great paintings, but I knew how to paint and Ivan Karp said I needed paintings, so I brought my skills together and it worked. My first classic Kostabi painting that had colors other than black and white was *Restaurant*, which was inspired by a drawing I made in a Mexican restaurant in Anaheim, California. I used muted reds, greens, and yellow ocher. My aim was simply to prove that I could successfully use color to evoke a soothing interior ambiance. Since then my color strategies have varied greatly. Sometimes I issue detailed memos to my assistants. Sometimes I restrict myself to the Mondrian formula of primary colors plus black and white. When I don't have a specific symbolic statement to make with

KOSTABI WORLD

12·18·1990

PAINTERS AND IDEA PEOPLE

THIS REQUIRES SOME OF YOUR OWN JUDGEMENT: DO NOT PUT "HALOS" BEHIND "INSIGNIFICANT" CONTOURS. FOR EXAMPLE:

YES HALO

NO HALO

NO HALO

YES HALO

THE HALO IS USED FOR DRAMATIC EFFECT TO DEFINE "IMPORTANT" PARTS OF THE PAINTING.

IF YOU FILL ALL THESE INSIGNIFICANT "HOLES" WITH STRONG HALOS THEN THE BACKGROUND WILL "BULGE FORWARD LIKE A SUFFOCATING WATER BALLOON."

EITHER ELIMINATE THESE CONTOURS AND LET THESE FORMS MYSTERIOUSLY MERGE WITH THE BACKGROUND. OR FILL THESE LITTLE NEGATIVE SPACES WITH THE APPROPRIATE FLAT COLOR THAT RECEDES.

THANK YOU

KOSTABI

colors, I may arbitrarily choose my favorites of the month. For a while in the 1980s I loved turquoise, chartreuse, mint green, and purple with red reflected light. Currently I have no favorite color. I like it as long as it's good.

✦ How do you know when it's good?

✧ **I rely on experience from trial and error but I still take surveys regularly to keep in check, because I know I'm not always right.**

✦ In *Mass Production* and *Automatic Painting*, you depict a black-and-white world that manufactures full-color art. What's that about?

✧ **At almost every level of the art world color is a marketing issue. Color equals money. Black-and-white paintings equal good reviews. Colorful paintings equal sales. Back in 1984, when I was twenty-four, I remember being in the lobby of 420 West Broadway, the most important art gallery building in SoHo. I overheard someone trying to sell a Milton Avery painting to the dealer, Larry Gagosian. Larry said, "Only if it's bright." That sentence stuck with me. Most recently, I was commissioned to**

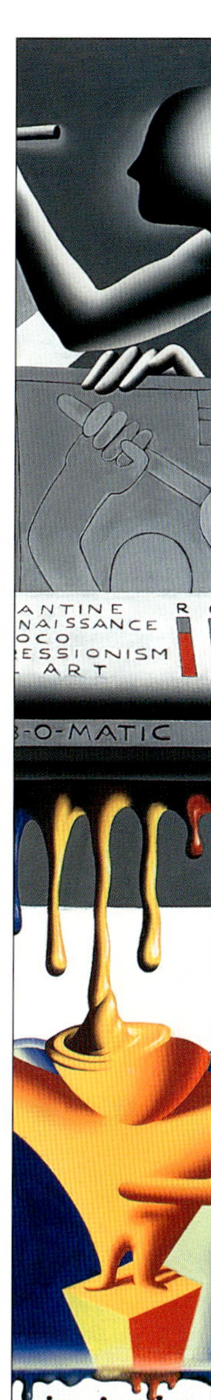

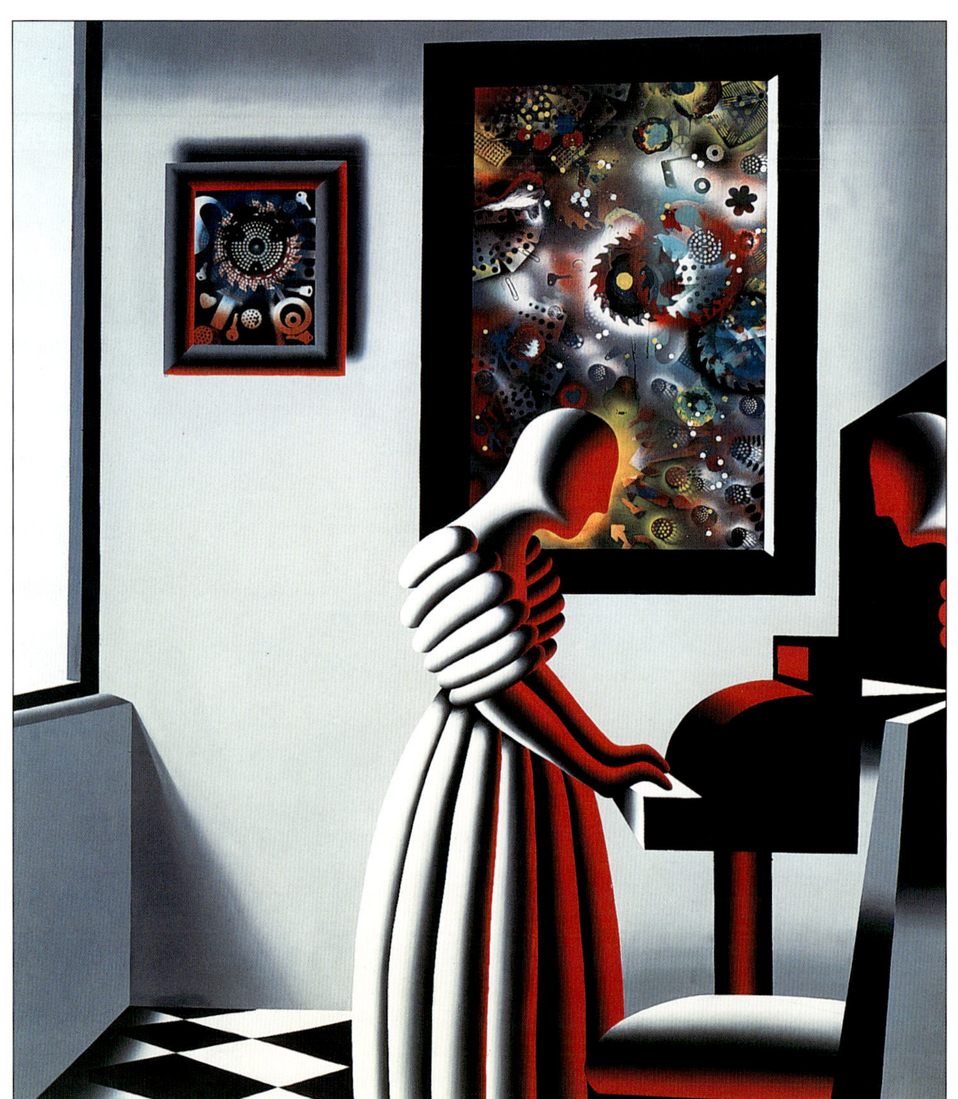

✧ **Requiem**
1987
Oil on canvas
84 x 72 inches
The Metropolitan Museum of Art, New York

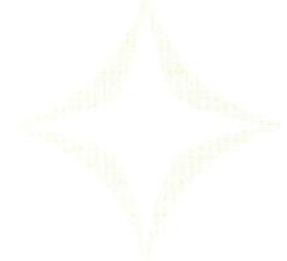

make eighty paintings for a collector in California. The stipulation was that each painting had to have at least twelve different bright colors. Together, they had to feel like a birthday party.

One time in Italy I made some intricate line drawings with black ink on white paper. I tried selling them to a dealer in Florence. He said, "They're beautiful but couldn't you just add a little color? Just a little? Then my clients will buy them." He had such a sad, begging face, and I had just gotten robbed because I foolishly left my wallet under the seat of my friends' car when we took a walk on the beach in Pietrasanta. So I agreed to add color. I bought three cans of spray paint, and gently sprayed a subtle mist of red, yellow, and blue over small parts of the line drawings, overlapping the colors and creating a rich veil which I thought would have made Paul Klee proud. The dealer's face lit up and he quickly produced a crisp stack of Italian lire.

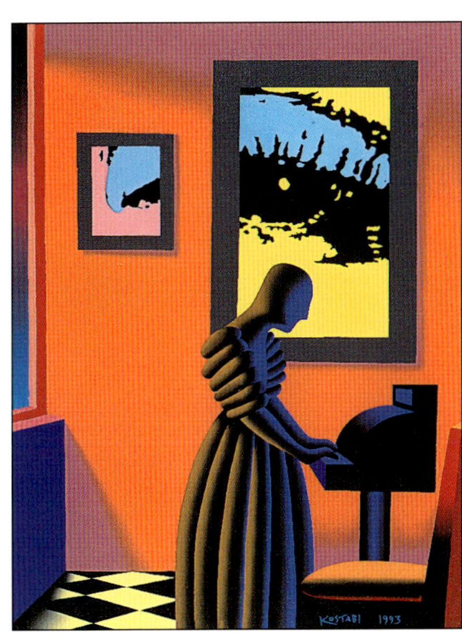

✧ The Eye of the Beholder
1993
Oil on canvas
24 x 18 inches
Collection of Michelle Ocampo

✦ People have praised your use of color in *The Eye of the Beholder*. Why is it so successful?

✧ **It successfully orchestrates colors that by today's standards would be considered hideous together: garish orange, drab olive green, baby blue, pink, mauve, and screaming yellow. It feels like a negative. Almost as if staring at it for a long period of time and then looking away would reveal a more logical color harmony. Also, the Warholian eye in the background is painted in a reductive style that faintly echoes Vermeer's premonition of photography. The painting is actually based on an earlier larger Kostabi called *Requiem*, which was based on Vermeer's *Lady Standing at a Virginal*.**

✧ page 91:
The Collector
1995
Oil on canvas
84 x 68 inches
Collection of Daniele Bevacqua

✦ You did another painting that deals with Vermeer's *Lady Standing at a Virginal* . . .

✧ **Actually I've done several.**

✦ I'm refering to *The Collector*, the one that shows Madame X, from the John Singer Sargent painting, turning away from the painstakingly accurate rendition of the original Vermeer in order to admire the Kostabi version.

✧ **Madame X had exquisite taste.**

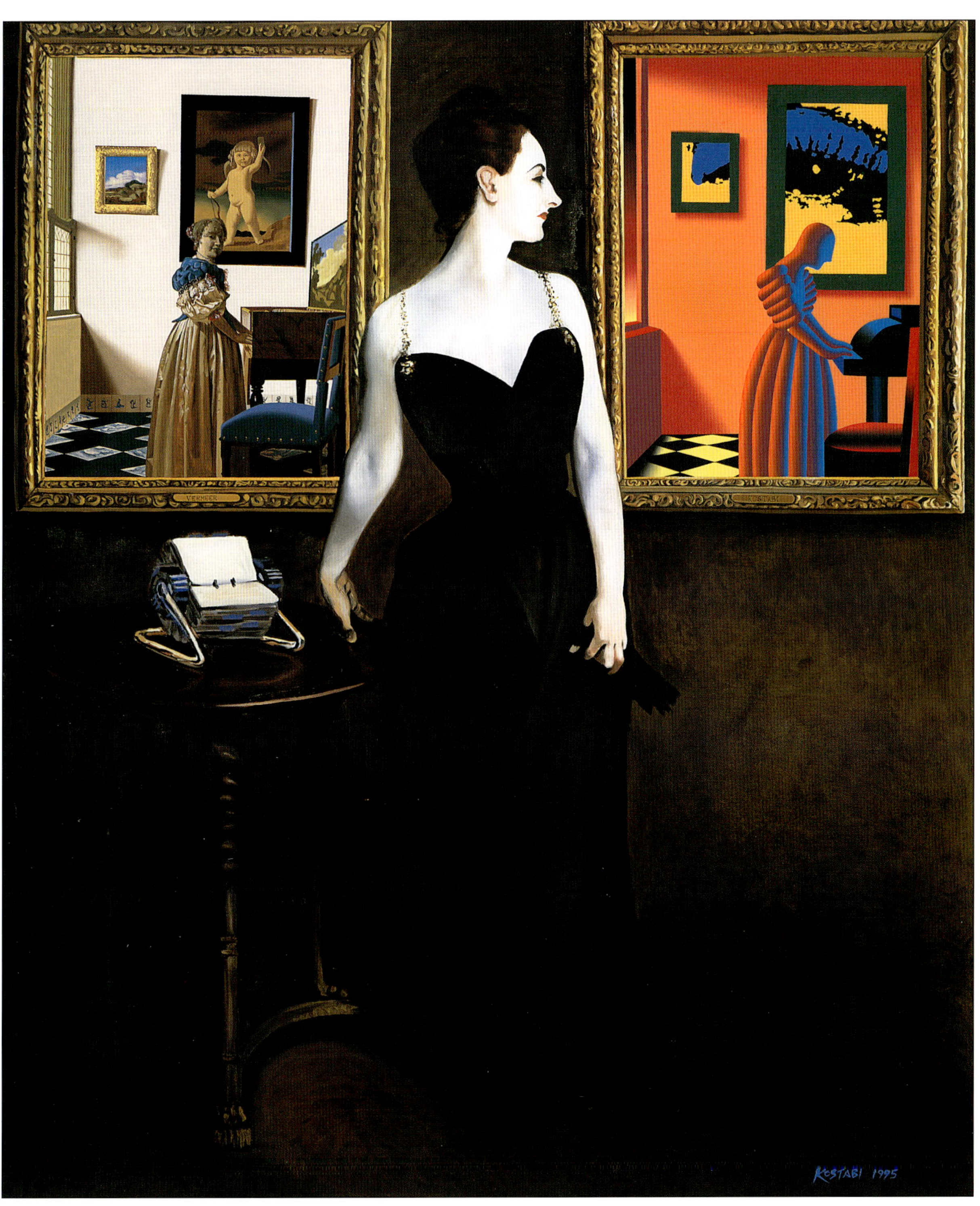
VERMEER
KOSTABI
KOSTABI 1995

✦ What about the lighting in your paintings?

✧ **I use strong side lighting, usually with a secondary light source from the other side. It's strong, high contrast, and looks good in print, even newsprint. The secondary light source is usually red. I use red because I know it has serious symbolic implications: danger, passion, blood, apocalypse. For a long time I resisted using the classic formula of black, white, and red because I thought it was too easy. I associated it with art students trying to look serious or trendy, by embracing the retro–Russian Constructivist look that was in vogue. But eventually I gave in, with paintings like *Upwardly Mobile*. Now I use every possible device in order to be more effective. Sometimes I juggle heavy symbolism to get a serious look, and sometimes I mock the juggling of heavy symbolism as a genuinely serious critique of juggling heavy symbolism. When you criticize others, people tend to close up and become defensive. When you criticize yourself, people listen.**

✦ Is your lighting inspired by film noir?

✧ **More by Caravaggio and by a desire for clarity through strongly defined form.**

✦ Why is clarity so important?

✧ **There's too much wishy-washy confusion and delusion in the world because of alcohol and drugs. I'm absolutely tired of it.**

✦ What about the shadows?

✧ **Shadows are rich.**

✦ Do your paintings have their own inner light?

✧ **You mean like they say about Matisse or Vermeer?**

✦ Yes.

✧ **I don't buy all that "inner light" stuff. Matisse got that look by using lots of bright colors and letting the white canvas show through. Since he didn't cover every square inch of canvas with opaque paint, the canvas feels like a powerful light behind the brush strokes, an illustration of inner light. But he certainly had a light touch.**

✦ And Vermeer?

✧ **Vermeer was just very knowledgeable and**

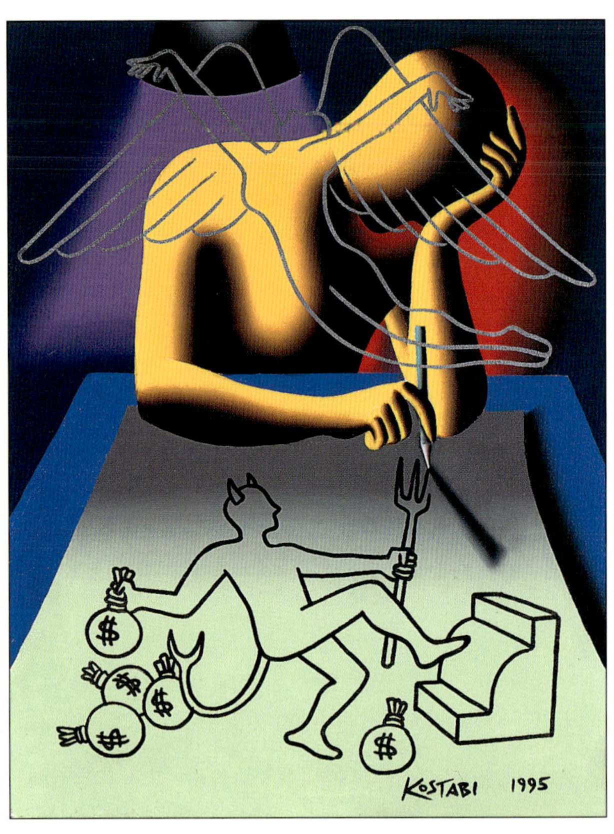

✧ **Diabolique**
1995
Oil on canvas
24 x 18 inches
Private collection

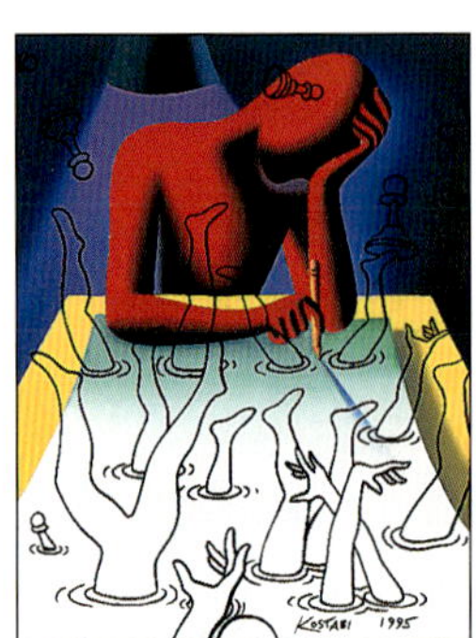

✧ **Liquid Paper**
1995
Oil on canvas
24 x 18 inches
Private collection

finished paintings that my assistants execute, as in *Open Season* and *Soul Kiss,* or I have them execute paintings with unresolved space in them specifically designed for my linear embellishments, as in *Liquid Paper* and *Diabolique*. I used this approach occasionally in the 1980s in paintings like in *Moses*, *Control*, or *Balzac*,

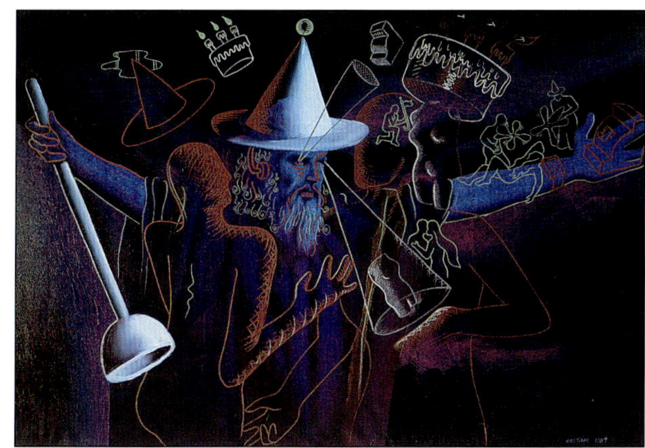

✧ **Moses**
1984
Oil on canvas
48 x 72 inches
Collection of Rick Wolfryd

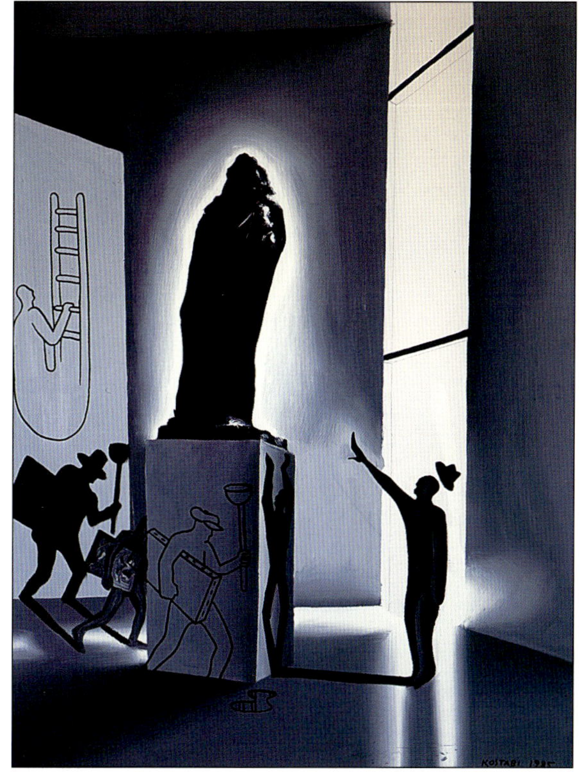

✧ **Balzac**
1985
Oil on canvas
48 x 36 inches
Private collection

but never to the extent I did in 1995. And lately I've been drawing on top of paintings I've found by anonymous Asian artists who use fake Westernized names to sell their paintings in Middle America. *S.O.S.* and *Dog and Pony Show*. If I draw directly on canvas,

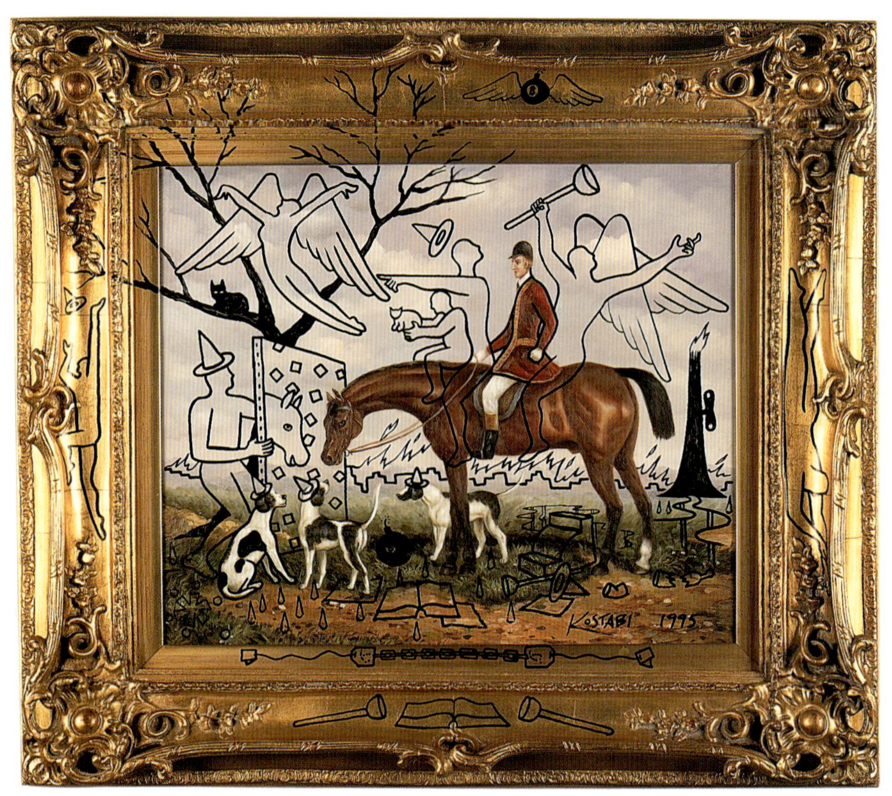

✧ **Dog and Pony Show**
1995
Oil on canvas
20 x 24 inches
Collection of Diane Sutter

it's much more likely to end up on a wall than if I draw on paper, which too often ends up in flat files. Ideas usually come from playing around. Some people in the art world actually look down on painters with lots of ideas. They try to dismiss the paintings as "idea dependent," "too narrative," or "too much like one-liners." They praise artists like Josef Albers or Franz Kline for their rigorous lifelong theoretical or spiritual investigation. They say, "Painting is not about ideas. Painting is about painting." Thankfully, art history has acknowledged genius idea-artists like Duchamp, Man Ray, and Magritte. Ideas are more memorable than sublime paint passages or breathtaking color harmonies. It's more memorable to say, "I liked the one with the crucified figure with a pacifier around his neck" than, "I liked the one where the blue blended into the red with the vertical yellow stripes on both sides."

✦ Do you ever sketch from life, or is everything created from your imagination in the studio?

✧ **I was asked to do a painting for a restaurant**

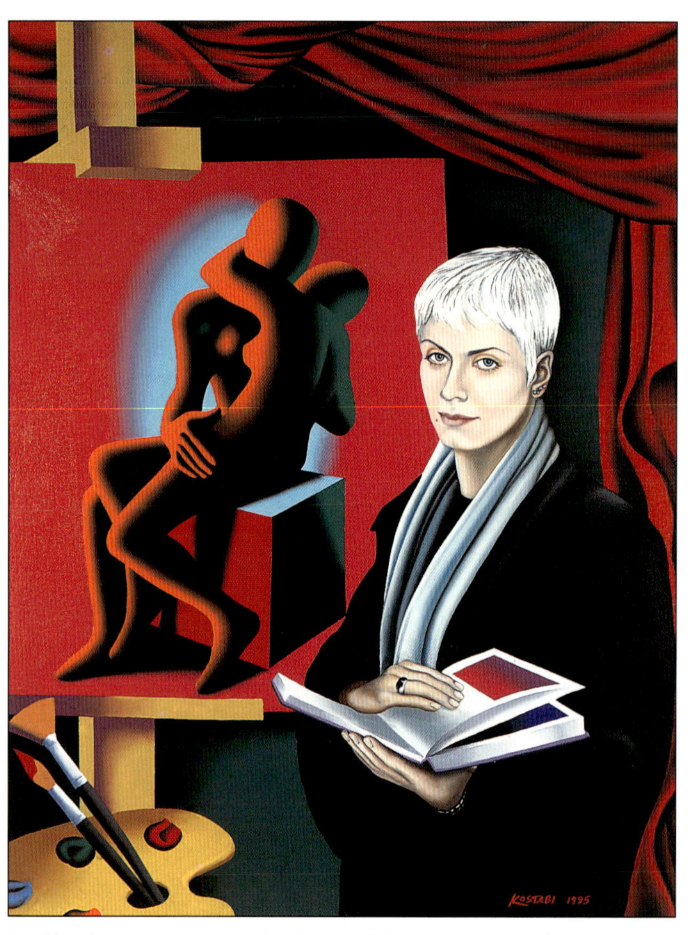

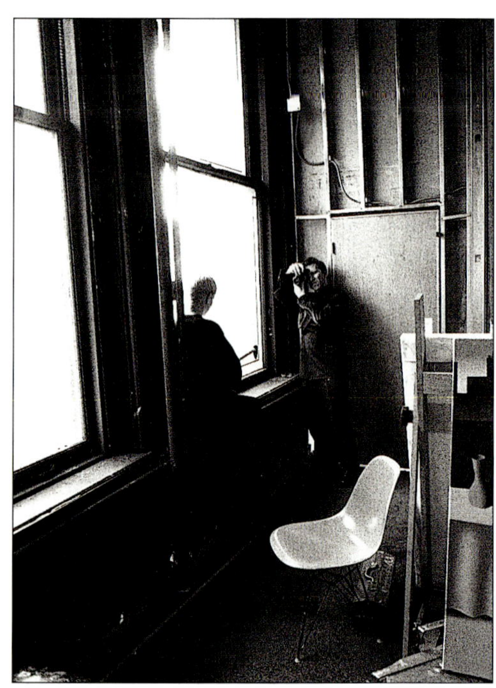

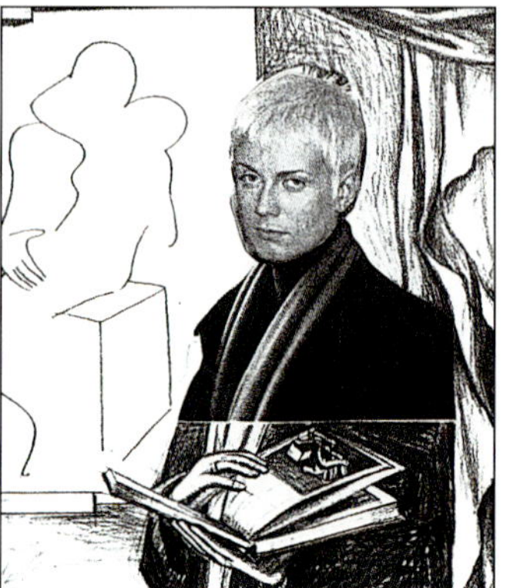

✧ **Monica**
1995
Oil on canvas
44 x 43 inches
Collection of Daniele Bevacqua

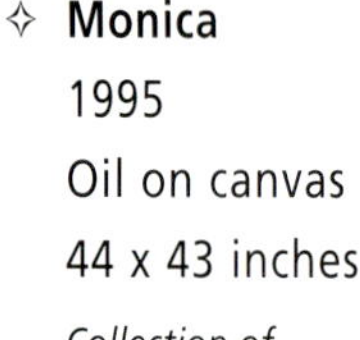

✧ above, right:
The artist photographing Monica Marongiu for her portrait in Kostabi World

✧ right:
Sketch for **Monica**
1995
Pencil on paper
Kostabi World

called Café Fiorello's, near Lincoln Center in New York City, and they suggested that I do a kitchen scene. They allowed me to go into the kitchen during one of their busiest times to witness the frenetic activity.

✦ Do you ever accept commissioned portraits?

✧ **Portraits can drive an artist crazy. Clients almost always want a portrait reworked. They call me up and say, "It's beautiful, but not quite what I had in mind." So, I try to oblige the client. I take the painting back and rework it until it's right. I usually incorporate a Kostabi figure with the realistically rendered portrait.**

It's a challenge. Some artists say, "I'll do portraits, but only if I have the final say. I'm the artist." A lot of people have that attitude. Maybe that's what made Rembrandt great, but I wouldn't be surprised if we discover that Rembrandt accommodated his clients.

✦ You've collaborated with other artists on several paintings. Why collaborate?

✧ **It opens up another creative universe for me.**

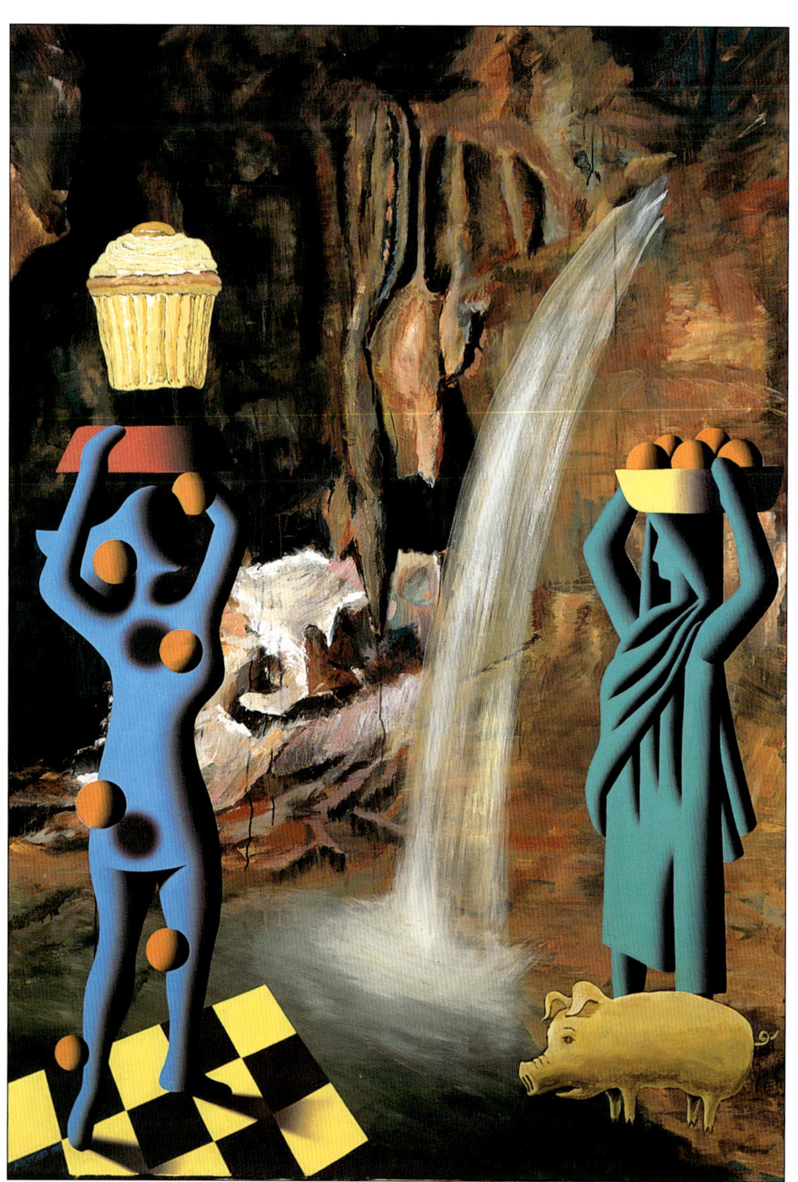

✧ *Collaboration with Tadanori Yokoo*
Two Cultures One Nature
1993
Oil on canvas
76 x 52 inches
Kostabi World

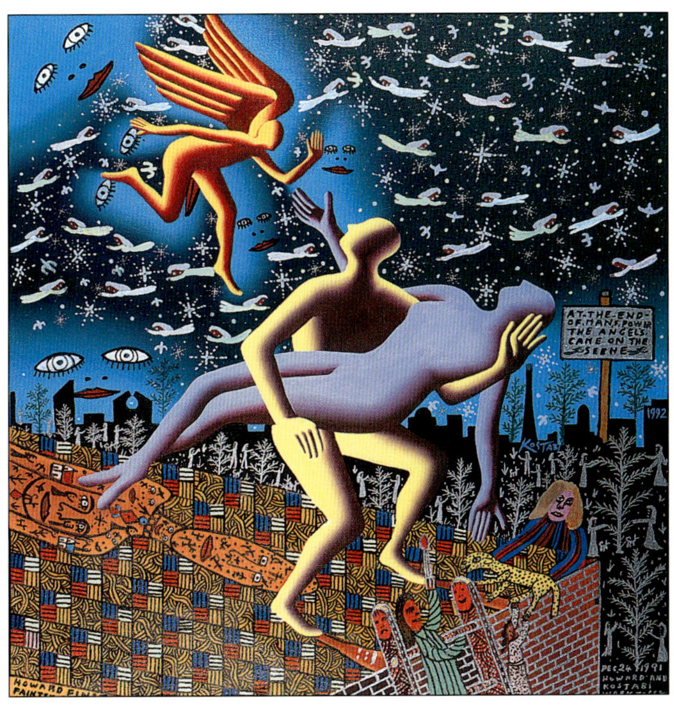

✧ *Collaboration with Howard Finster*
25th Hour
1991
Oil and paint marker on canvas
28 x 26 inches
Private collection

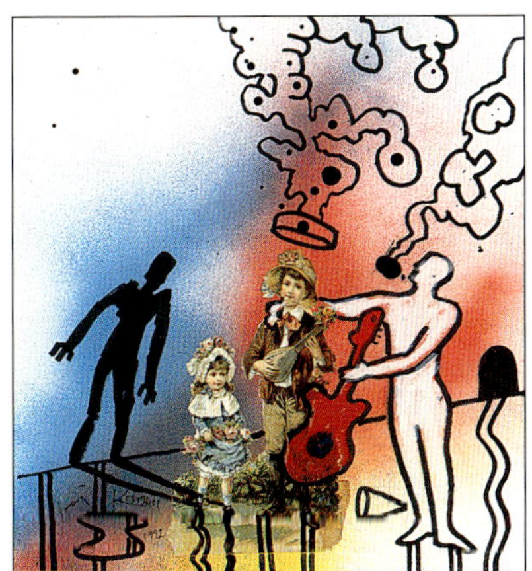

✧ *Collaboration with Enrico Baj*
A Present from the Future
1992
Paint marker, spray enamel, oil pastel, and collage on paper
10.5 x 9.5 inches
Collection of the artist

IS DIFFICULT

I learn about artists, and they learn about me. I get new ways of thinking about art.

✦ How does a collaboration work?

✧ **There are different kinds of collaborations. Sometimes I send the artist an unresolved or unfinished painting to complete and send back. I might add a few finishing touches and we both sign it. At other times I'll request a half-finished work that I can finish. Occasionally we work on a canvas at the same time. Or we'll send it back and forth many times until it's finished. Sometimes we'll sketch together and simultaneously come up with a drawing that finally gets painted in one of our studios. So it opens up a whole new world artistically. I can't leave out the fact that it's also good for exposing each of us to the other painter's audience. When I collaborate with Enrico Baj, I get his admirers looking at my work and he gets my fans looking at his.**

✦ What are your ideas about about composition?

✧ **No fancy cropping or clever hidden triangles. I like clarity and matter-of-factness. Many of my**

compositions end up containing classical triangular structures, but these find their way in by intuition. I try to balance and overlap circles, squares, and triangles in a dynamic way that emphasizes clarity and is subservient to the picture's overall intention.

✦ Did you learn this in art school?

✧ Most of my knowledge comes from experience and years of looking at art, but art school was very important. One important technique that I learned in art school was the value of using a clearly defined foreground, middle ground, and background. Monet capitalized on this abstract device in almost all of his paintings. There's a famous Monet called *La Grenouillère,* a painting of a popular boating and bathing resort with a café on a covered raft floating in the Seine. The main visual ingredients are water, boats, a dock, and people. Renoir made a painting of the same scene. The story goes that both artists painted at the same location at the same time, standing side by side. Although beautiful, the Renoir is compositionally uneventful while the Monet springs to life because he confidently

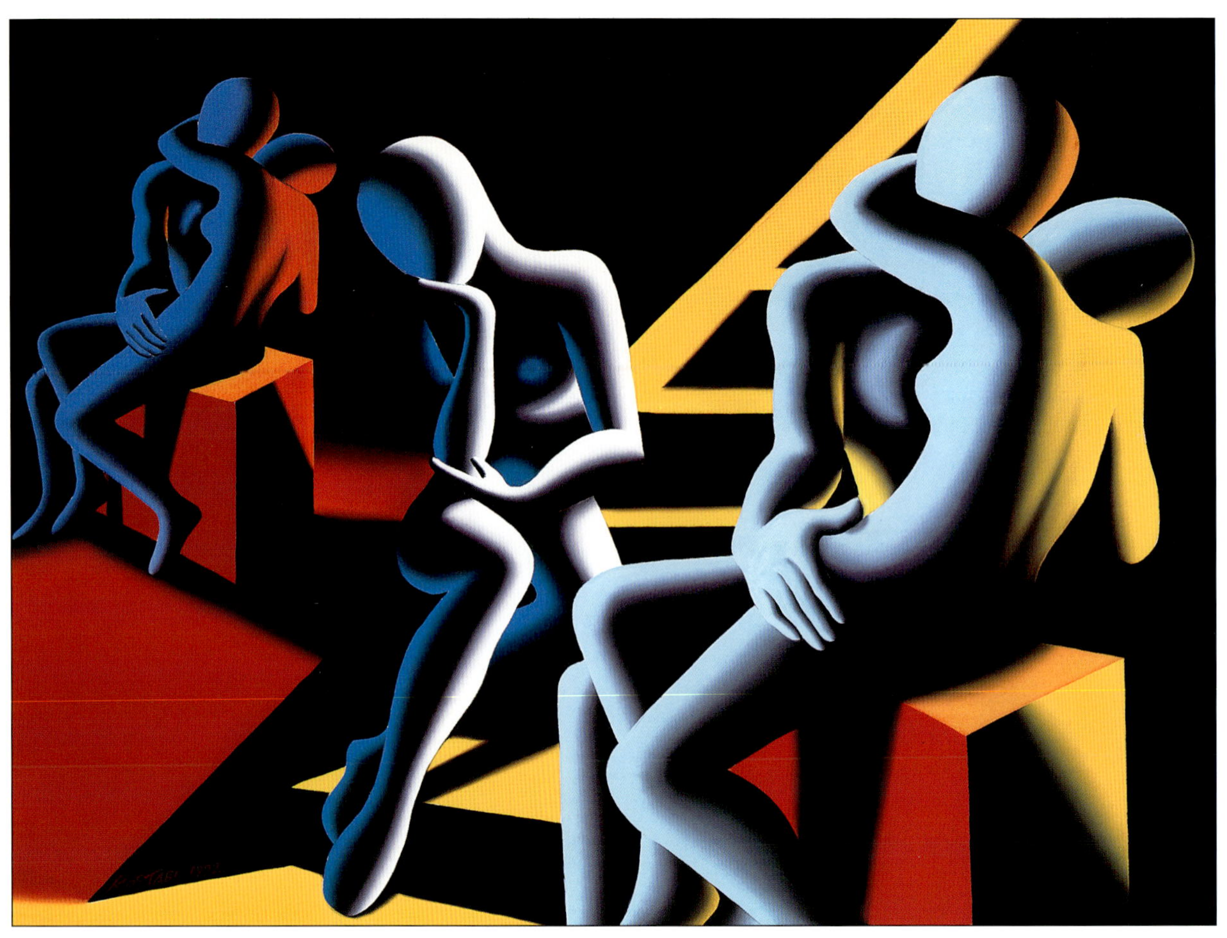

✧ **The Languor of Love**
1992
Oil on canvas
36 x 48 inches
Private collection

whipped reality into shape and made it obey his compositional rule of clearly defining foreground, middle ground, and background. It is said that nature never makes a bad composition, but sometimes it takes human nature to make it better. My painting *The Languor of Love* is a good example of foreground, middle ground, background clarity. Basically, for a Kostabi painting to be successful, the composition must be bold, clear, and no-nonsense. In other words, the whole head should be in the picture even though there's no eyes, nose, or mouth.

✦ How important is the title?

✧ Paramount. *Untitled* is a blatant sign of artistic lethargy. Contemporary artists who use it are admitting to laziness and a lack of imagination, blowing a major opportunity to add punch to their artistic statement, and creating an annoying inconvenience for their dealers, collectors, promoters, and archivists. If an untitled work of art is any good, the public eventually gives it a title (which the artist may not like) the same way the public has renamed several historical works. Rembrandt's

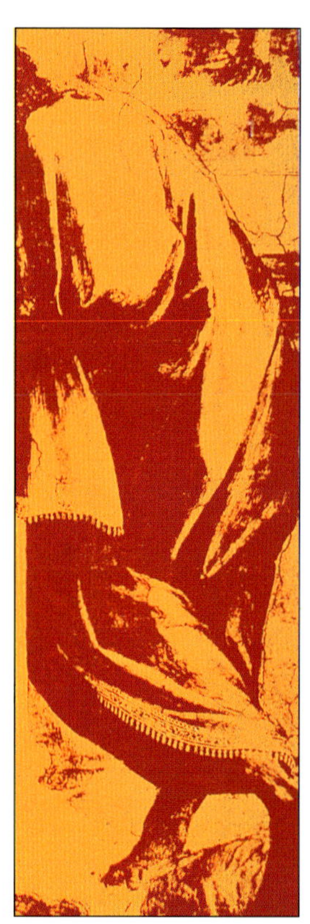

"Nightwatch," "Whistler's Mother," and the "Lipstick Building" come to mind. Modern cleaning has revealed that Rembrandt's "Nightwatch" wasn't even a night scene. But if you establish a title to begin with, you're less likely to end up with an inaccurate interpretation. Even a number is better than *Untitled*.

✦ How do you come up with your titles?

✧ **Originally I named them by looking at the finished painting. Usually the title just popped into my head. For many years I've used a titling person, the poet and translator Joachim Neugroschel. Art critic Robert Pincus-Witten titled about fifteen of my paintings, and film critic Eric Monder, who used to be my secretary, titled several in 1987. I've had several other guest titlers, random visitors whom I'd spontaneously enlist into our titling sessions. My brother, Paul, titled one of my most famous paintings, *Use Your Illusion*, which became an album cover for Guns N' Roses. But Joachim titled hundreds of paintings. Several great ones, like *The***

***Blossoming of Vulnerability*, *Secrets of the Psyche*, and *Upwardly Mobile*.**

✦ Titles are usually thought of as defining or giving meaning to a painting. What is the connection between your titles and the original ideas of your paintings?

✧ **Titling is a separate verbal art that complements the idea. An idea can be fully born and out of the womb before it's named. I'm like a parent who names a child after getting a good look at it.**

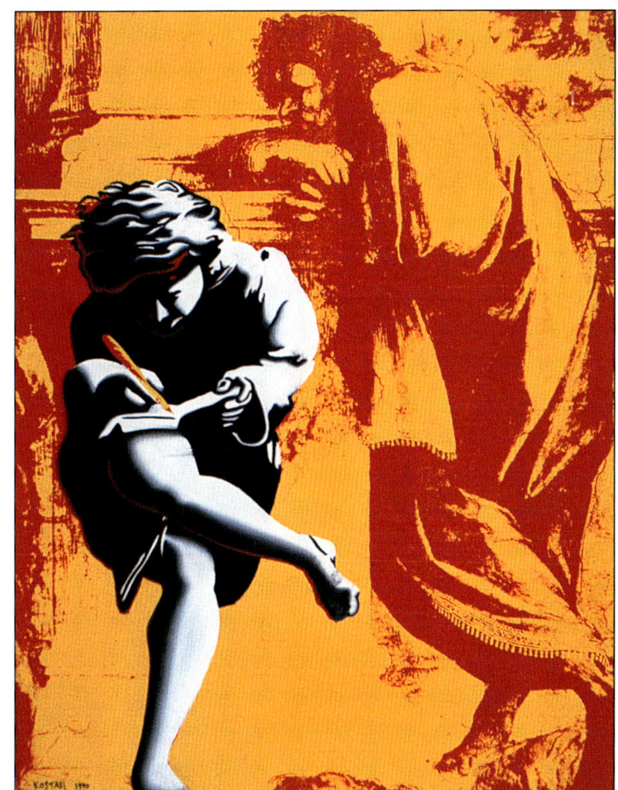

✧ **Use Your Illusion**
1990
Oil on canvas
48 x 36 inches
Collection of Axl Rose

✦ How do you find the right title?

✧ ***Find* is the key word. It's as if the perfect title for any painting already exists somewhere out there in the silent field of infinite possibilities. And it's just a matter of finding it. It's not a case of good titles versus bad titles, it's a matter of right and wrong. Some titles are definitely wrong while others are**

DO YOU

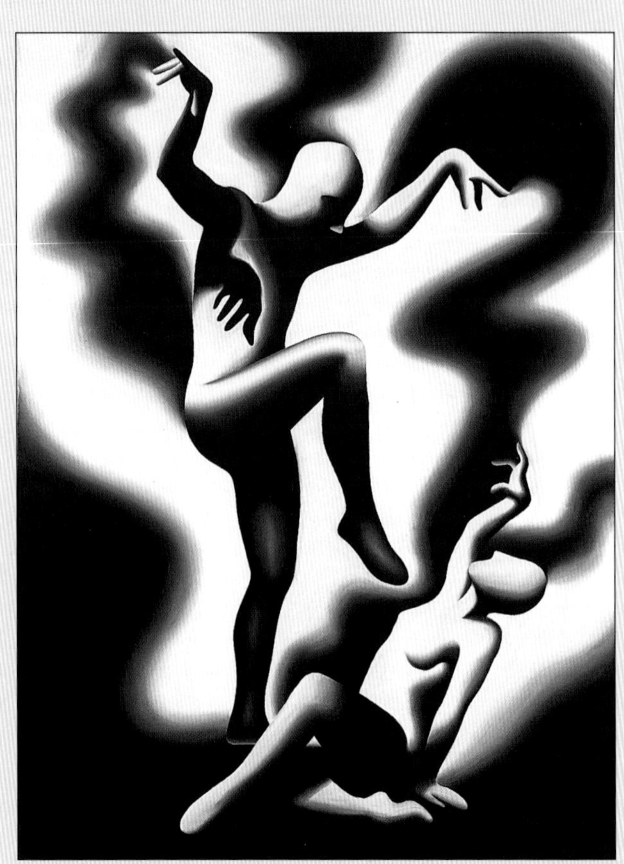

right. And some are more right than others. A title should add without giving away. It should evoke rather than describe. And it should be memorable. In the early 1980s most of my titles were either one word or a full sentence. After I started using other people to title paintings, I got in the habit of creating two-word titles, which now dominate my oeuvre. This is probably the influence of Hollywood movie titles like *Indecent Exposure*, *Midnight Cowboy*, *Being There*, and *Batman Forever*. Hollywood loves two-word titles. Often I test the quality of a title by asking myself, "Would I go to see a movie with that title?" And so I've ended up with two-word titles like *Blue Oblivion*, *Useless*

***Knowledge*, *Above Cologne*, *Greenwich Avenue*, and *Enough Already*.**

✦ Do you ever change titles?

✧ **Yes. Sometimes even after the work has been published in a book or magazine. I'm constantly improving. In the mid-eighties critics praised my titles because they wickedly called attention to my persona. Titles like *Paintings Are Doorways into Collectors' Homes*, *The Merely Rich Buy Art—the Truly Rich Buy Artists*, *Take the "L" out of Play,* and *Say Less and Say Yes*. They were really just quotable Kostabisms worthy of publication but arbitrarily attached to paintings. Later I gave these paintings more appropriate titles that enhanced the work. And I put the Kostabisms on signs that hang in Kostabi World.**

✦ How important is irony in your paintings?

✧ **Irony in late-twentieth-century art is like gold was in previous centuries. The more gold in a painting, the more money it was worth. Today the more irony in a painting, the more it's worth in intellectual currency.**

✧ page 112:
The Blossoming of Vulnerability
1987
Oil on canvas
84 x 60 inches
Ronald Feldman Fine Arts, New York

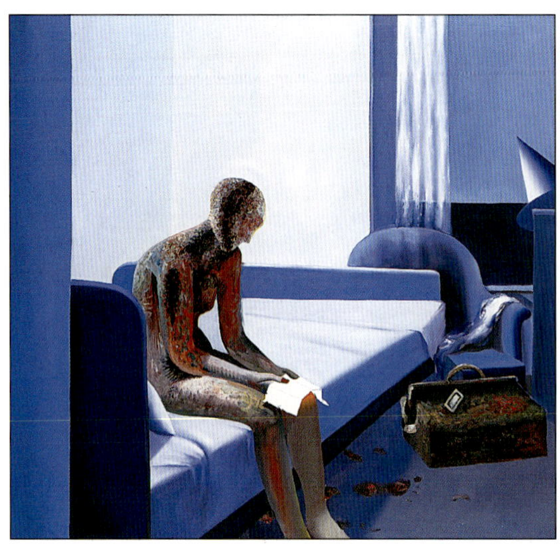

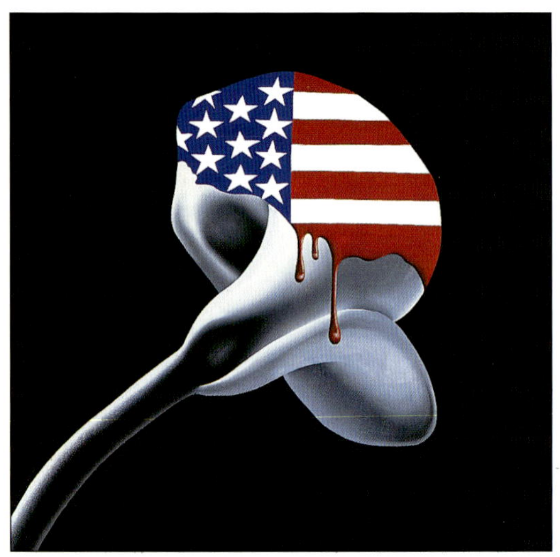

✧ left:
Blue Oblivion
1991
Oil on canvas
60 x 64 inches
Collection of Ray Medieres

✧ right:
Enough Already
1989
Oil on canvas
48 x 48 inches
Collection of John B. Koegel

✦ What's your definition of irony?

✧ **Irony is the incongruity between the actual result of a sequence of events and the normal or expected result.**

✦ What are some examples of irony in your paintings?

✧ **The facelessness in general is ironic. With all our technology and accumulation of rich cultural history, we live in a world fearing individual identity. So we join a herd and wear identical costumes, be it punk, Wall Street, designer, preppy, grunge, whatever. It's all an effort to be comfortably faceless. In**

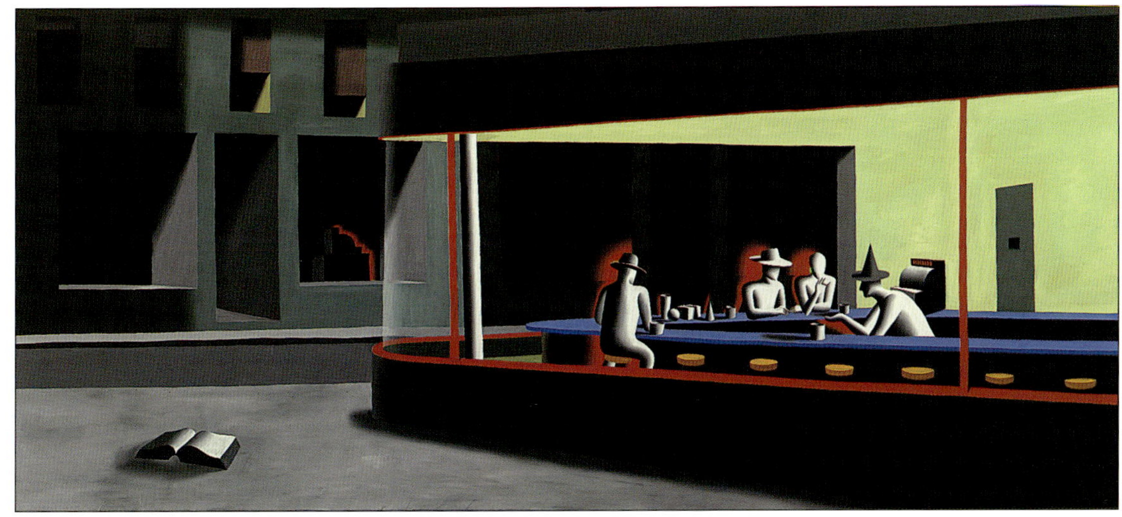

✧ **Greenwich Avenue**
1986
Oil on canvas
7.5 x 17 feet
Collection of Rodney Sheldon

my restaurant scenes like *Culinary Chaos*, the cooks in the kitchen prepare food and serve it up but no one has a mouth. No one has the means or time to devour all the information and culture we buy. Who really reads the *New York Times* cover to cover? It would take all day. And the Sunday paper would take all week. Most of it gets thrown out, unread. Who reads all the books on their shelves? Who wears all the clothes in their closet? We have the technology and raw material to cook more than enough food for the whole world. And it gets

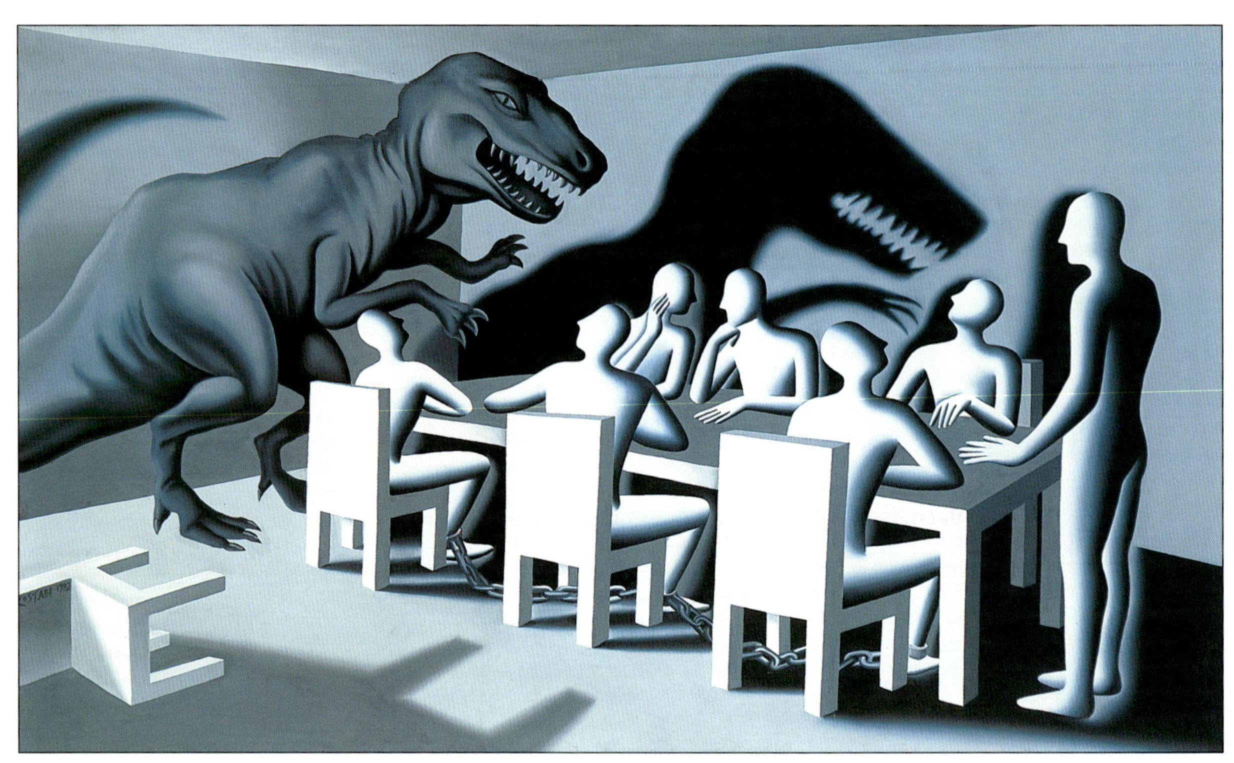

✧ **Extinction**
1989
Oil on canvas
54 x 90 inches
Kostabi World

cooked. But a third of it never gets to anyone's mouth. Why? Because there are no mouths. We are Kostabi figures. We embrace a singular emptiness. Our power is like that of a lightning bolt that enters the earth, immense power dissipated in an instant. We steal only from ourselves. Our Buddha contemplates the unplugged appliance. We drink from empty goblets. The umbrellas are open but no rain falls. People watch TV, but the screen is blank. The world in my paintings is comfortable and familiar, but we have no place in it. It is our world, but we are not there.

✦ Could you talk a little about your painting *Extinction*?

✧ **Yes. A dinosaur has replaced the Chairman of a faceless Board. Primitive and powerful, a perfect leader for the modern-day corporate giant.**

✦ And now we come to the signature. You sign all your paintings, don't you?

✧ **Yes, and my hand is tired. It's an absurd activity. Talk about irony. It's very ironic that the founder of a successful art studio is reduced to signing his name over and over again, day in and day out.**

Paintings, prints, drawings, contracts, autographs, and checks. It's a primitive system of authentication that will eventually be obsolete, but it's the only system we have right now, so I play the game.

✦ But you don't have to sign your paintings on the front. Most major contemporary artists don't. They believe the signature is the ego visually interfering with the integrity of the art.

✧ I don't buy that at all. If they have so much selfless integrity by not signing the front of their paintings, they lose it all by boldly signing their prints and drawings on the front. It's conceptually incorrect. Sloppy thinking. And when they get arrogant and condescending toward artists who sign their paintings on the front, it becomes embarrassing. How ironic that art by definition is associated with creativity, freedom, and individuality, and yet artists play by so many art world rules in order to be taken seriously. Don't sign your paintings on the front. Don't talk openly about money (unless it's cleverly cloaked in theoretical jargon). Don't be seen talking to anyone outside your clique. I figure if Picasso and Duchamp could sign their paintings

on the front, then why can't I? Vermeer was an art dealer. And Duchamp maintained his friendship with Dali even though the bully critic André Breton threatened to excommunicate any surrealist who associated with Dali. Duchamp's historical stature wasn't harmed. Also, I personally enjoy seeing signatures on masterpieces in museums. It's another artistic challenge. Where to put it? How big? What color to use? It's informative. It's part of the art game. People like it. Why fight it?

✦ But don't you think some people buy your work for the signature alone? Because you are a brand name?

I do all the signatures myself. I put a lot of care and effort into each letter. If someone wants to pay me ten thousand dollars for my signature alone, I'd be happy to oblige them.

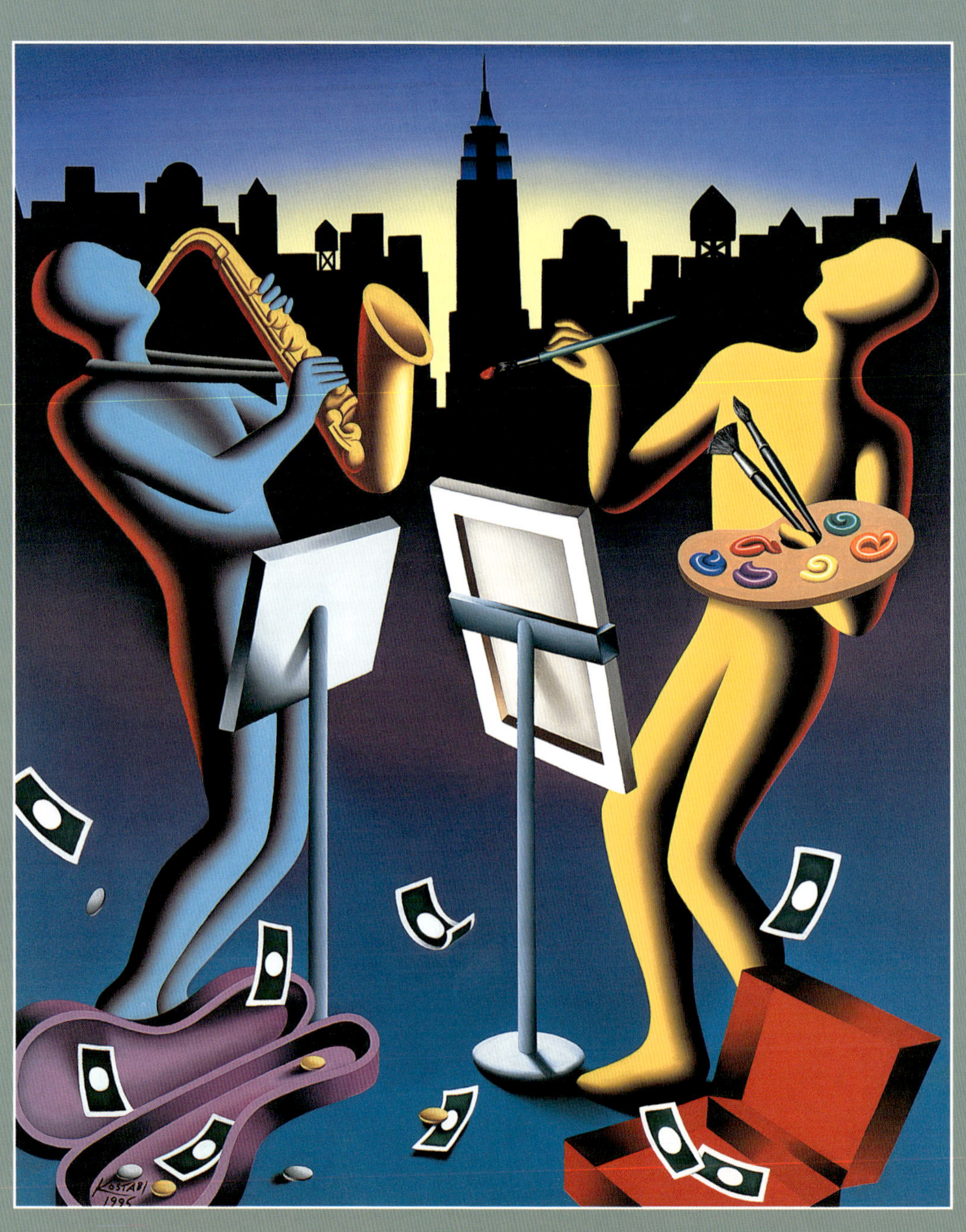
KOSTABI
1995

CHAPTER ✧ FIVE

RECURRING THEMES

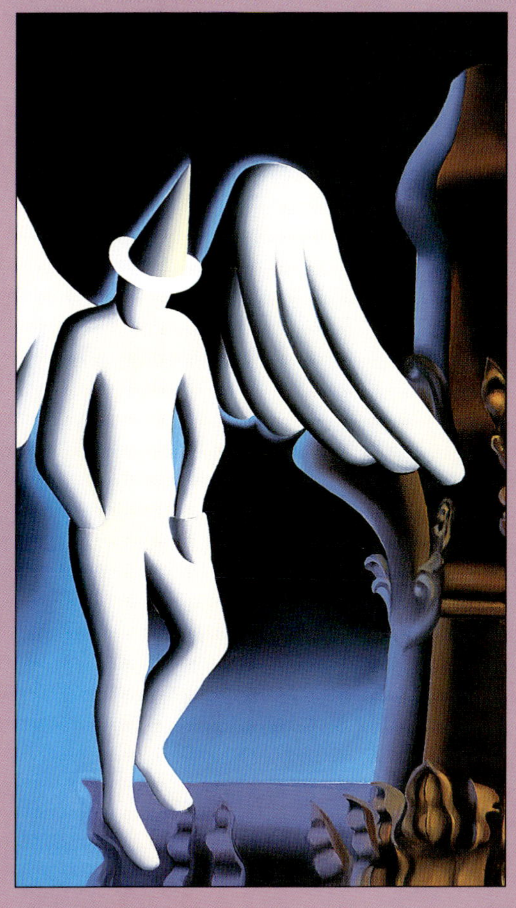

✦ Why do you paint images of loneliness?

✧ **I like the beauty of loneliness. A lonely person is a vulnerable, melancholy creature waiting to be touched by another, as in the painting *Upwardly Mobile*.**

Above Cologne depicts a lonely angel trying to find his place in the material world. He adopts the body language of mortal loneliness. Head down, hands in pockets, he tries to make contact with ornate architecture, a beautiful artifact of materialism, rather than the spirit that created it. His feet try to stand on the monument but they never truly connect. _The Creative Process_ shows a lonely artist sitting at the drawing board, wearily creating figures who suddenly come to life and leap off the paper. But instead of having created his dream

✧ page 120:
For Love or Money
1995
Oil on canvas
54 x 44 inches
Collection of Emanuele Dibbia

✧ page 123:
Above Cologne
1991
Oil on canvas
50 x 50 inches
Kostabi World

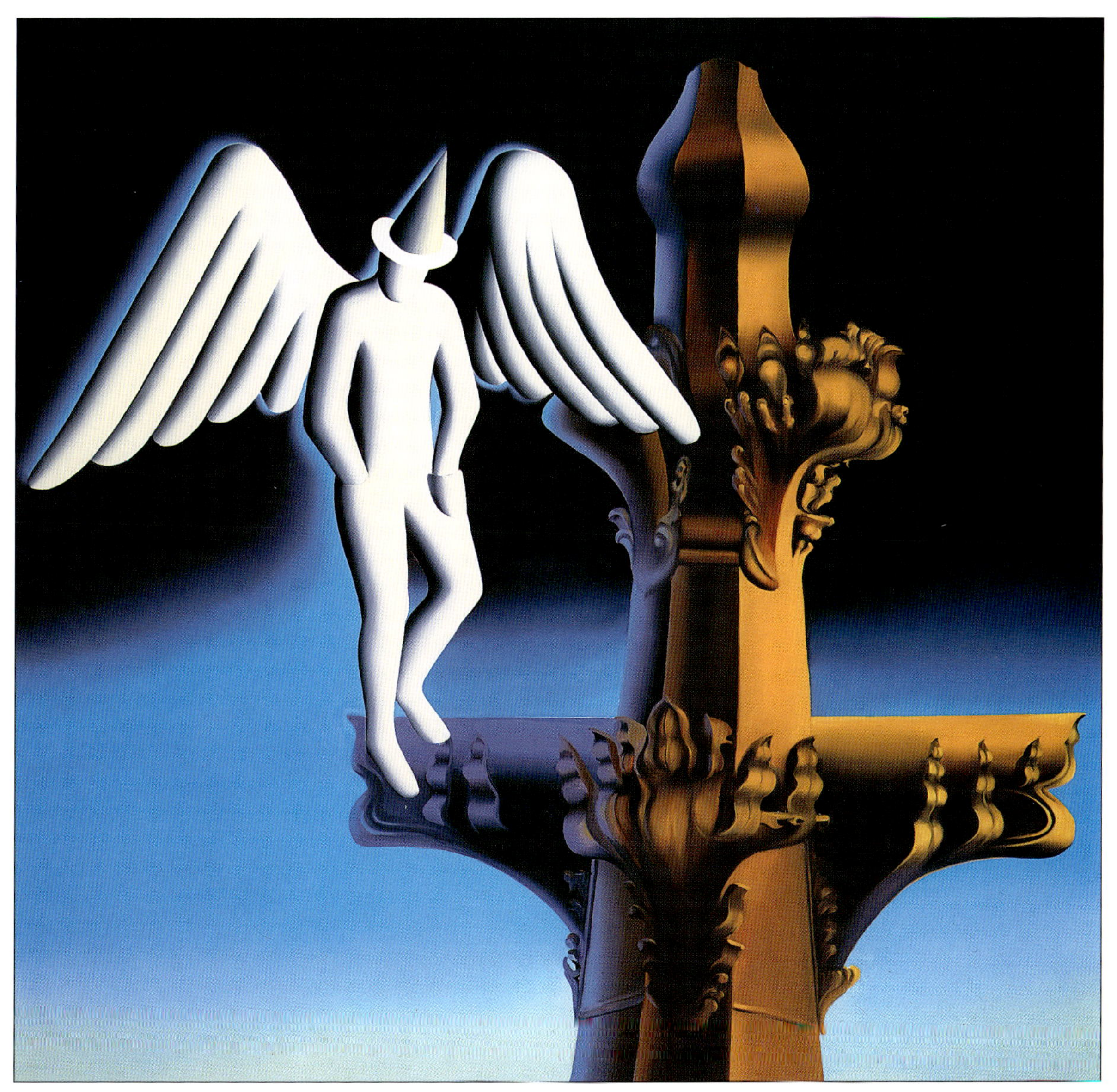

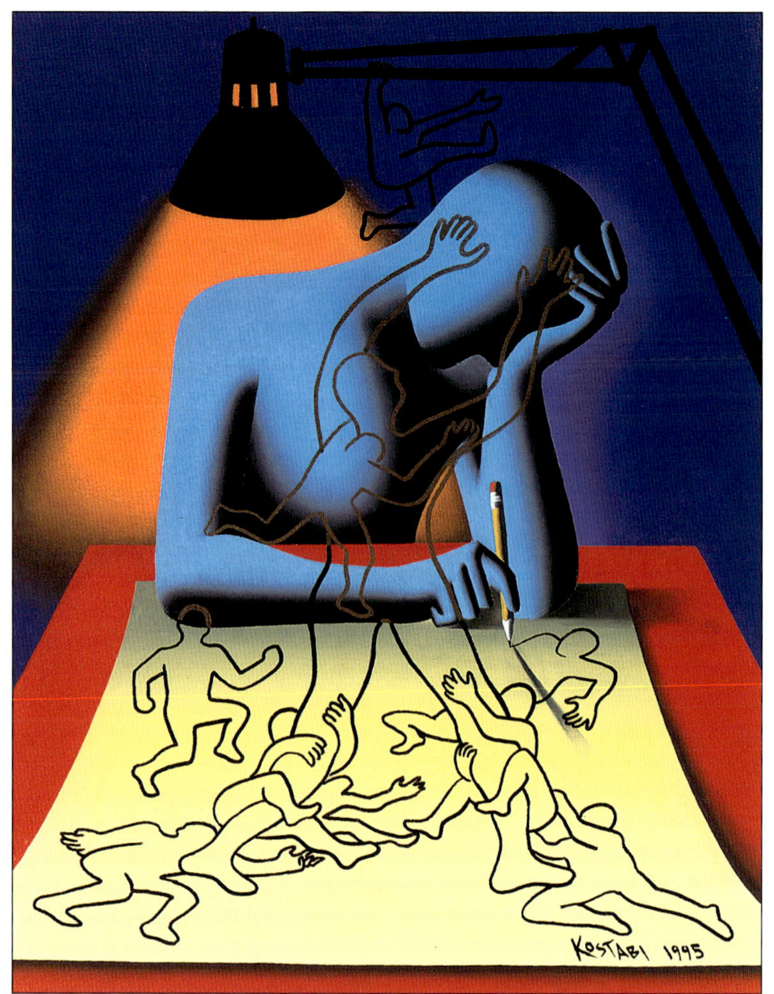

✧ **The Creative Process**
1995
oil & paint marker
on canvas
24 x 18 inches
Collection of Kristi and Wayne Schweizer

woman, as in *Pygmalion and Galatea* by Jean Léon Gérôme, this twentieth-century slave draws his nightmare of domestic anarchy: a dysfunctional family, with needy children frantically clinging to a desperate mother who reaches out for help from the artist as he compulsively creates more chaos.

✦ Many of your paintings are inspired by Edward Hopper, who is also known for depicting twentieth-century loneliness.

✧ I admire Hopper's achievement of perfectly capturing the bleak beauty of mid-twentieth-century American alienation. In some ways things have gotten worse, and depending on how you look at it, even more beautiful. I believe my work, with its facelessness and extreme architectural minimalism, takes Hopper one step further. When I deal with Vermeer, I deal with the mythology of value that surrounds Vermeer's work. When I deal with Hopper, I feel genuine artistic kinship. A continuum. I believe he would approve. I subtract in order to add.

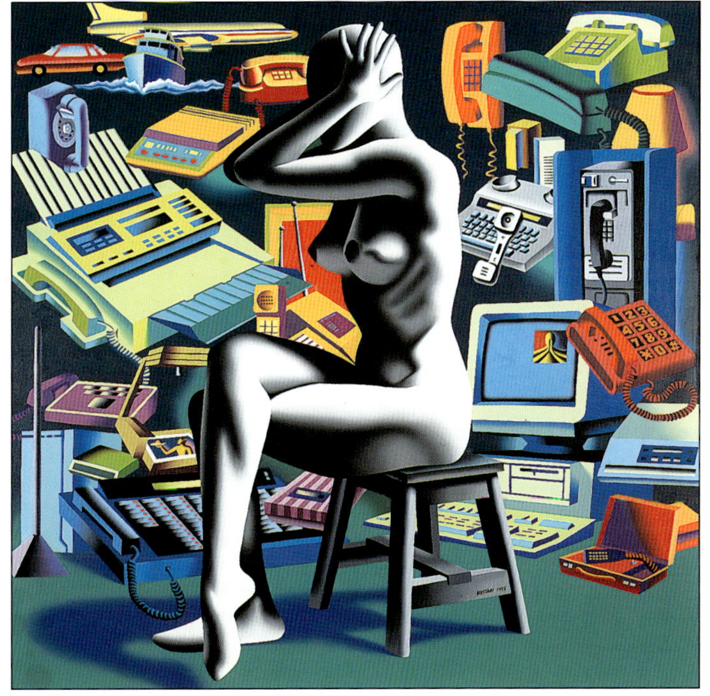

✧ **The Information Age**
1995
Oil on canvas
84 x 84 inches
Kostabi World

MY OWN SC

✦ In *The Information Age* you seem to be blaming technology for the anguish and alienation that the nude female is experiencing.

✧ **She's a metaphor for Mother Nature. Modern technology and attitudes about physical perfection have forced her into a kaleidoscope of communication that she can't take anymore.**

Too much technology is driving people crazy. Just when you think you've caught up and bought the latest video camera, the latest cellular phone, the latest computer, it's been replaced by something more advanced. Many of my paintings are a reflection of society's love-hate relationship with technology. It's on everyone's mind. For instance, I was riding uptown and a cabdriver suggested that I do a painting of two people making love while wearing headphones plugged into the same Walkman radio. So I painted *Lovers*.

✦ An interesting interpretation of technology and alienation.

✧ **I just did what the cabdriver told me to do.**

✦ Do you use computers to help you create?

✧ **No. Computers have been around for several**

ENE GOING

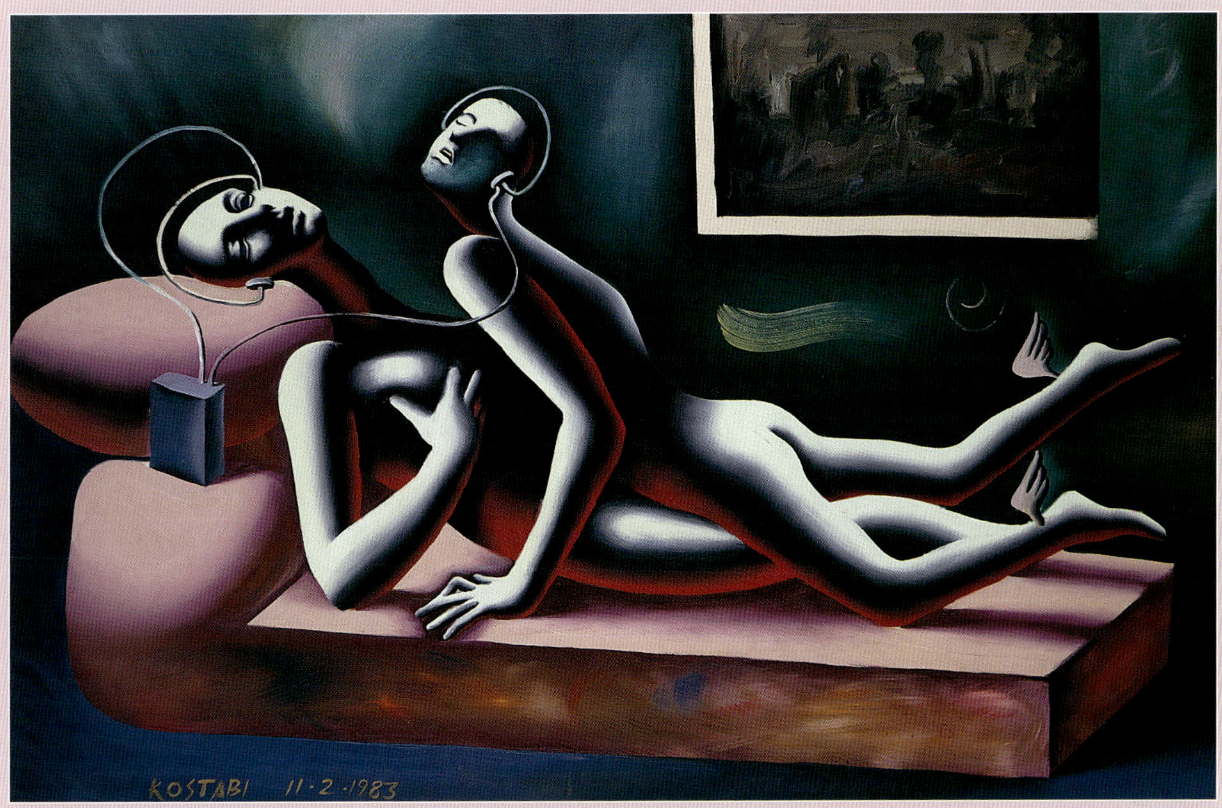

✧ **Lovers**
1983
Oil on canvas
48 x 72 inches
Marrs Gallery, Tokyo

decades now and I have yet to see a single piece of computer art that has knocked me out. I can see using computers to crank out multiple color variations of a sketch, but the finished painting would still be executed by a human. In art, humans are still the best computers.

✦ The world of business has been a recurring theme in your work, starting with your early drawings in 1979. What was the impetus for a nineteen-year-old to do sketches that parodied corporate board meetings?

✧ I was flipping through the pages of an encyclopedia and I found an illustration of a conference room. I thought it looked cool. I remembered hearing grown-ups complain about the absurdity and tedious bureaucracy of the corporate world. Of course, I hadn't made that direct observation myself, but I liked the idea of poking fun at the adult world. So I copied the drawing from the encyclopedia and added my own faceless humanoids. The first one I did shows a headless Board of Directors, and a Chairman of the Board carrying their heads in his arms. In a sequel, I sketched the Chairman

tossing heads out to the Board members. Another sequel has the Chairman again throwing heads, but no one's trying to catch them. When the grown-ups saw them, they said things like, "Wow! You're a genius! That's exactly what it's like! How do you have so much insight at such a young age?"

✦ And you were just interpreting what you overheard.

✧ **I didn't think it was a big deal. I mean, I knew**

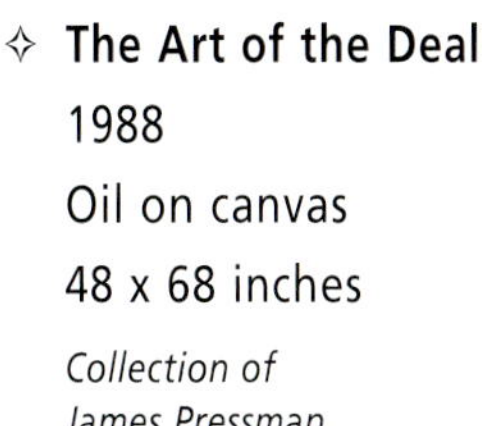

✧ **The Art of the Deal**
1988
Oil on canvas
48 x 68 inches
Collection of James Pressman

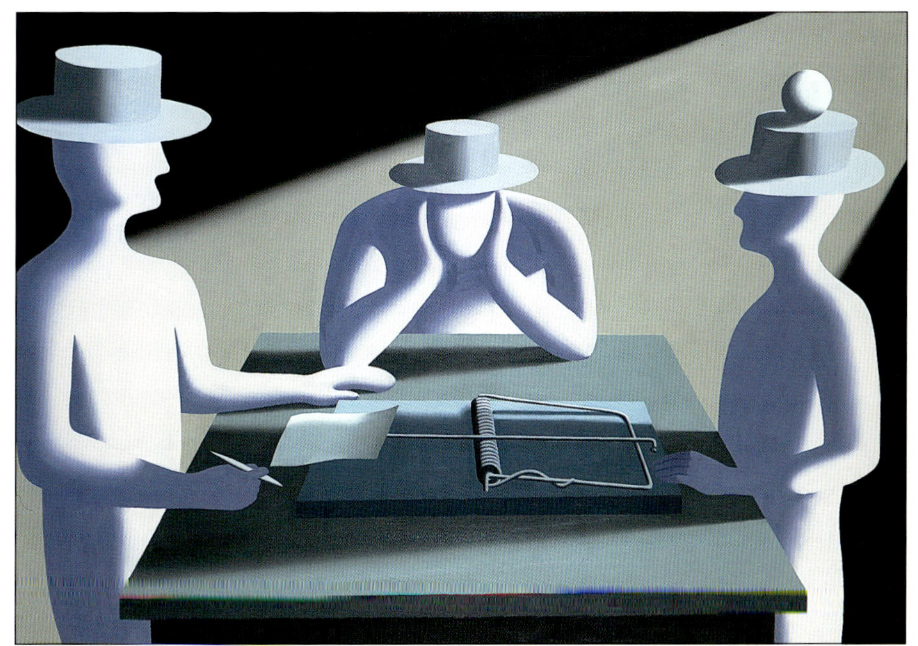

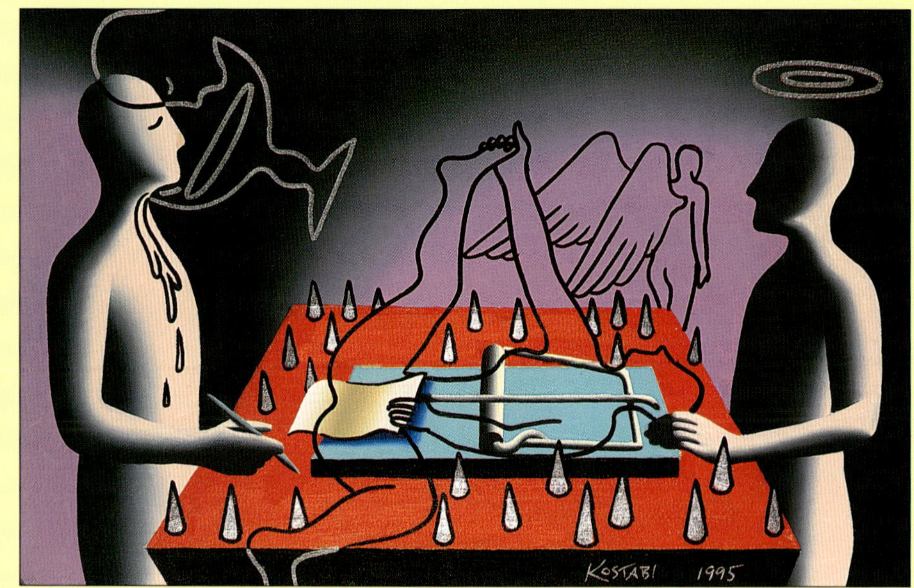

✧ **The Art of the Deal (Body or Soul)**
1995
Oil on canvas
16 x 24 inches
Private collection

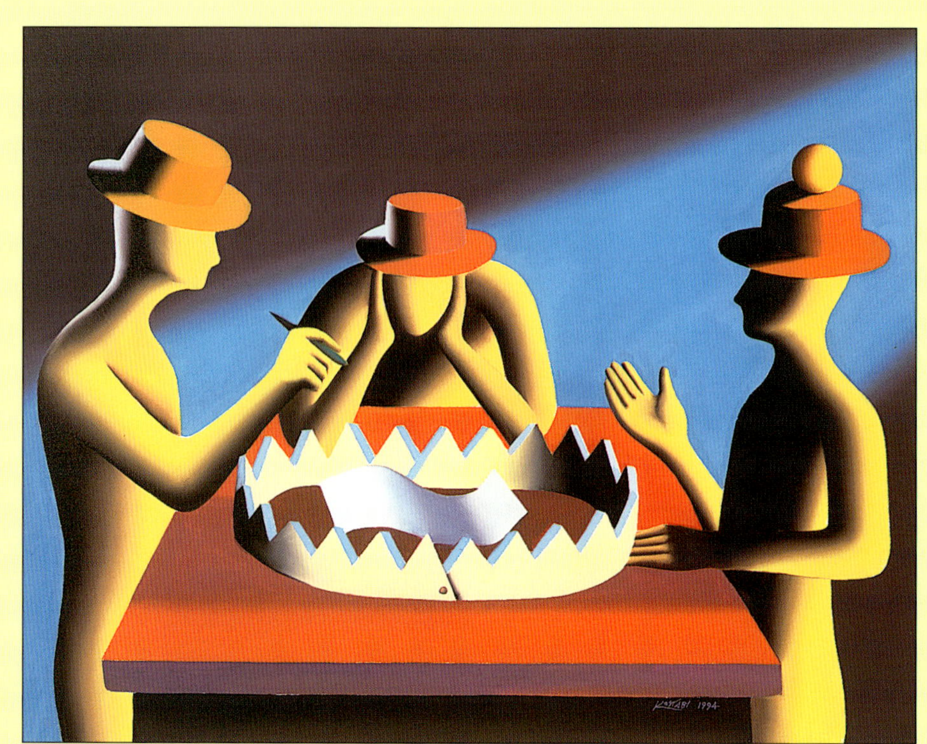

✧ **The Art of the Deal (Queen's Gambit Accepted)**
1994
Oil on canvas
24 x 30 inches
Private collection

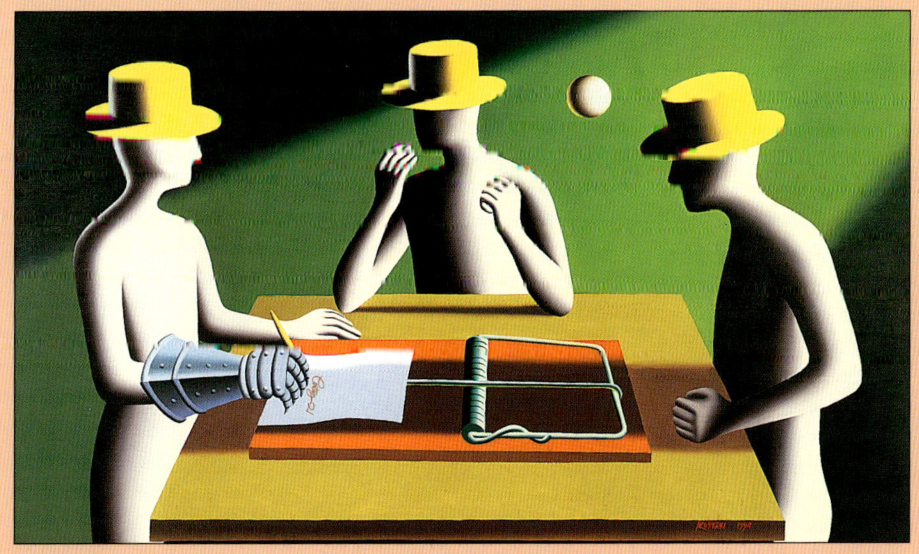

✧ **The Art of the Deal (Robatsch Defense)**
1994
Oil on canvas
18 x 24 inches
Collection of Raymond Gindi

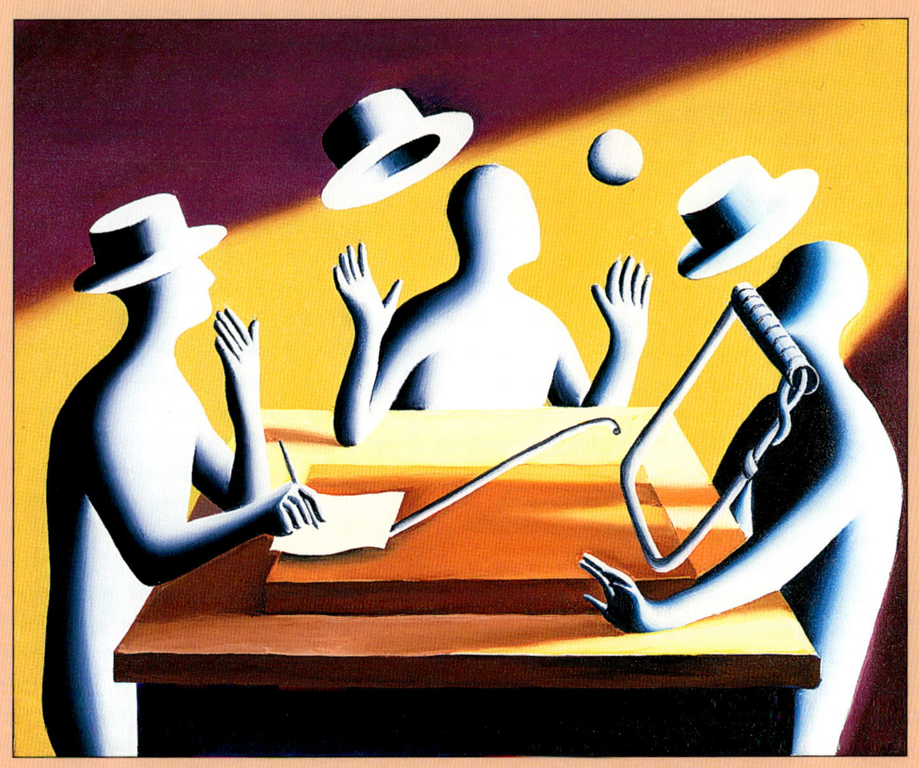

✧ **The Art of the Deal (Upset)**
c. 1992
Oil on canvas
48 x 68 inches
Private collection

✧ **First, Last, and Security**

1988

Oil on canvas

69 x 84 inches

Private collection

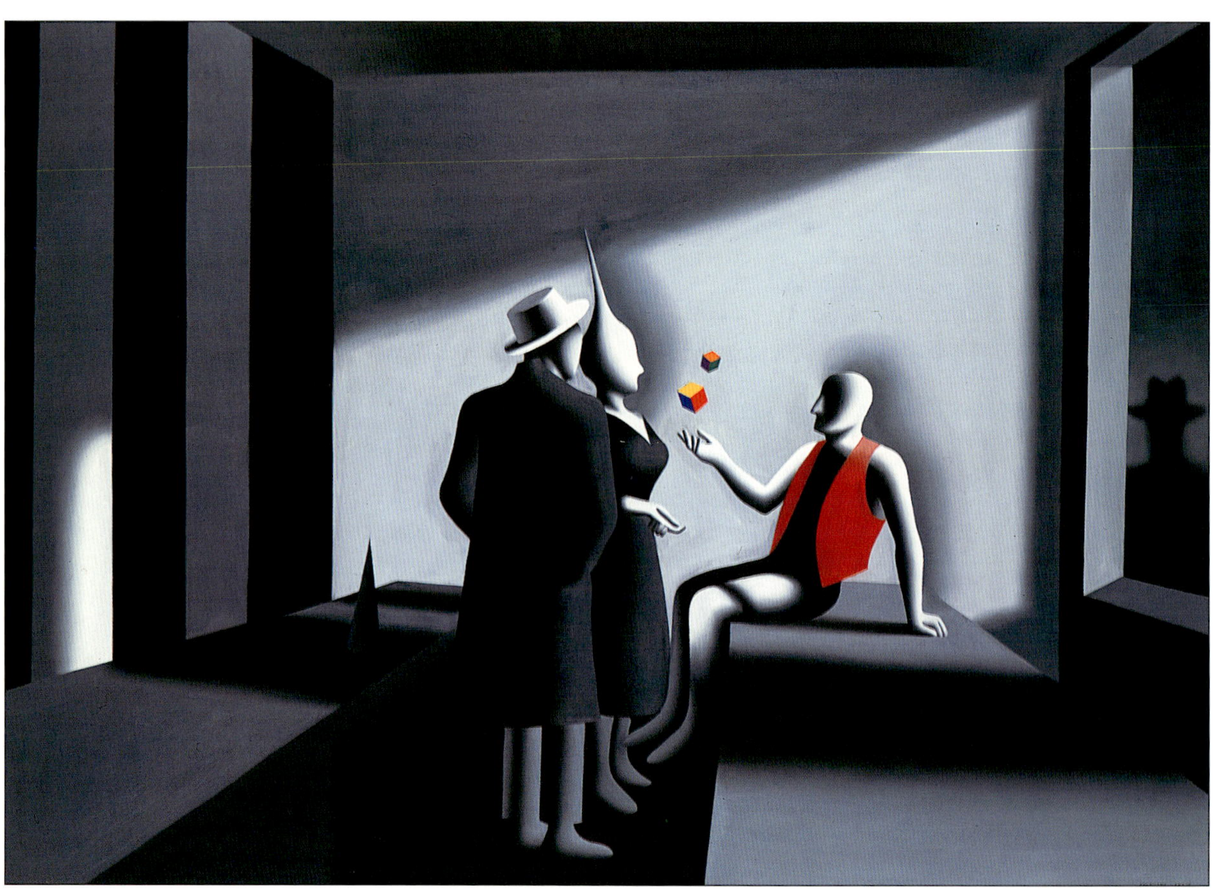

they were good drawings. I just didn't think that making fun of business in a clever way constituted genius. But I didn't complain. I kept making more. They turned out to be my entrée to the art world. My first dealer, Molly Barnes, sold those drawings to movie producers in Hollywood. Then I was commissioned to design the menu for Ma Maison, which was Hollywood's "in" place for power lunches. Before me, David Hockney had been the menu designer. Hockney is an artist whose success helped fuel my own ambition.

✦ You've done several paintings that reflect your personal experiences in the business world.

✧ **I've been ripped off by dealers and I've always been reluctant to sign exclusive deals, so my *Art of the Deal* series probably reflects my own personal anxiety about signing contracts. I've moved seven times since coming to live in New York, so my painting, *First, Last, and Security*, which is based on Edward Hopper's *Conference at Night*, is an acknowledgment of those seven real estate deals.**

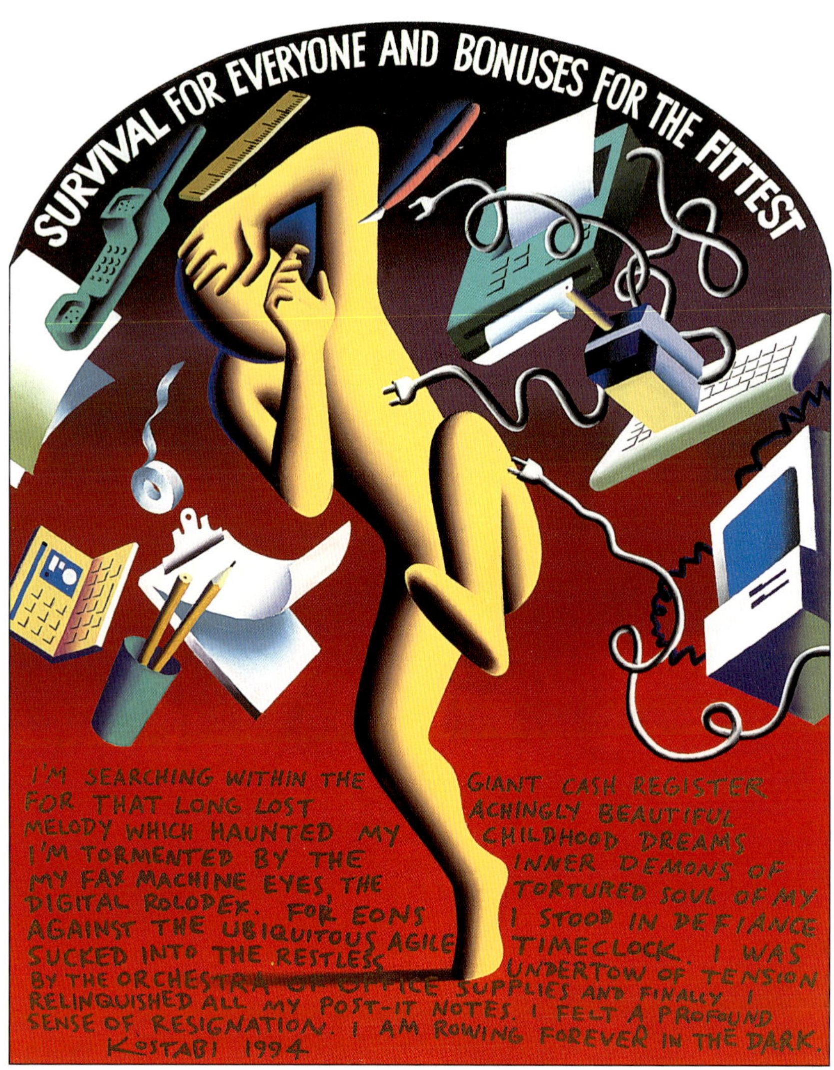

✧ **Office Deluge**
1994
Oil on canvas
28 x 22 inches
Kostabi World

✦ What about your painting *Office Deluge?* It shows a figure overwhelmed by a rain of office supplies: pens, Post-it notes, a fax machine . . . You've been accused of being a phony artist, in reality just a businessman. Is that painting a personal statement about your frustration at being principally involved in the business end of the art world?

✧ **No. It's a parody of phony spirituality as well as a parody of those who replace spirituality with business and technology. Some people are so consumed by business that it becomes a spiritual thing. And others are so consumed by spirituality that it becomes a business thing. With regard to your comment about my being more businessman than artist, that's factually inaccurate. I spend 10 percent of my time doing business and 90 percent of my time creating art. That's probably the same ratio as most successful artists. I just choose not to hide my 10 percent.**

✦ Is it significant that *Office Deluge* has text? That's rare for your work, isn't it?

✧ **I was asked to make an emblem painting for a show at Yale University, where a group of** contemporary artists were asked to re-interpret the ancient tradition of the emblem. Emblems usually combine words with imagery. I wrote, "I'm searching within the giant cash register for that long-lost achingly beautiful melody which haunted my childhood dreams. I'm tormented by the inner dreams of my fax machine eyes, the tortured soul of my digital Rolodex. For eons I stood in defiance against the ubiquitous, agile time clock. I was sucked into the restless undertow of tension by the orchestra of office supplies, and finally I relinquished all my Post-it notes. I felt a profound sense of resignation. I am rowing forever in the dark."

I got most of the Tortured Soul verbiage from a music lecture I attended at the 92nd Street Y. I love it when people earnestly use that kind of over-the-top language. While at the lecture I copied down all the key buzzwords and later wove them in with business iconography instead of historical music anecdotes.

✦ What about your business-related painting called *Secrets of the Psyche (Currency)*?

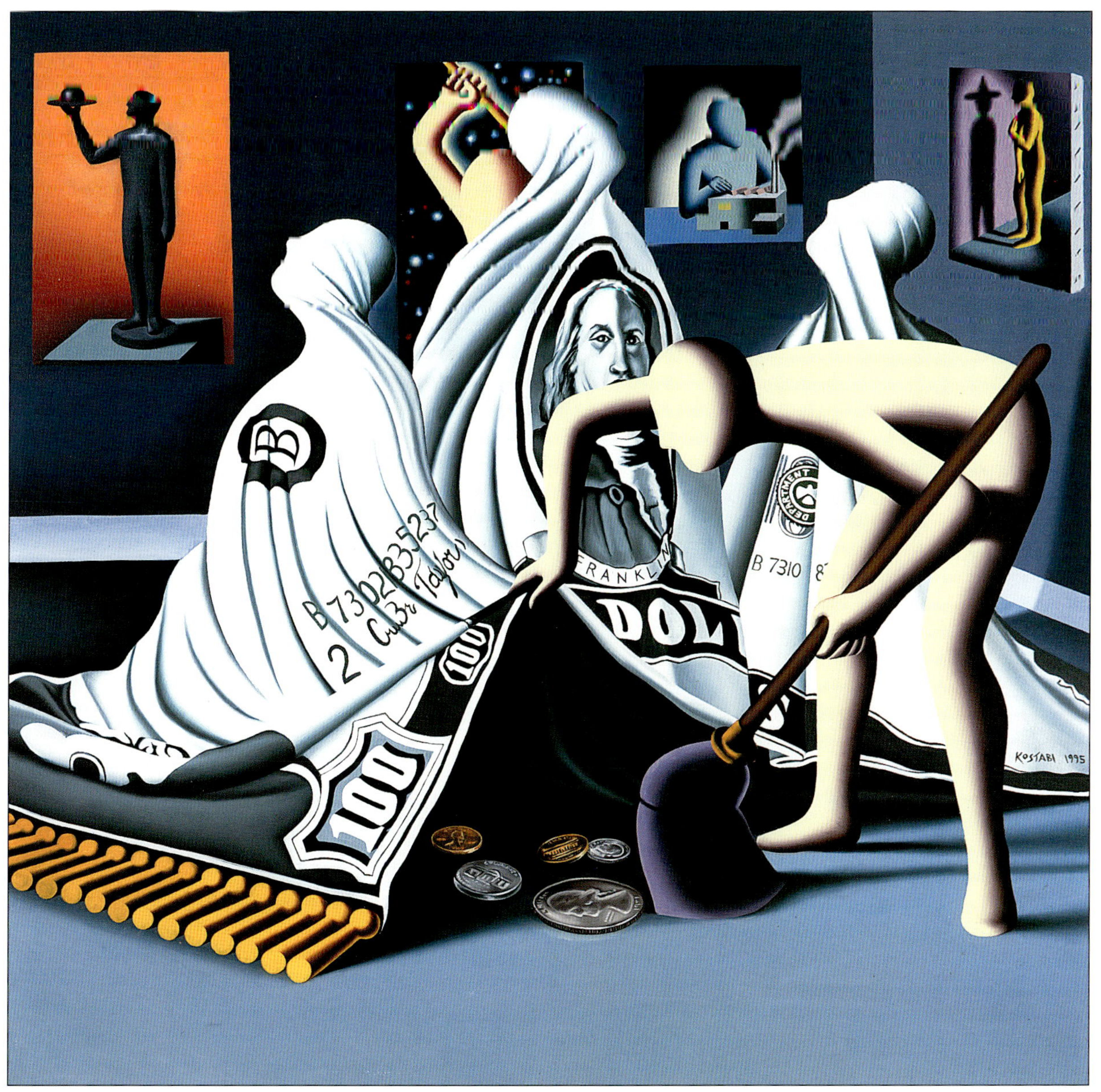

✧ **Secrets of the Psyche (Currency II)**

1995

Oil on canvas

48 x 48 inches

Private collection

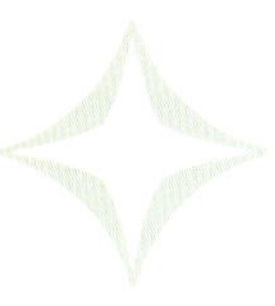

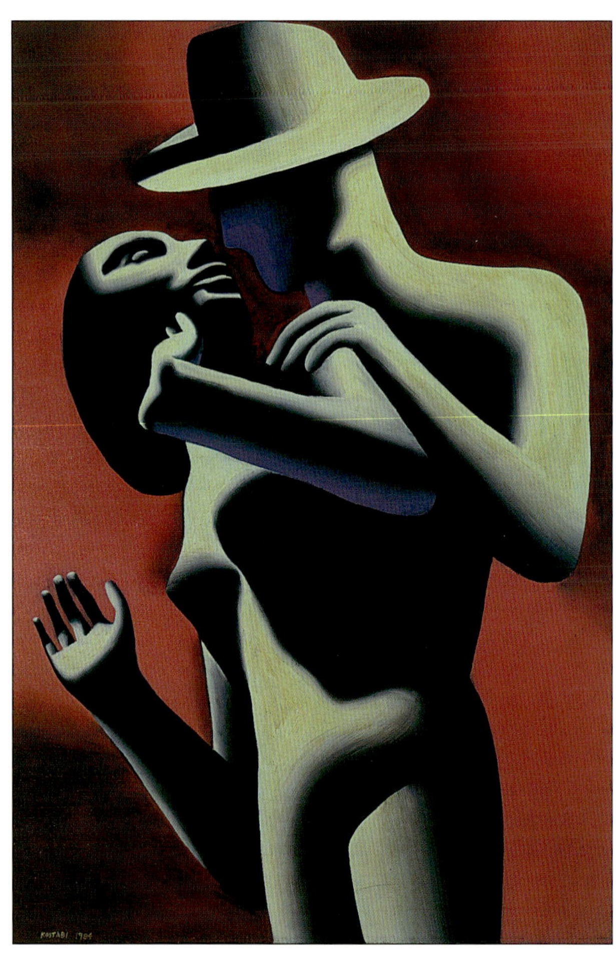

✧ I Go for a Man with an Adam Hat
1984
Oil on canvas
74 x 48 inches
Alpha Cubic Corporation

✧ **It's a more complex and ambitious version of a 1993 painting with the same title, which was stolen from the Kostabi World Gallery in 1994. The fact that it was stolen drove me to make the larger, better version. The original was painted by Yuriy Tenman, second-place winner in a painting contest that I held. Yuriy came up with the idea of sweeping coins underneath the money rug. Money beneath money. (Jennifer Tull executed the new version reproduced here. I frequently ask Jennifer to make new and improved versions of existing paintings.) It shows a materialistic society hopelessly trying to conceal its obsession with money in the trappings of culture. The setting is Kostabi World.**

✦ Assembly-line art is one of your recurring themes.

✧ **Basically I'm illustrating my own mythology. Gauguin moved to Tahiti and his paintings, while great works of art in themselves, also function as illustrations of his mythology. My creation of Kostabi World is like Gauguin's move to Tahiti, or like Van Gogh's cutting off his ear. A self-portrait of Van Gogh with a bandage on his ear has additional value because it illustrates his mythology.**

✦ Is your mythology the creation of repetitious assembly-line art?

✧ **To use the word "repetitious" as a pejorative adjective is to ignore major contributions by Warhol and other important twentieth-century artists. Repetition is a hallmark of modernism. Repetition is to the twentieth-century artist what perspective was to the Renaissance artist.**

✦ Do you have any personal feelings about assembly-line art?

✧ **I love the idea of industry. My painting *The World According to Mark* is an expression of pure joy. Kostabi World is my favorite place.**

✦ Romance has been a recurring theme in your work, going back to paintings like *Lovers*, *I Go for a Man with an Adam Hat*, *The Blossoming of Vulnerability*, and more recently in paintings

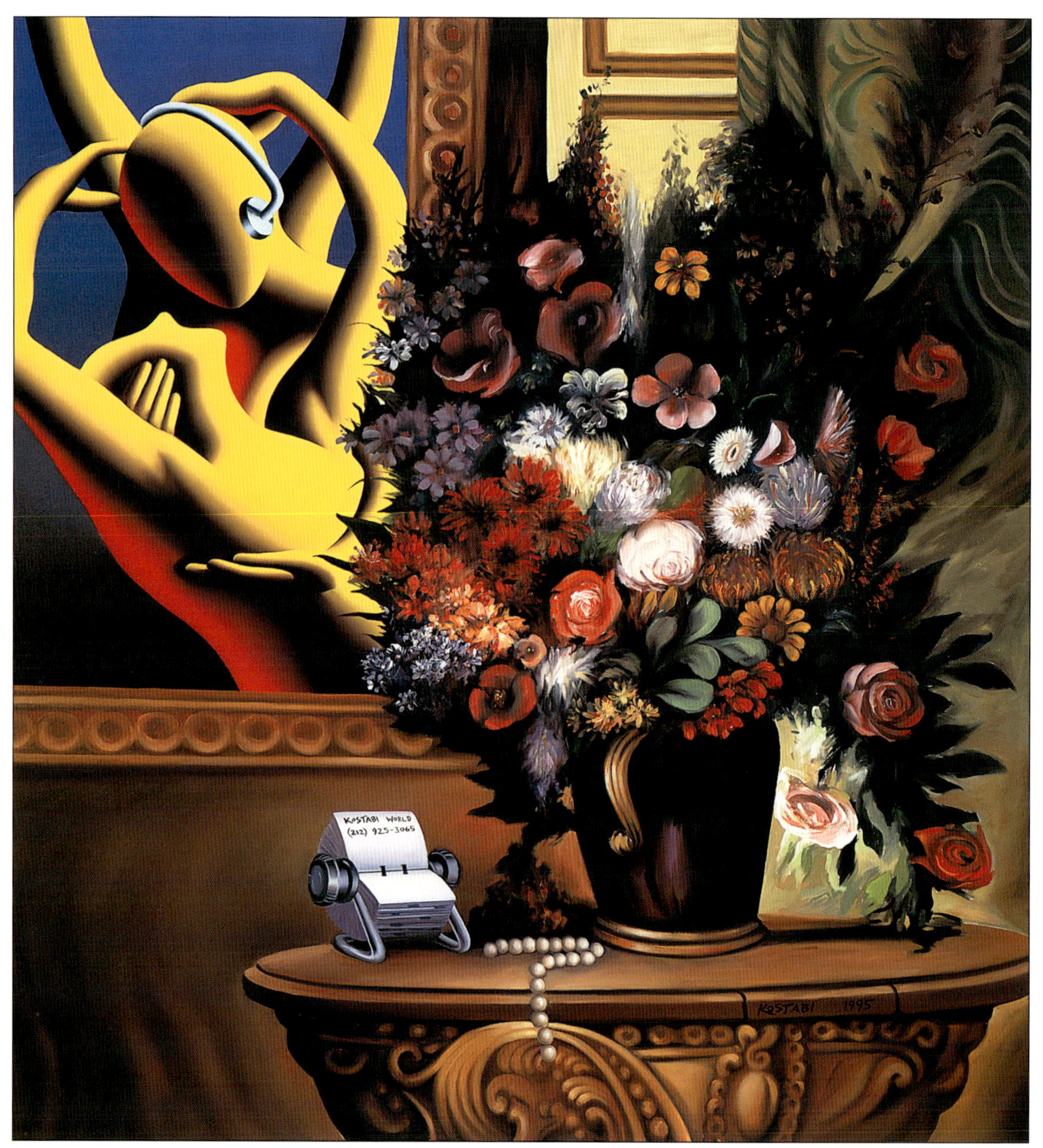
KOSTABI WORLD
(212) 925-3065
KOSTABI 1995

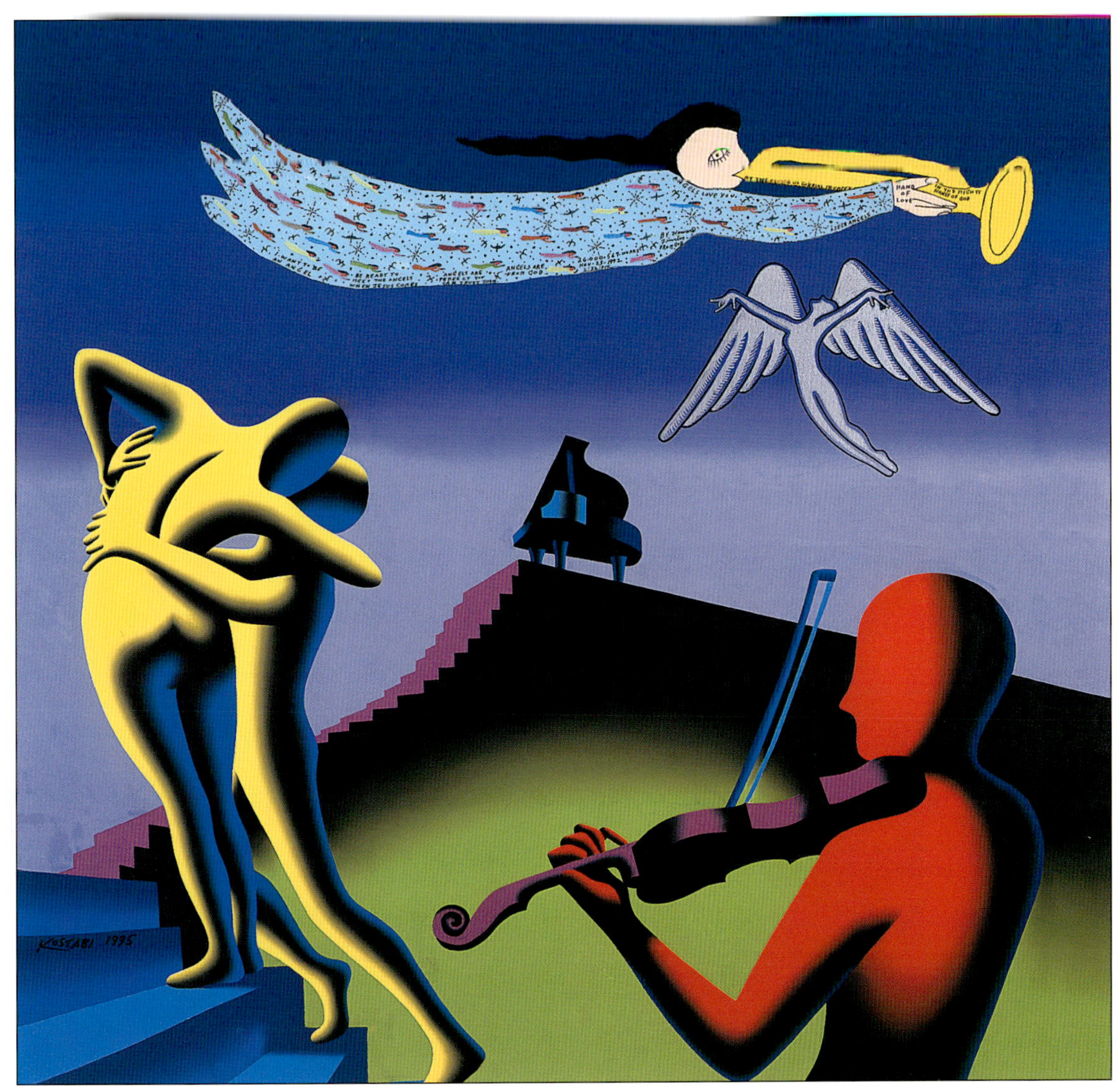

✧ page 140:
A Perfect World
1995
Oil on canvas
66 x 60 inches
Collection of Daniele Bevacqua

✧ *Collaboration with Howard Finster*
The Ascendence of Love
1995
Oil on canvas
64 x 64 inches
Collection of Anton Dorner

like *The Languor of Love*, *A Perfect World*, and your recent collaboration with Howard Finster, *The Ascendence of Love*. Is romance for you just another aisle in the department store of culture, something you churn out, the way pop musicians routinely churn out love songs?

✧ **No. I genuinely believe that love is the highest possible state of enlightenment. Next to making money.**

✦ Be serious. Why is your painting called *The Languor of Love* so popular?

✧ **I believe the central figure is a metaphor for the modern woman contemplating the merits of an independent career, symbolized by the stairs, versus a passionate love life that might lead to the overwhelming responsibilities of traditional motherhood.**

✦ What motivates you to frequently quote imagery from art history?

✧ **It varies . . . Homage, spoof, study, expansion, or to update. Sometimes I just like a composition and I want to use it as a structure for my own iconography. Like a jazz musician playing a standard**

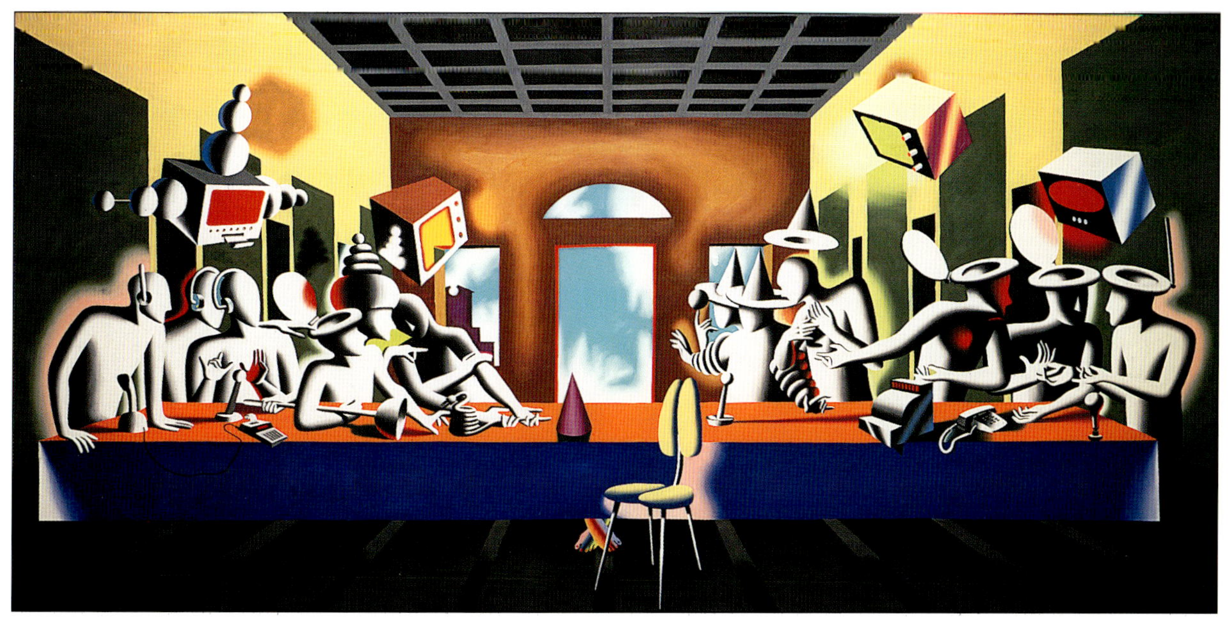

✧ **The Last Supper**

1986

Oil on canvas

10 x 20 feet

Collection of
Rodney Sheldon

melody, but clearly in a unique way. That's how I approached *The Last Supper*. It was neither homage, spoof, nor study. It certainly is an update with the televisions, calculators, and telephone, but my intention was to use the composition as a scaffolding on which I could playfully unleash my imagination. Some of my art history references are very obvious while others are rather obscure. For example, few people would spot the source for *I Go for a Man with an Adam Hat* as a Hugo Robus sculpture. No one has ever said to me, "I know you got your *On the Edge* image from a Rockwell Kent woodcut." But it's easy to spot my references to Hopper, Vermeer, or Leonardo da Vinci. Sometimes even I don't know. For example, when an assistant at Kostabi World won first prize in my *Secrets of the Psyche* painting contest, I thought he invented the architecture in the background. A year after I

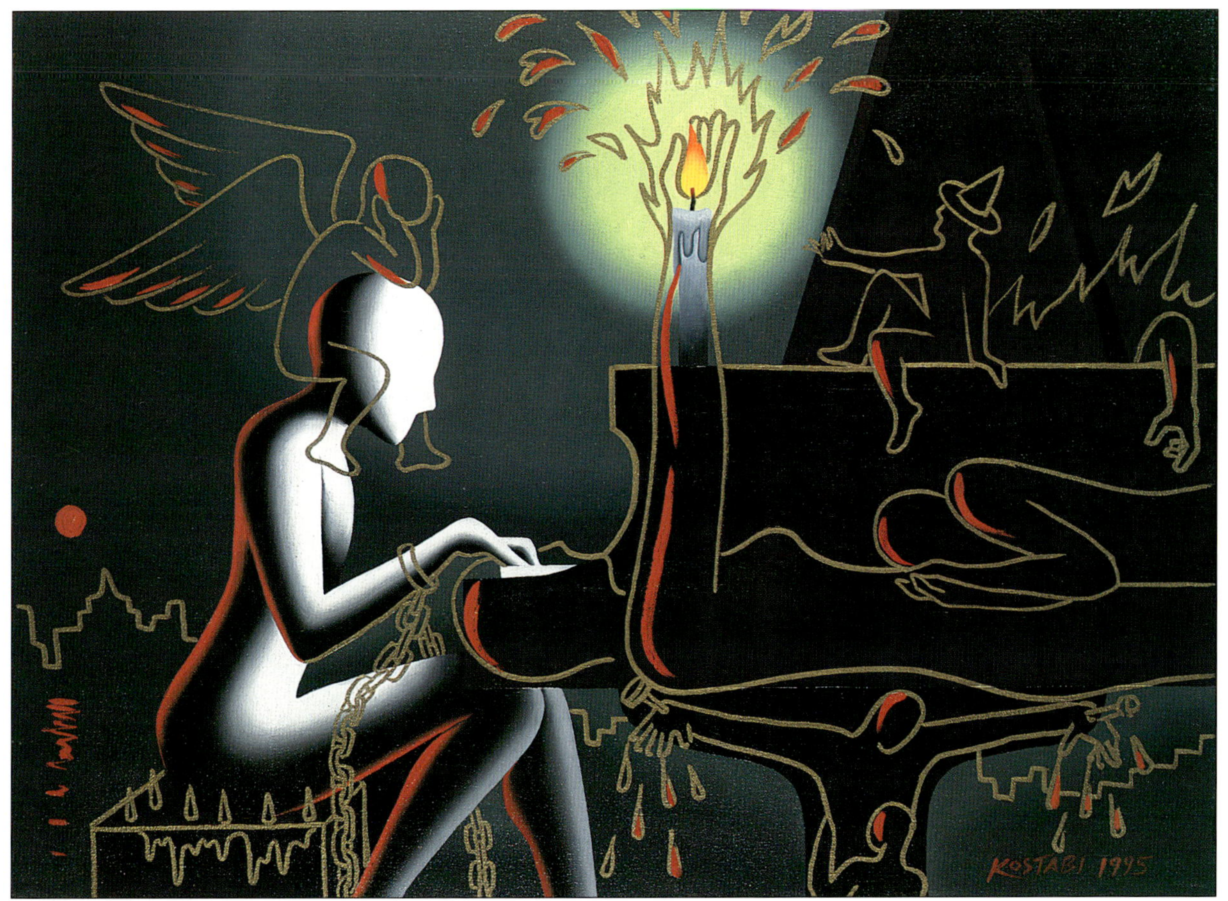

✧ **Improvise the Night Away**
1995
Oil on canvas
18 x 24 inches
Collection of Stella Alvarado

✧ page 151:
Concentration
1994
Oil on canvas
54 x 44 inches
Collection of Edward M. Eglowsky

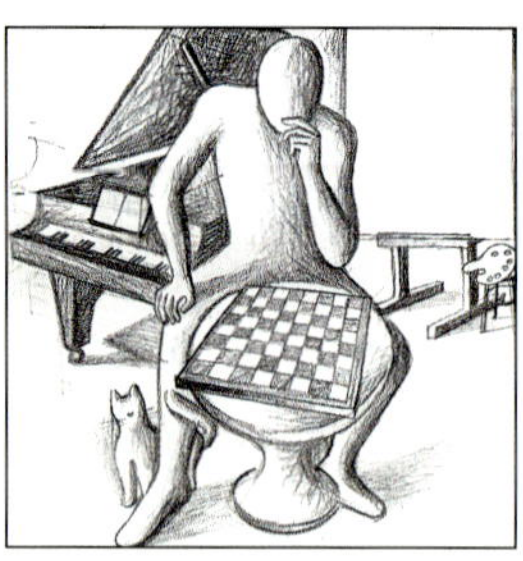

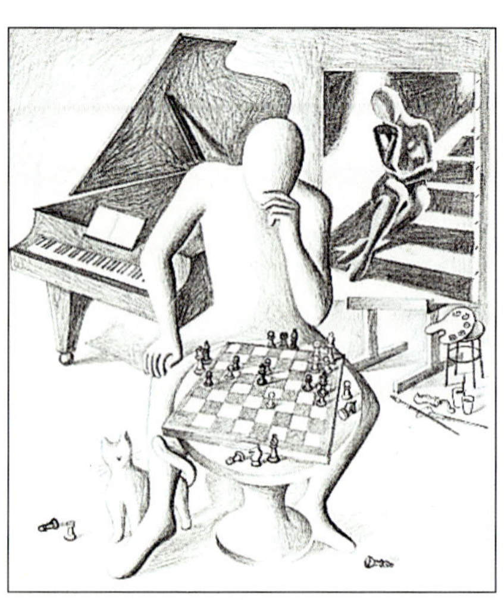

✧ above, left:
Study for Concentration I
1994
Pencil on paper
12 x 9 inches
Collection of the artist

✧ above, right:
Study for Concentration
1994
Pencil on paper
12 x 9 inches
Collection of the artist

signed the painting, I visited the Metropolitan Museum's "Early Dali" show. I discovered the source was a 1924 Dali painting called *Port Alguer*. It shows a church in Cadaques, which was Dali's childhood Parthenon.

✦ Is there a danger in relying so much on art history to inspire your imagery rather than on your own experience?

✧ **My priority is making good, interesting paintings. I'll use whatever it**

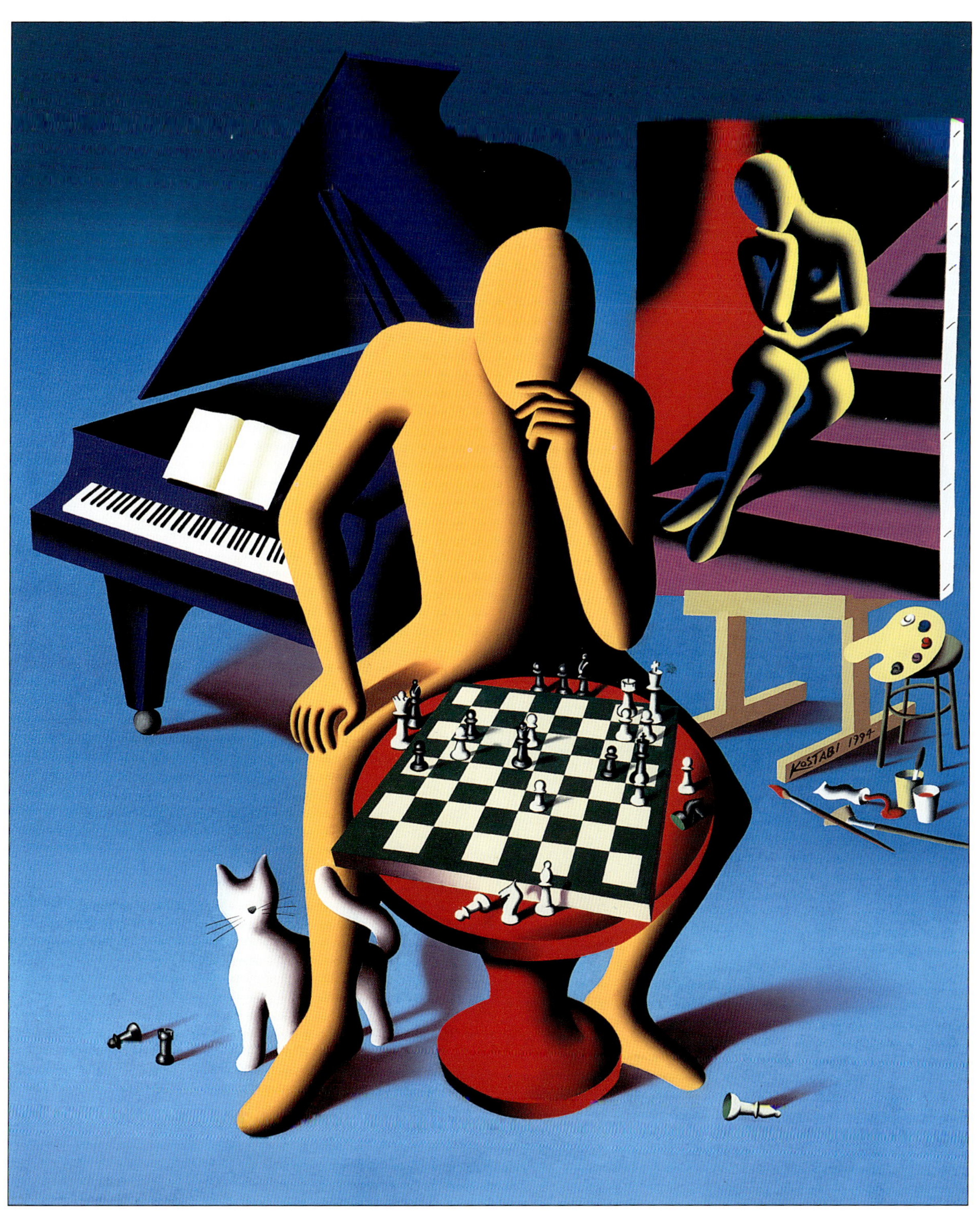
KOSTABI 1994

takes. And, it *is* my own experience. I love art history. I love going to museums. That's how I spend my time.

✦ Musical imagery is a recent development in your work, as seen in paintings like *The Cellist*, *Violin Concerto*, *Concentration*, *Absolute Ensemble*, and *Improvise the Night Away*. Why music suddenly?

✧ It's a visual acknowledgment of my new commitment to music. I've composed piano music since 1975 but I made a conscious decision in the late 1970s to put my music career on hold so I could focus on my career as a visual artist. Since 1994 I've devoted several hours a day to music, so naturally it has surfaced as imagery in recent paintings. *Improvise the Night Away* shows a lonely pianist, battling with inner demons through his music, hoping to create his ideal woman. He wishes her to be his source of light and affection, but he has also created his own chains that lock him eternally to the piano.

✦ Chess is another frequent subject in your paintings. What's that about?

✧ **I played chess when I was a teenager, and then about three years ago my assistants began playing at lunch every day and I got hooked again. Now I get chess lessons once a week from Lev Alburt, a Russian Grand Master. It's almost like going to a guru.**

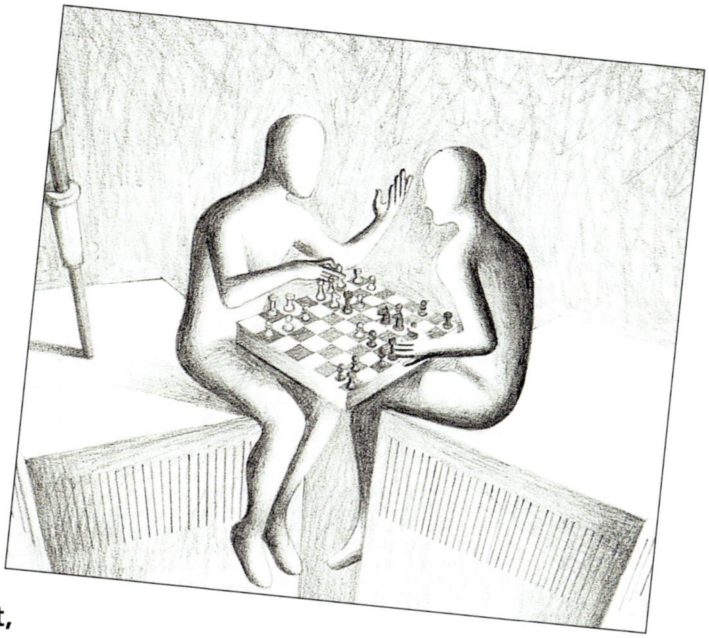

✦ Why chess?

✧ **Chess has become my metaphor for art, business, and life.**

✦ Can you explain in more detail?

✧ **Chess is a game, and art is a game. I learn about art, business, and life when I play chess. In the past, I've had a tendency to compound a mistake by becoming anxious and speeding up. Chess has taught me that when you make a mistake, it's time to slow down. A beginning chess player will become frustrated, speed up, and make matters worse. I've learned to slow down in life as well, evaluate my**

✧ Sketch for
Grandmasters
1995
pencil on paper
12 x 9 inches
Kostabi World

position based on the new situation and take the time to figure things out before I make the same mistake again. It's just one of the lessons I've learned.

✦ Anything else?

✧ Get all your pieces on the board. Control the center. Develop your pieces. As an artist, it was very important for me to get my art pieces on the board, to be visible. That's why I didn't turn up my nose at showing in restaurants or movie theater lobbies. My pieces were out there on the playing field, rather than back home waiting for that one big break at Leo Castelli's Gallery. I didn't wait for Castelli. I got my pieces on the board immediately. In art, it's important to establish your position, like in chess. Knights on the rim are dim. On the rim, a knight can only move to a maximum of four squares. But a knight in the middle of the board can move to eight. The piece is more powerful, simply because of its position. I've learned to get the pieces to the center of the board, or to places where they control the center. It's better in the long

✧ page 155:
Grandmasters
1995
Oil on canvas
64 x 48 inches
Collection of Richard and Kathy Wentz

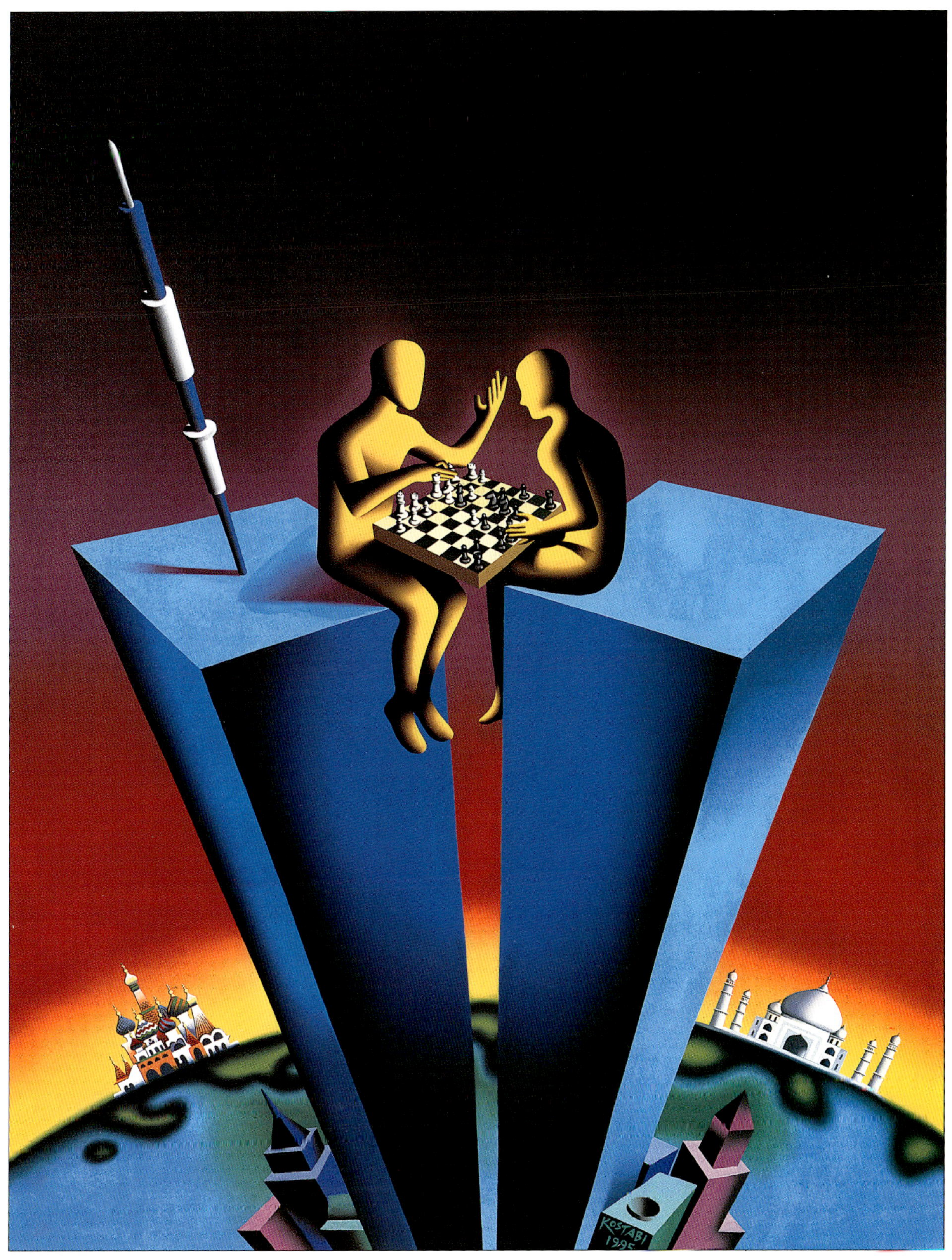
KOSTABI
1995

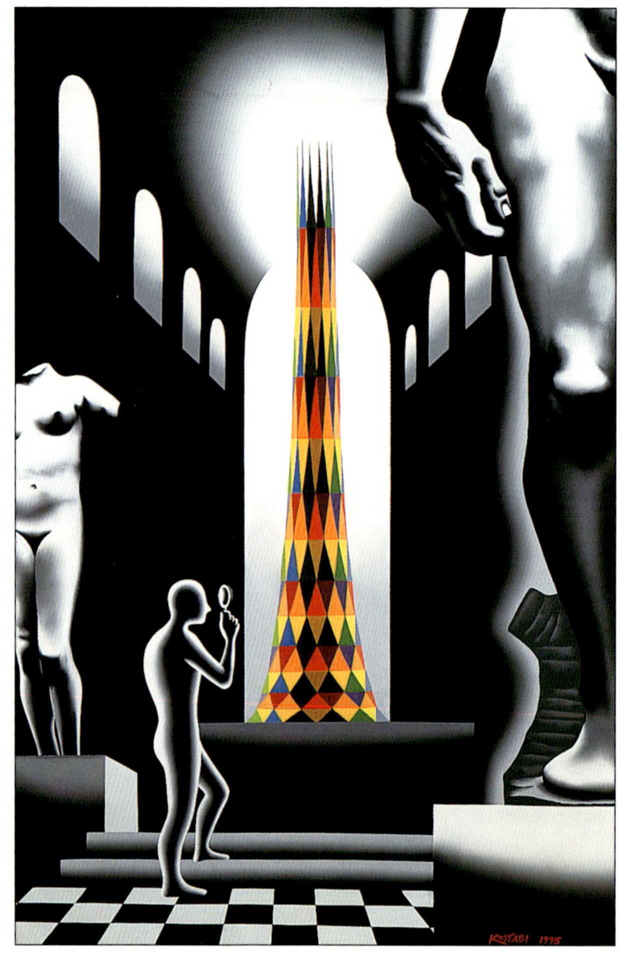

✧ **Inspection**
1995
Oil on canvas
72 x 46 inches
Kostabi World

run to show your art in a movie theater in Manhattan than in a bona fide art gallery out in the sticks. The center of the art world is New York. For an artist, obscurity is dangerous.

Another rule I learned is to castle as soon as possible. Put your king into safety and develop your rook.

✦ I don't understand.

✧ The king is ultimately the most powerful piece on the board, like the artist's soul, but it must be protected during the opening and middle game. It comes into play in the endgame, like in Rembrandt's soulful late self-portraits. As for my media antics, they're equivalent to castling. They are maneuvers that keep my king, and my soul, well protected.

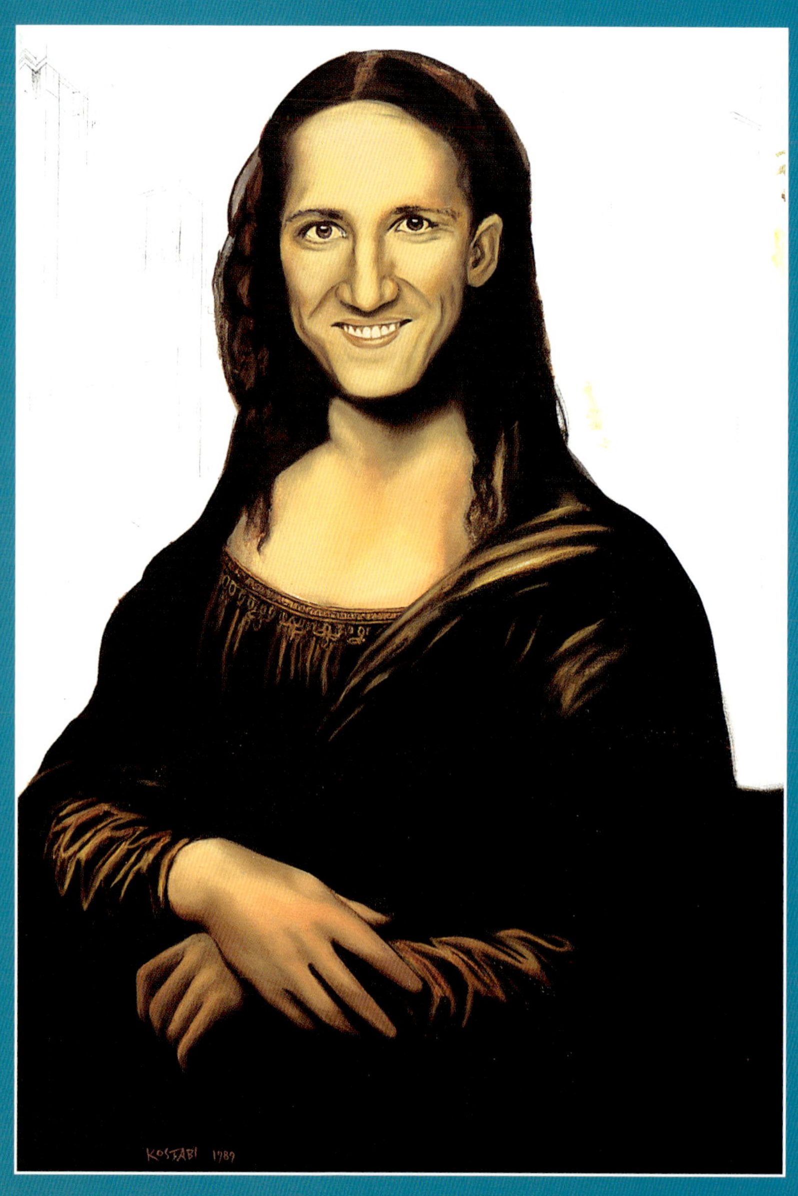
KOSTABI 1989

CHAPTER ✧ SIX

How To Become A Rich And Famous Artist

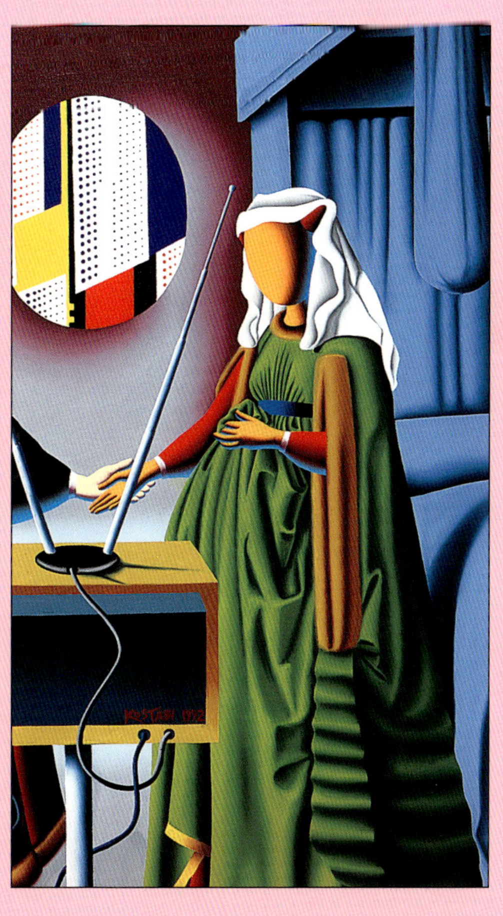

MAKE GREAT ART

✦ How do you make great art?

✧ **Only do what you love. People will admire you for it. They'll look up to you. Nobody wants to follow a drudge who's always complaining about a day job or the corrupt system that prevents the artist from succeeding. Don't waste your time doing anything except what you love doing. And do it enthusiastically because enthusiasm is contagious. I used to have day jobs. I was a custodian, a stock clerk, a sign designer, and a receptionist. I never complained about them. I learned from them. And I loved the paychecks, which I used to buy Frank Zappa albums.**

Complaining isn't productive, because even

✧ page 158:
The Woman in Me
1989
Oil on canvas
54 x 36 inches
Collection of Peter Sugleris

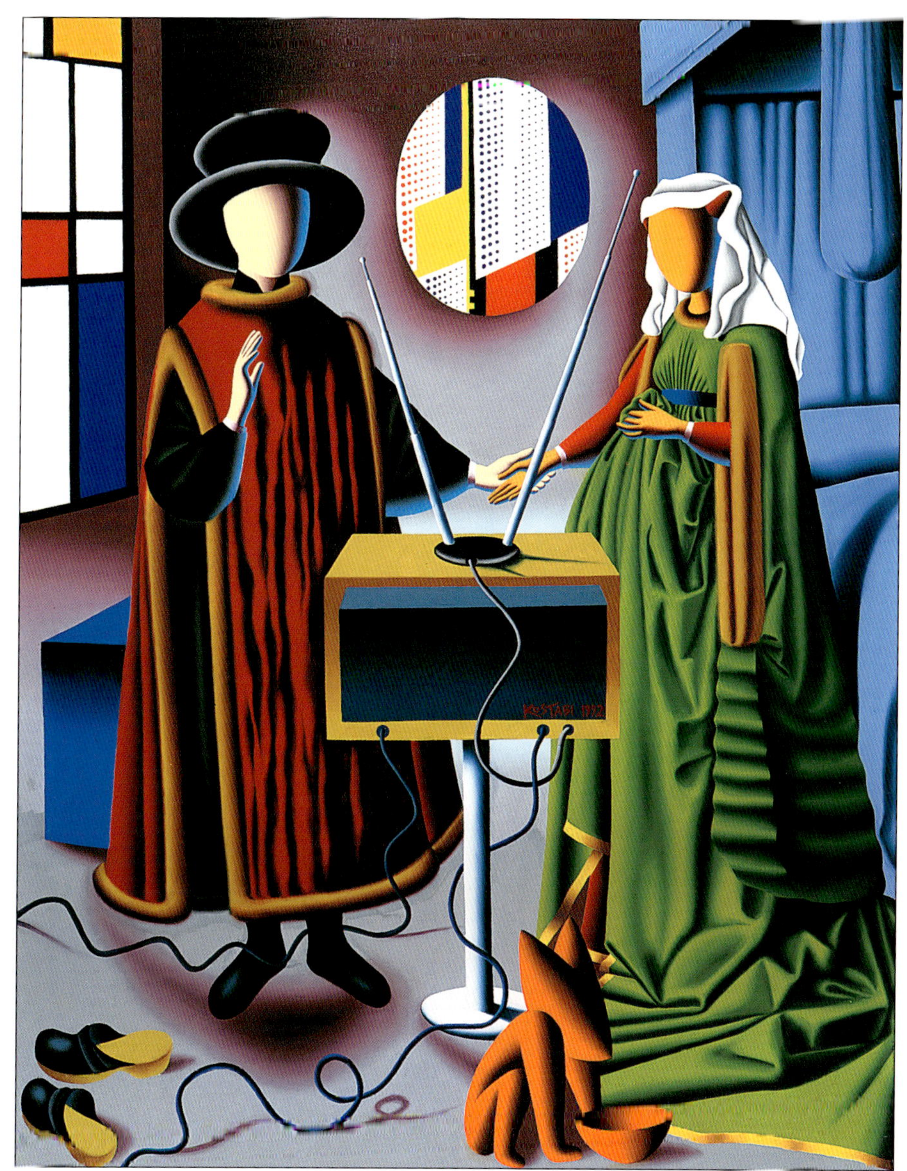

✧ **A Marriage of Convenience**
1992
Oil on canvas
48 x 36 inches
Europa Art Gallery
West Bloomfield, Michigan

LIVE IN NEW YORK

✦ Is it absolutely necessary to live in New York?

✧ **You could probably break one or two of the rules and still make it. But it's much easier if you don't. Why swim upstream? New York is the center of the art world. It has the densest concentration of galleries. It has more major museums than any other city in the United States. All the major American art magazines are published in New York. It simply has the most opportunities.**

✦ How do you take advantage of New York once you're there?

✧ **Visit the major museums regularly. Visit the major galleries and all the important experimental galleries and alternative spaces. Read the major art magazines. Read *New York Times* art reviews every Friday and Sunday.**

CIRCULATE

✦ What do you mean by "circulate"?

✧ **The goal for any artist is to have a show. You can't get in by making appointments, showing**

shine. Allow yourself to be their audience. They'll love you for it. It's important to get dealers to visit your studio. I can't stress this enough: do not make appointments at galleries. The way to attract dealers is to attend the art openings and art parties. Get to know people. Once they know you, other artists will recommend you to a dealer. That's why it's so crucial that you meet and mingle, not only with powerful dealers, but with fellow artists as well. For instance, one of the first times I went to an opening I met

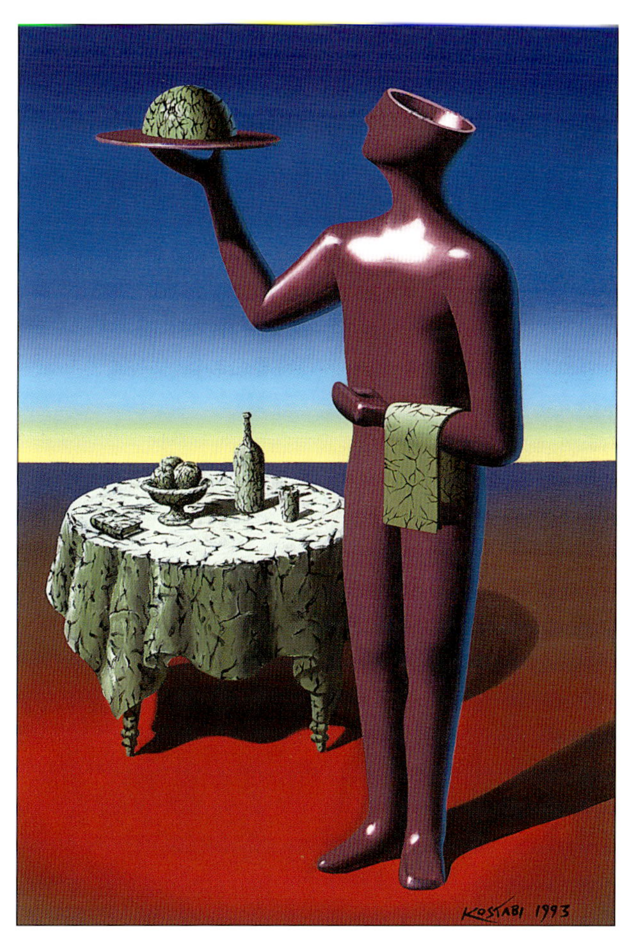

✧ **Service (Magritte)**
1993
Oil on canvas
24 x 16 inches
Kostabi World

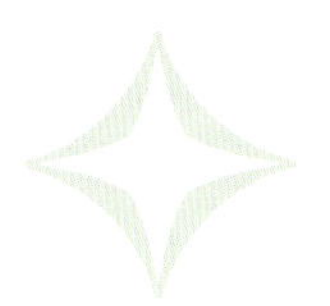

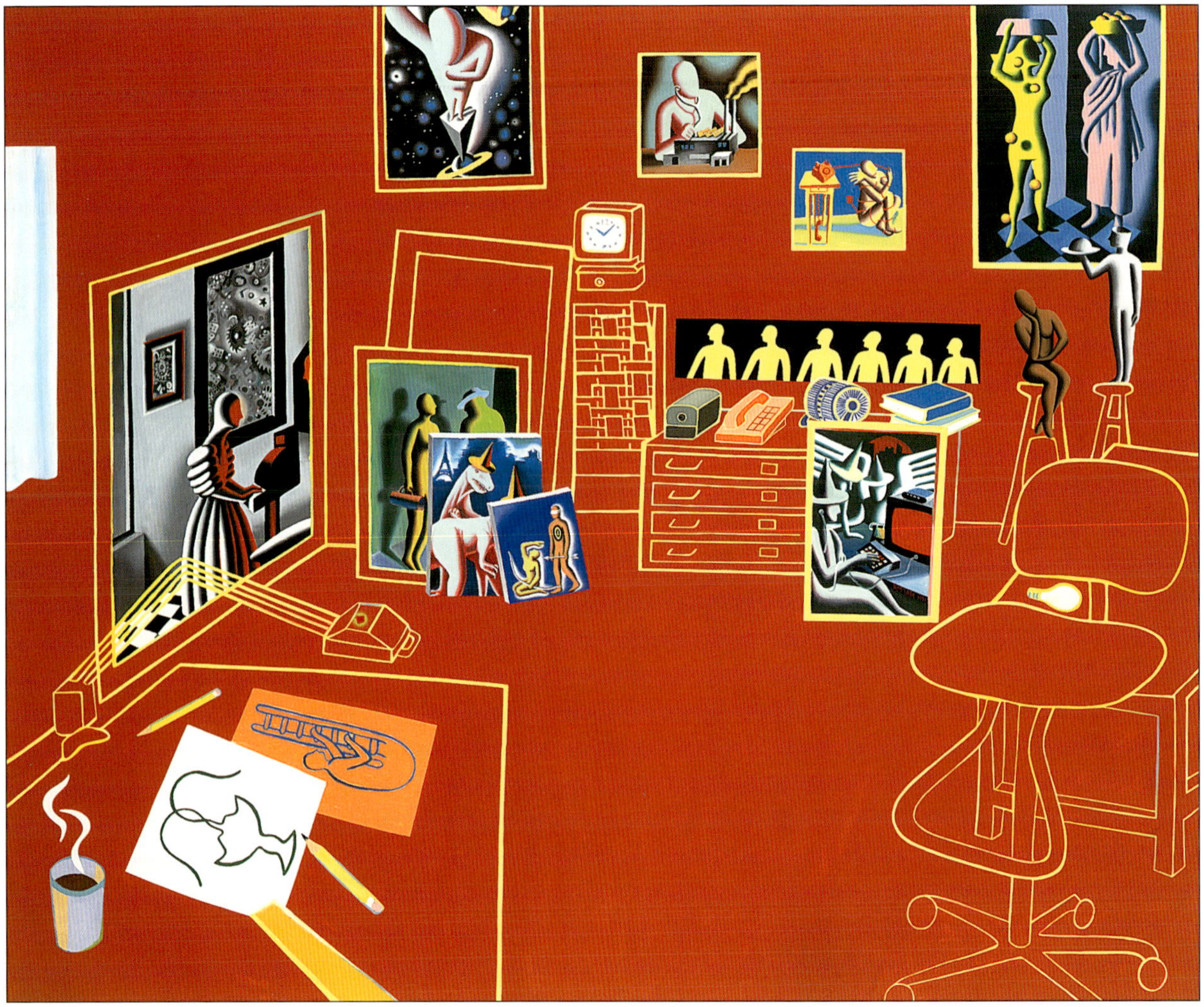

✧ **Red Studio**

1991

Oil on canvas

72 x 86 inches

Kostabi World

Rick Prol. He was in the same position I was. We became both friends and rivals, and it wasn't a bad thing. We began getting shows together and sharing notes on what to do and what not to do. I found it was very helpful to be around someone who, like me, was just beginning to get noticed. Circulating in the art scene can also lead directly to sales. It's possible that if you're around enough, dealers will notice you, get curious, and introduce themselves. This happened to me in the mid 1980s, when I was going to literally every opening I heard about. So was Larry Gagosian, a major Los Angeles art dealer, who at that time was just beginning to circulate in the New York art scene and who now is one of the most powerful art dealers in the world. We kept seeing each other all over SoHo. I was at an opening at Leo Castelli's Gallery when Gagosian walked over to me and said, "I'd like to go to your studio." He didn't even ask my name. He knew

✧ page 171:
Jacket for DIFFA
1994
Oil on denim

who I was because he'd seen me around so often and knew that I was part of the scene. We made an appointment and a few days later he visited my studio. In a matter of minutes he purchased ten paintings and a group of drawings. Right then and there, he paid for the drawings with a stack of crisp, new one-hundred-dollar bills. For the paintings he cut me a check for fifteen thousand dollars. In 1985 getting fifteen thousand dollars was for me like getting a million dollars today. It was that dramatic, it really happened that fast, and it was purely a result of having been seen at openings. Of course, he had to like my work, but it was almost as if he was buying whoever he thought was hot, whoever was doing the art dance. Even now, attending openings is crucial to my continued success. At a recent Kenny Scharf opening at the Tony Shafrazi Gallery, I met an Italian dealer named Alex Mantice, who came to my studio and bought over two hundred major paintings from me. Those paintings would still be in my racks collecting dust if I wasn't out there making the rounds. Circulating

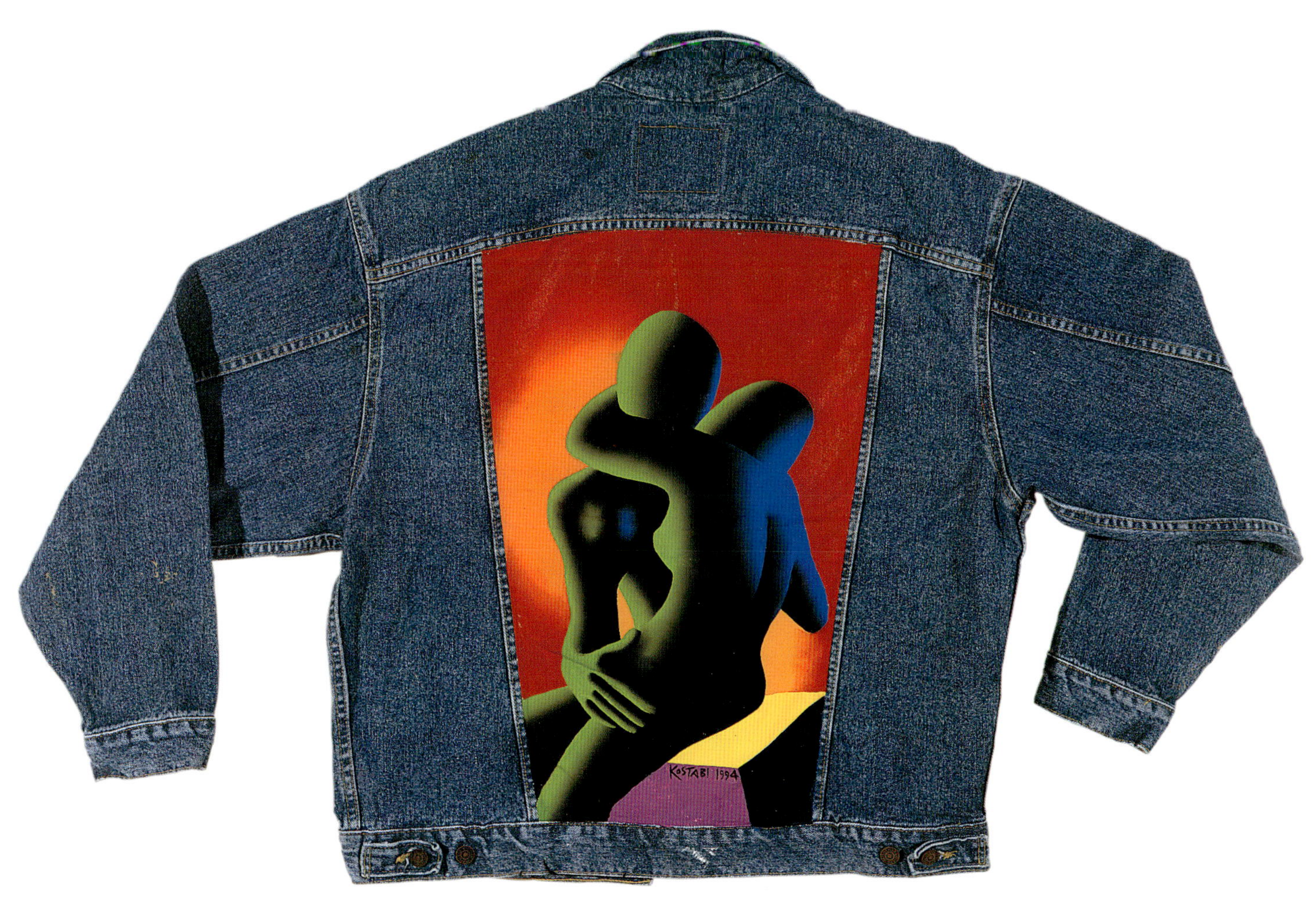
KOSTABI 1994

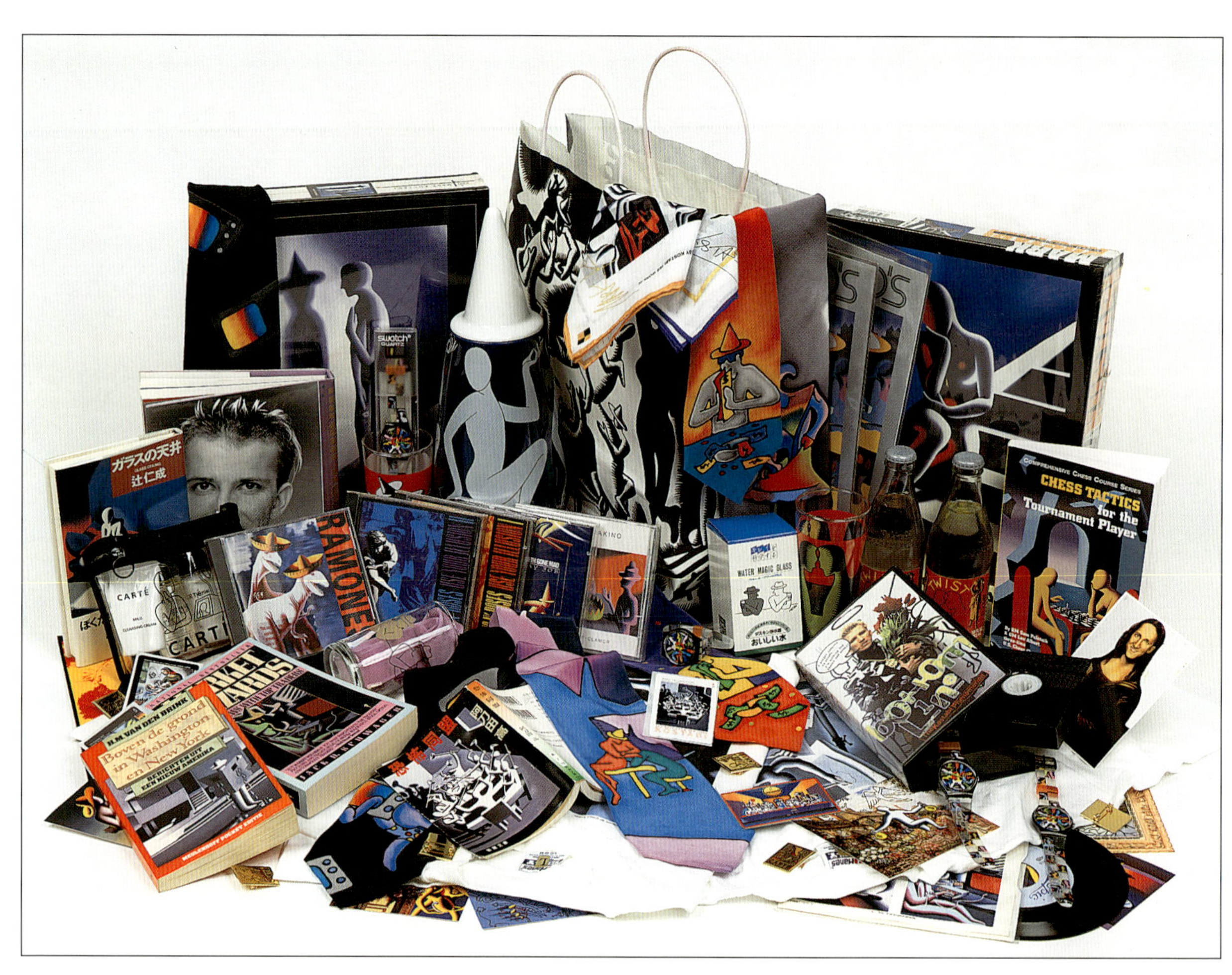
ガラスの天井
辻仁成
swatch
RAMONES
WATER MAGIC GLASS
おいしい水
COMPREHENSIVE CHESS COURSE SERIES
CHESS TACTICS for the Tournament Player
H.M. VAN DEN BRINK
Boven de grond in Washington en New York
CARTE

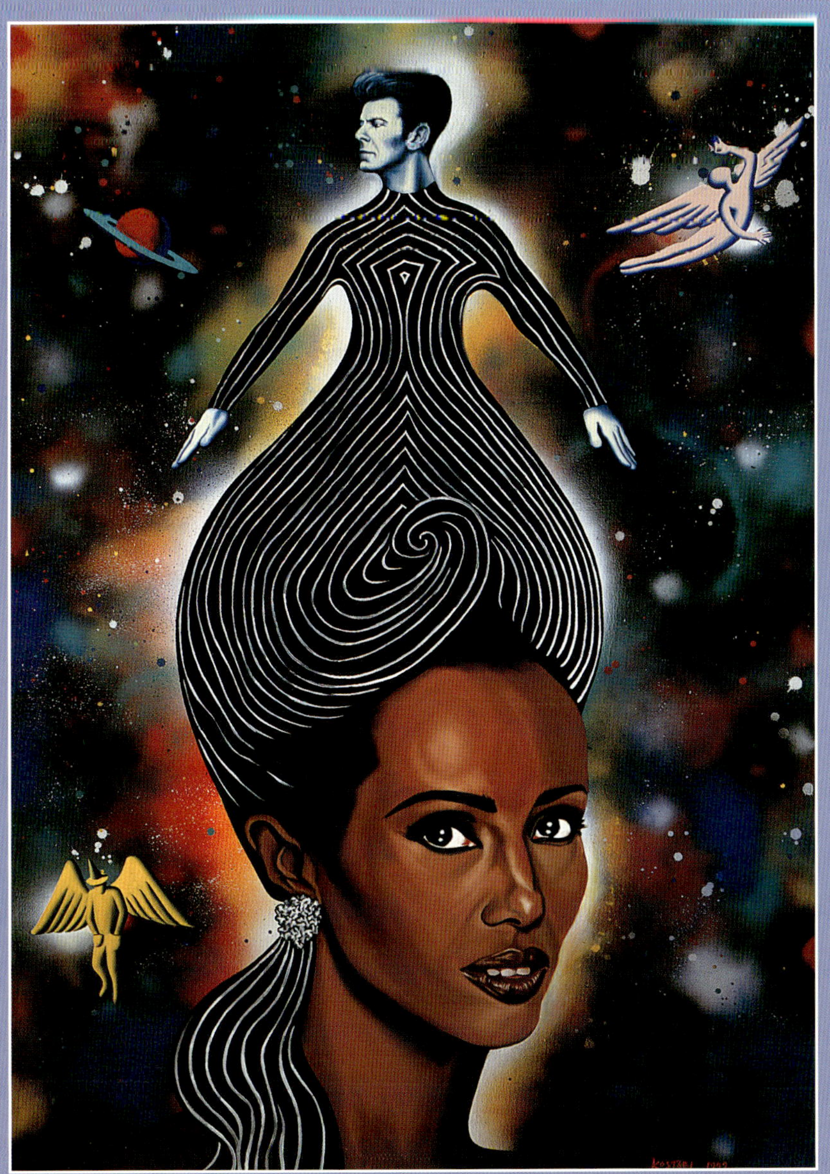

✧ **Seeing Stars**
1992
Oil on canvas
72 x 48 inches
Collection of David Bowie

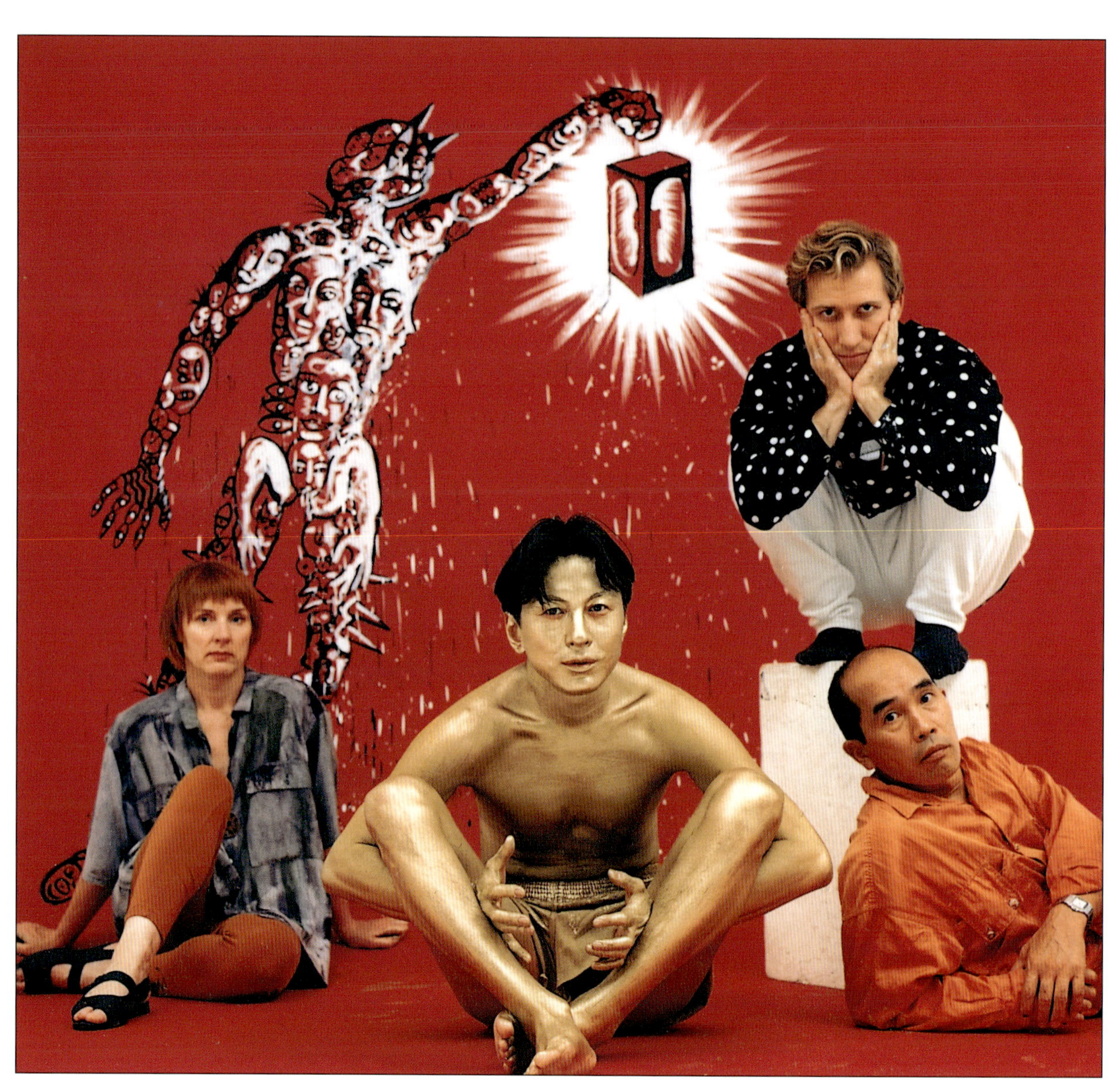

also leads to publicity. In 1987 I crashed the opening of the Whitney Biennial. Only a select few are invited to museum openings and, although I was well known by then, I was not among them. However, I knew that I deserved to be there and that I belonged there, so I went to the Whitney and talked my way in by telling them I had left my invitation at home. Once, to get into the Louise Bourgeois opening at the Museum of Modern Art, I sneaked an invitation off the desk. At the Whitney opening I ran into a journalist, Matthew Rose, whom I knew from other openings. He hadn't seen me in a while and he asked me what I was doing. I told him that I had hired assistants to paint for me. I didn't think it was that shocking. It never occurred to me that this was newsworthy, since most artists have assistants. I was just being honest about it. Rose told me he wanted to come over and see my studio. He was intrigued by the fact that I had assistants openly painting my paintings and idea people developing ideas for them. A week later a full-page article appeared in *New York* magazine,

✧ page 174: Linda Mason, Masami Matsui, Mark Kostabi, and Seiichi Tanaka from the collaborative portrait book ***Tanaka Mason Kostabi.*** Photo by Seiichi Tanaka.

and the major papers followed. This all came from being at an opening. It would never have happened if I didn't circulate.

✦ How do you find out about art openings?

✧ **The *Gallery Guide*. Listings in the *New York Times* and the *Village Voice*. Ads in *Artforum*. You can call the galleries and ask. Eventually you find out by word of mouth and you get on mailing lists. Art parties and studio visits are also very important.**

✦ How do you find out about art parties?

✧ **When you start attending art openings, you'll hear about art parties, which usually take place in an artist's loft or a collector's home. Usually you'll tag along with an invitee the first few times.**

✦ What about studio visits?

✧ **The four most important words an artist can say to another artist are, "Let's trade studio visits." It's**

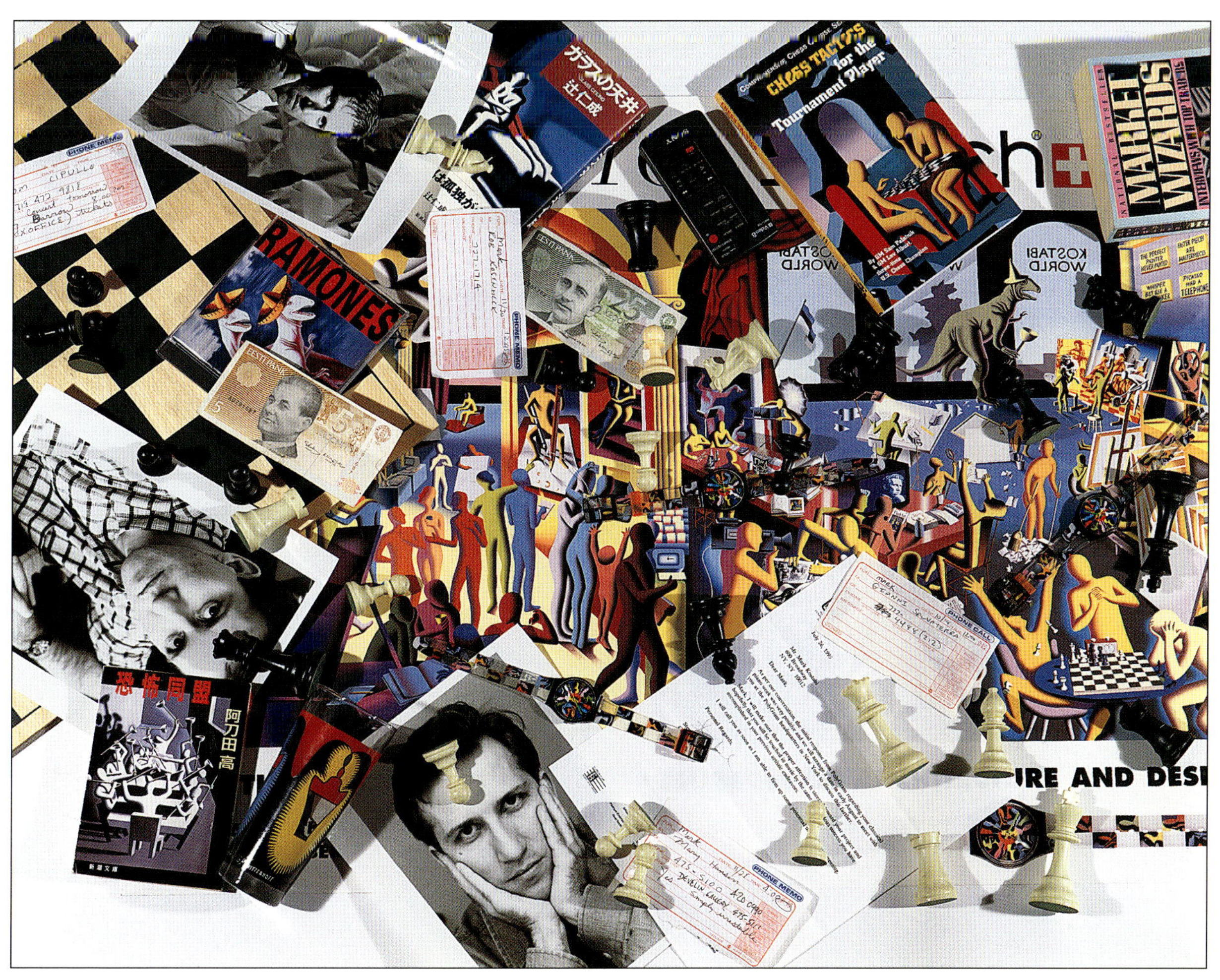
ガラスの天井
辻仁成
CHESS TACTICS for the Tournament Player
MARKET WIZARDS
RAMONES
KOSTABI WORLD
EESTI PANK
PHONE MEMO
恐怖同盟
阿刀田高
IRE AND DESI

important to build a support system with other artists. They give you credibility with dealers. And they are a valuable source of information and inspiration.

The classic studio visit usually proceeds like this: you arrive. You ring a buzzer or call from the corner. A key is thrown down in a sock. You walk up a wide, dark, creaky wooden staircase. Once you're in the studio, you compliment the space, the light, the artist's decision to conceal the beautifully antiquated columns with uncompromisingly severe sheetrock so they won't distract from the art. Then you are offered tea. You accept. You pet the cat and sit in one of the two wooden chairs and you begin looking at the paintings. You compliment the sensitive nuances here and there. If you are a real painter type, you speak in terms of whether things in the painting "work" or not. You discuss "events" within the painting. You discuss "belief systems." If you are looking at minimalism, you always

✧ page 179:
Jeans for Energie
1994
Oil on denim

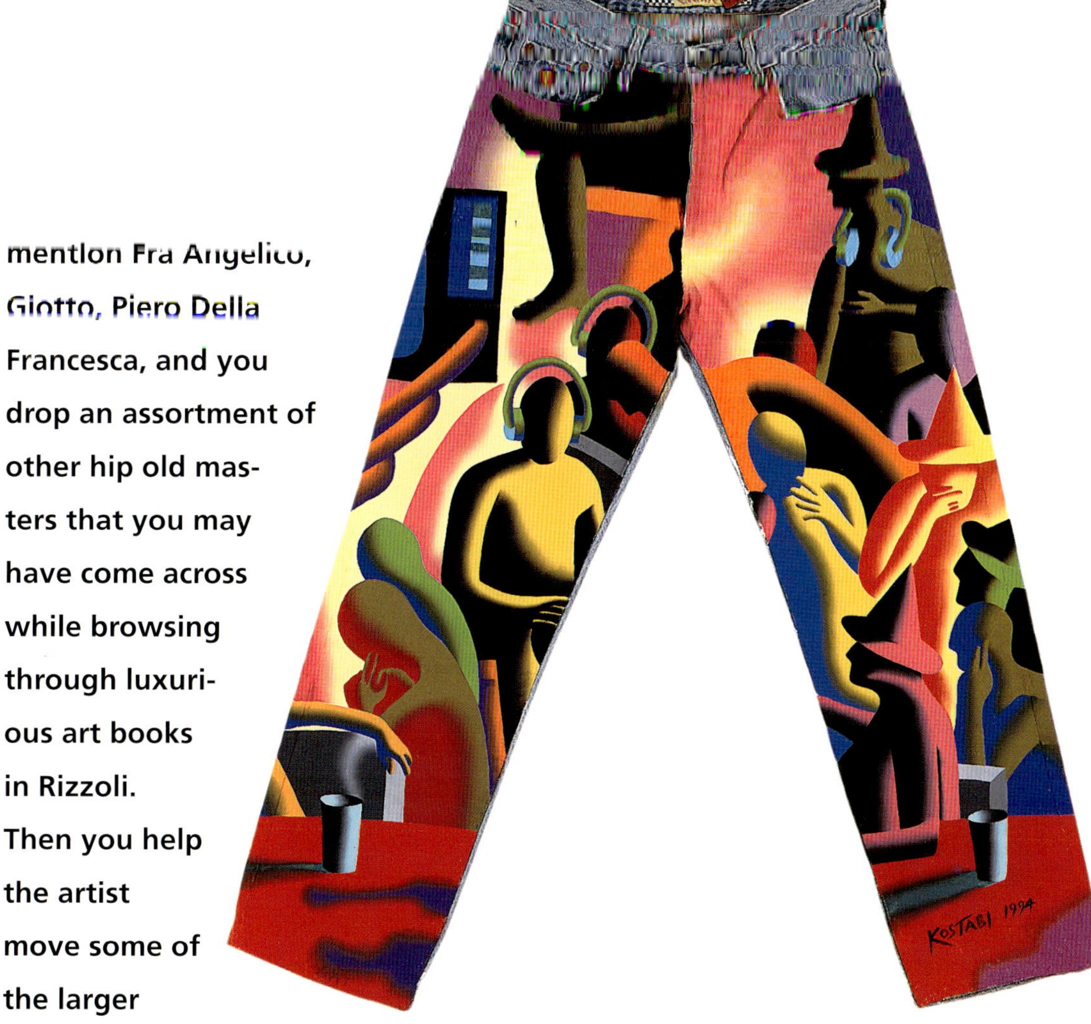

mention Fra Angelico, Giotto, Piero Della Francesca, and you drop an assortment of other hip old masters that you may have come across while browsing through luxurious art books in Rizzoli. Then you help the artist move some of the larger paintings for better viewing. You discuss the upcoming show, you confirm the artist's wisdom at leaving out the large pink one. You acknowledge a few friends or acquaintances you have in common. Or, if you are both already selling, you might use a

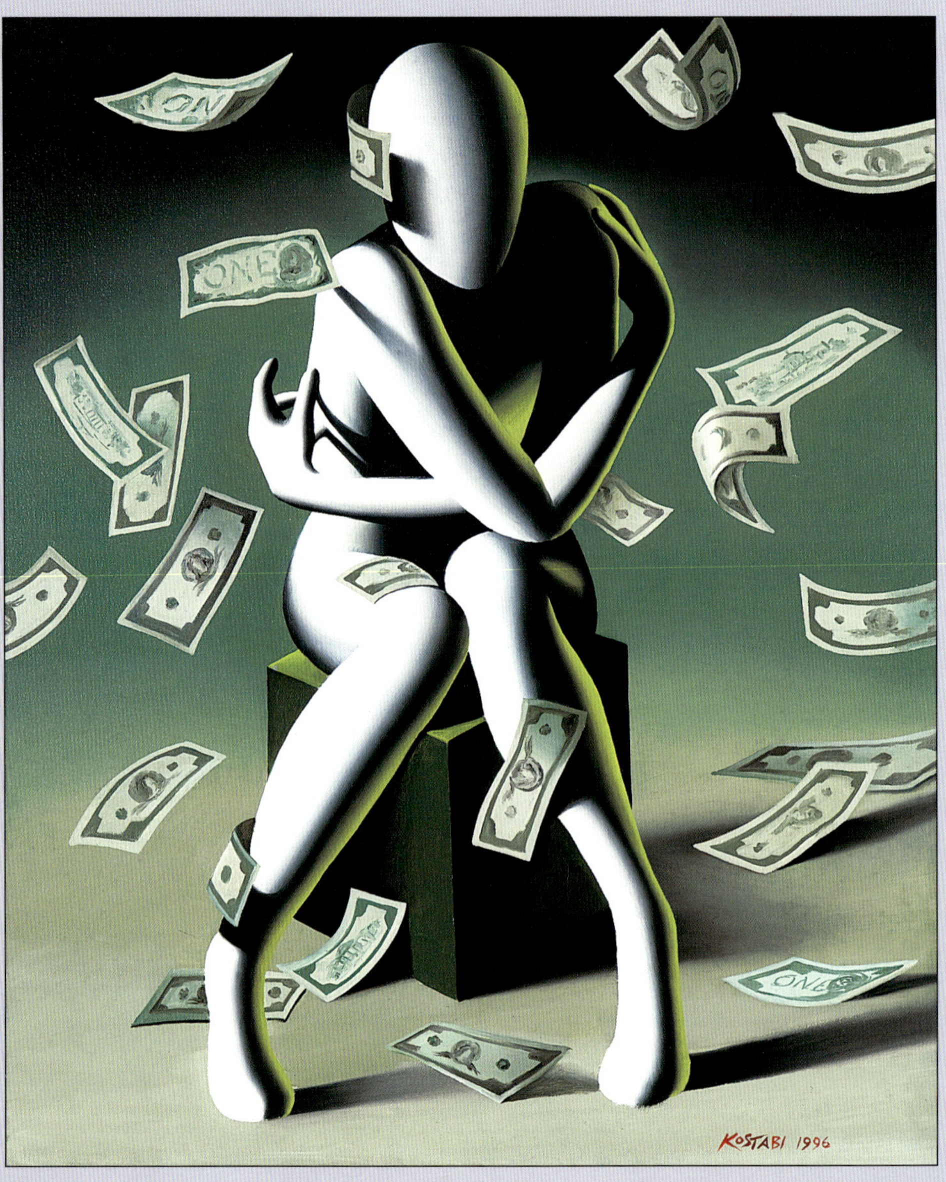

✧ **Cubic Euphoria (Green Day)**
1996
Oil on canvas
30 x 24 inches
Private collection

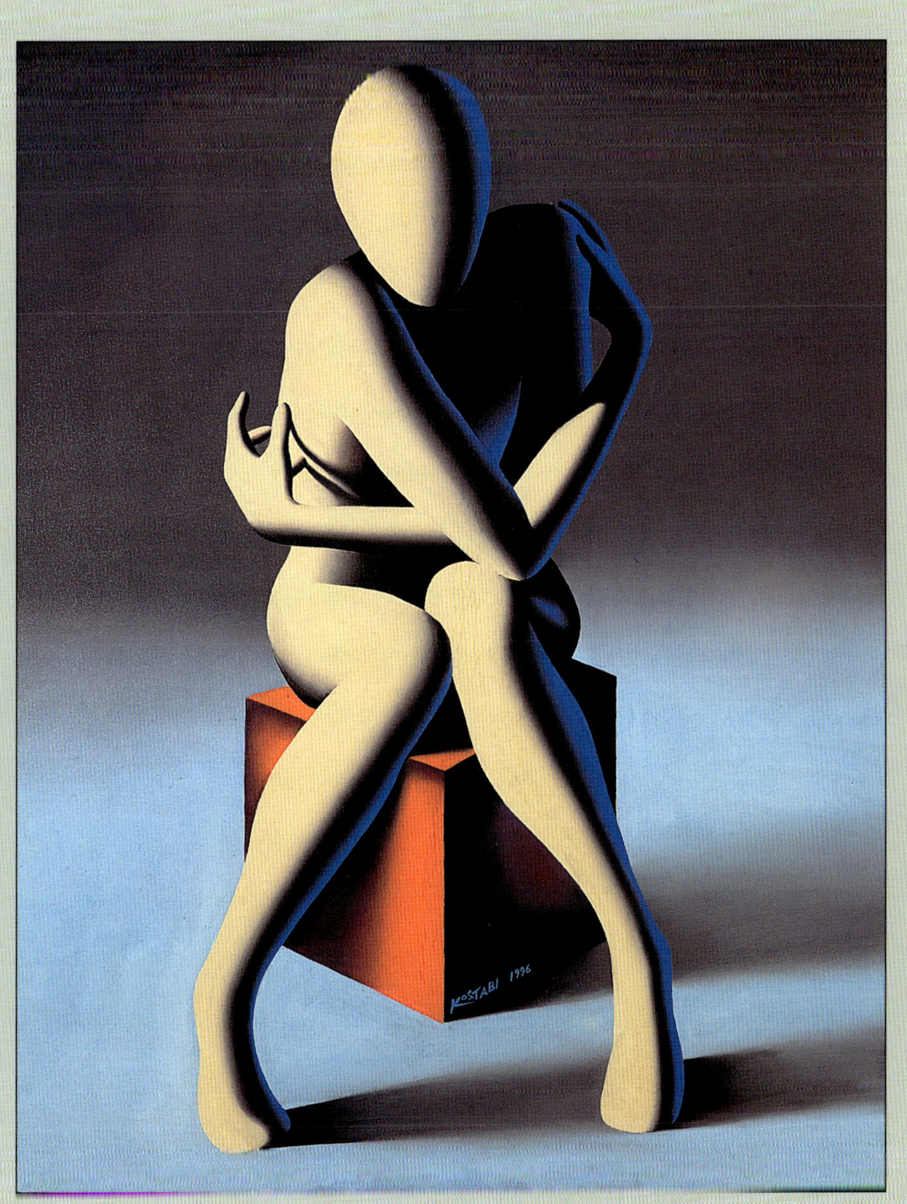

✧ **Cubic Euphoria**
1996
Oil on canvas
40 x 30 inches
Kostabi World

term like "mutual collector." You mention Mary Boone's latest remodeling of her gallery skylight, Larry Gagosian's latest power move, and by then it should be time to leave.

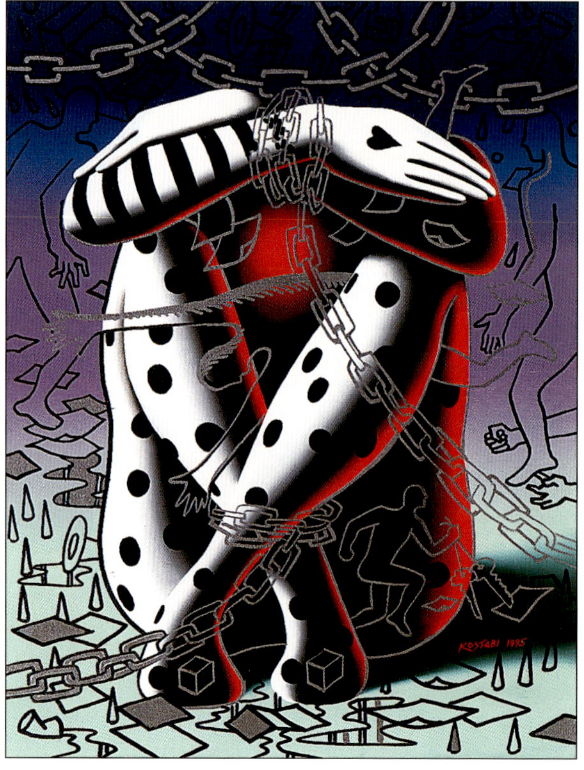

✧ **He Who Has the Key**
1995
Oil on canvas
24 x 18 inches
Private collection

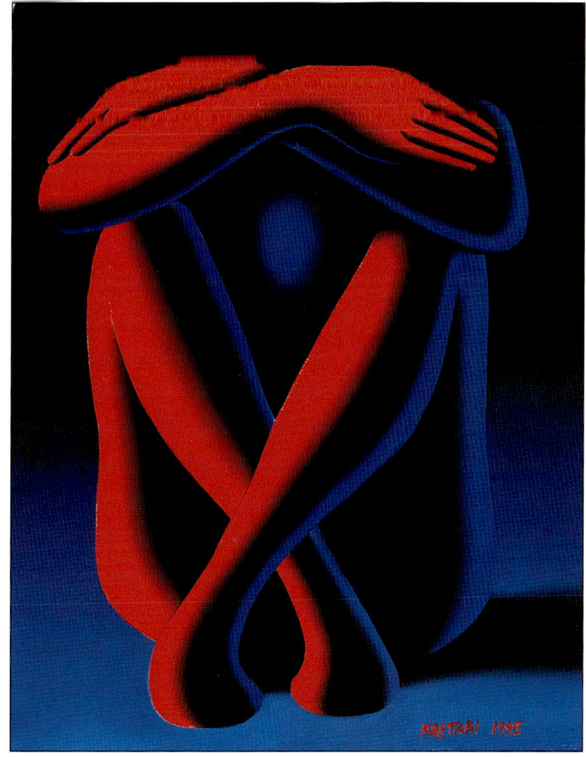

✧ **Inner**
1995
Oil on canvas
24 x 18 inches
Collection of
Michelle Weidman

✦ How did you get older, more established artists like George Segal and Philip Pearlstein to praise you in *New York* magazine? It's not like you saw them at all the openings and hung out together at the Red Bar in the East Village.

✧ **True. This brings me to another trick of**

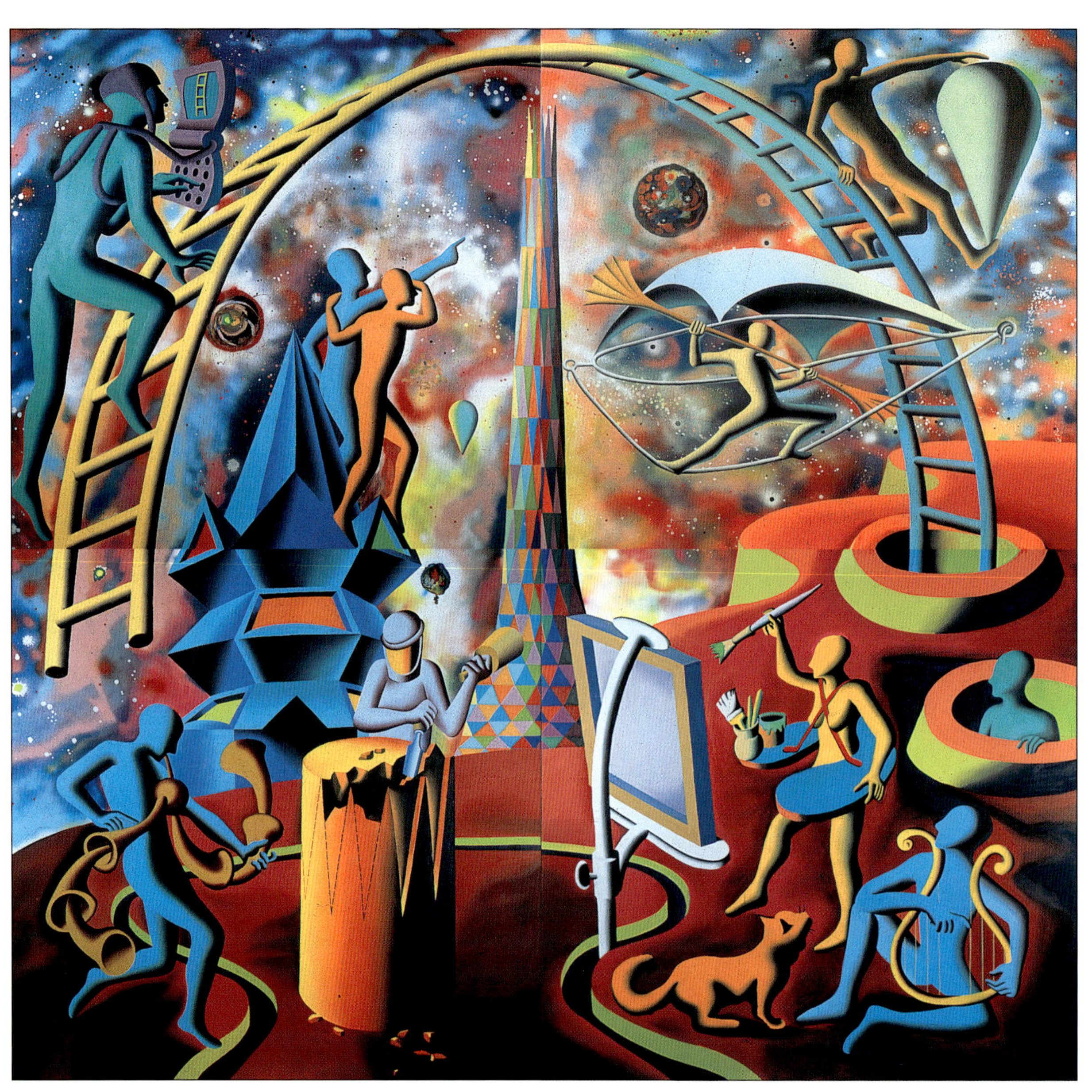

circulating. Call up your favorite artist and say, "I like your work and I'd like to meet you." That's exactly what I did with the sculptor George Segal in 1983. He said, "You've caught me off guard," and invited me to his vast chicken coop studio in New Jersey. I spent over an hour looking at and discussing his work. Eventually, he asked me about my work, at which point I produced my slides. In these types of situations, only talk about your own work or show your slides when asked. Let the star shine first. Otherwise, you're just another pushy artist. He was genuinely surprised and impressed by the work. We talked for a while longer. He warned me about the bullies of the art world, and then he drove me to the bus station. A few years later he agreed to write the introduction to a book of my line drawings called *Office Suite*. He compared me to Franz Kafka and Charlie Chaplin. He never asked for payment. Many years later, a journalist who was doing a cover story about me for *New York* magazine asked me for names and phone numbers of close friends and famous artists who might

✧ page 184:
Celebration of Infinity
1992
Oil on canvas
14 x 14 feet
Collection of Vincenzo Pellegrino and Renzo Tarocco

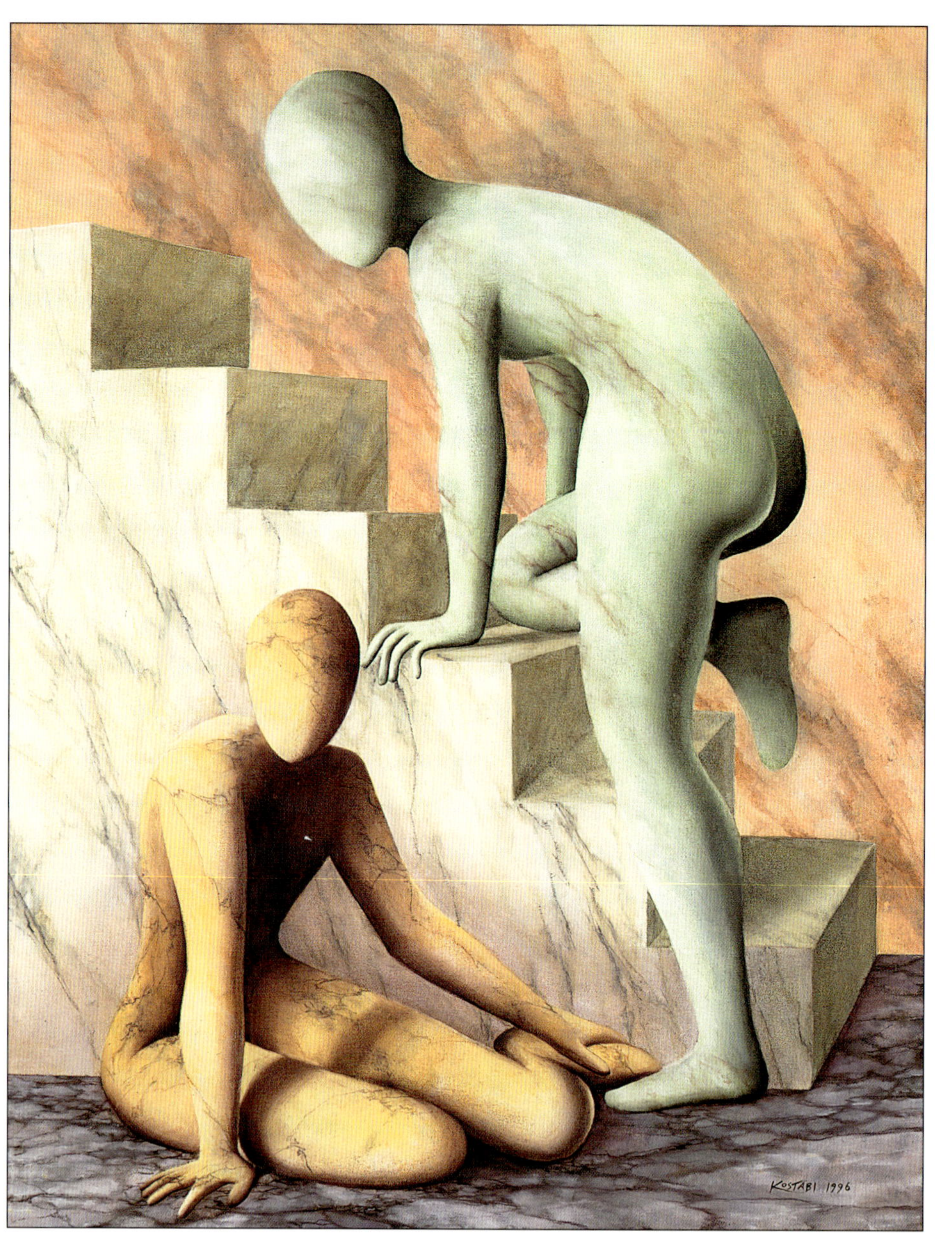

✧ **Marble Fable**
1996
Oil on canvas
40 x 30 inches
Kostabi World

provide a quote about me. I gave him George Segal's and Philip Pearlstein's phone numbers. I knew Philip Pearlstein because at one time we both had studios in the same building. Both artists were extremely kind in their comments about me. And I will always return the gesture. Not that either of them needs my endorsement. It's just an example of how artists are often instinctively supportive of other artists, especially if they're nice to each other.

✦ Do artists ever call you up out of the blue?

✧ **Yes. And sometimes they misinterpret the advice. Once someone called and said, "I read an article about you and I'm taking your advice, so I'm calling you. Can I visit your studio?"**

"Why do you want to visit me?" I asked.

"Because you're a marketing genius and I like the way you piss off the art world. I'd like to get some advice from you."

"Am I one of your favorite artists?"

BUY ARTIST

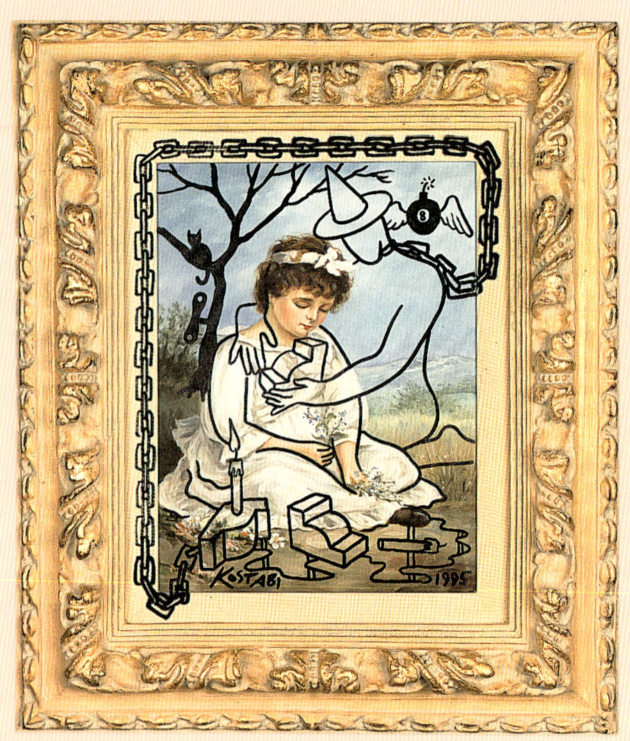

✧ **A Lesson Well Learned**
1995
Marker & oil on canvas
12 x 16 inches
Collection of Hugh and Kristin Fast

"No, not exactly."

I imagine he was actually thinking, "No. Your work sucks. But you're rich and famous and I deserve to be rich and famous and I intend to use you for whatever I can get."

I told him that my advice was to call up your *favorite* artist . . . It's important to be sincere.

BE PROFESSIONAL

✦ "Be professional" is obvious advice. Can you be more specific?

✧ **Everyone would agree that it's unprofessional to get drunk at a business meeting. Art openings and art parties are thinly veiled business meetings, so it follows that you shouldn't get drunk at an art opening or party. Don't be pretentious. It's a turn-off. If you don't know something, it's a golden opportunity to let someone give you advice. People who give you advice usually end up being your supporters. Don't be afraid to show your naïveté. Don't interrupt. Listen. To listen is to acquire. To** speak is to give away. Look at the person to whom you're talking. A classic mistake that art world hustlers make is to look around the room while they are having a conversation with someone in order to find another person who they believe is more important. This is insulting and it's stupid, because you never really know who's who. B-list people frequently become A-list people and they don't forget. If you're not satisfied with the person you're talking to, end the conversation politely and move on. Otherwise, give them your full attention. When you meet people at openings, don't shove invitations into their faces the moment you meet them. It makes you look like a beginner and makes people think you're treating them as part of the herd to be rounded up. Instead, develop and maintain a mailing list. Mail your invitations, or have your gallery mail them one to three weeks before the opening. This makes people feel infinitely more special,

✧ page 191:
Transfigured Night
1995
Oil on canvas
24 x 18 inches
Collection of John and Mary Box

because you took the time to think of them and spent money on a stamp. Although it's better to mail them, it's okay to give out invitations in person, but only after the recipient expresses some interest first. As in, "What have you been doing lately?" or "Do you have any shows coming up?"

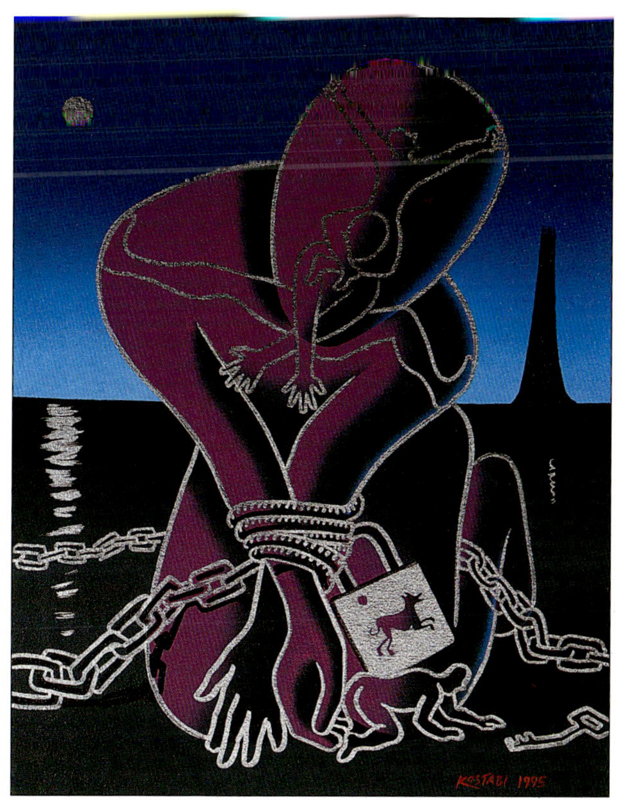

Unless the show is two days away, it's still better to say, "Yes, would you like me to send you an invitation?" This will usually lead to your getting another address for your mailing list.

✦ What does having a story have to do with art?

✧ **Van Gogh cut off his ear. Gauguin went to Tahiti. Picasso went to the bullfights. Chris Burden shot**

himself in the arm. Beethoven was deaf. Mozart was a child prodigy. Kostabi doesn't paint his own paintings. These anecdotes have very little to do with the work of the artist. And yet more people know the stories than know the work.

✦ That's an interesting point, but I have a feeling that your example of "Kostabi doesn't paint his own paintings" arguably has a lot to do with your work. You've done so many paintings about factory-made art and the creative process at Kostabi World, like your recent painting *The Rhythm of Inspiration*.

✧ page 193:
Whiffle
1995
Paint marker & oil on canvas
24 x 18 inches
Collection of Davide DiMaggio

✧ **In the grand scheme of things my paintings about Kostabi World constitute a miniscule fraction of my entire oeuvre. Van Gogh also painted self-portraits showing his bandaged ear, and while anecdotally interesting and valuable, simply depicting the bandage is not what made Van Gogh's work great.**

HAVE A STORY

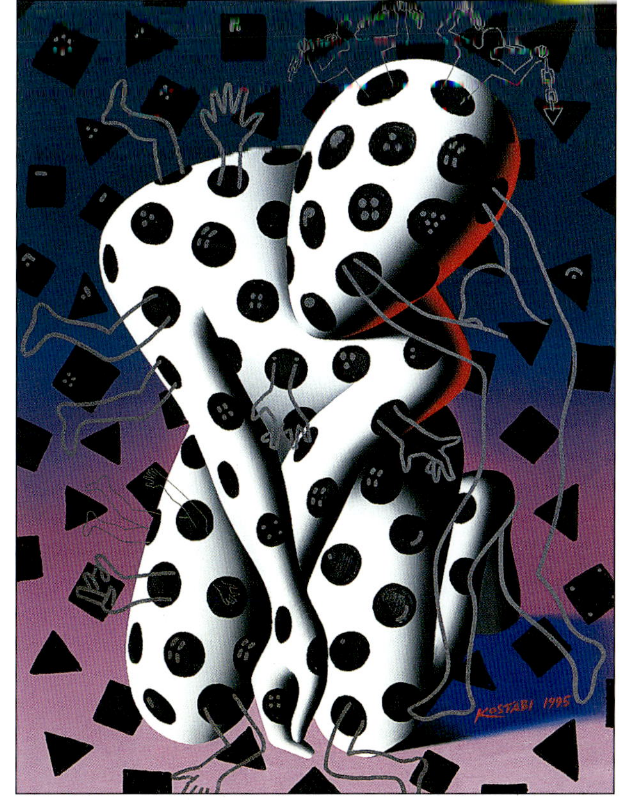

✦ What if you don't have a story?

✧ **Don't cut off your ear! But it does help to have interesting anecdotes to color your mythology. Even if your life is boring, that could be your angle.**

"His work is so interesting and yet his life is so dull."

Make it duller and play it up. But most likely you have a story, especially if you live in New York. You get a story pretty fast here. At one time I had nothing to say about myself or my work. The work was good and it attracted journalists, but they didn't write much about me because I couldn't deliver at the interview. One day I decided to do

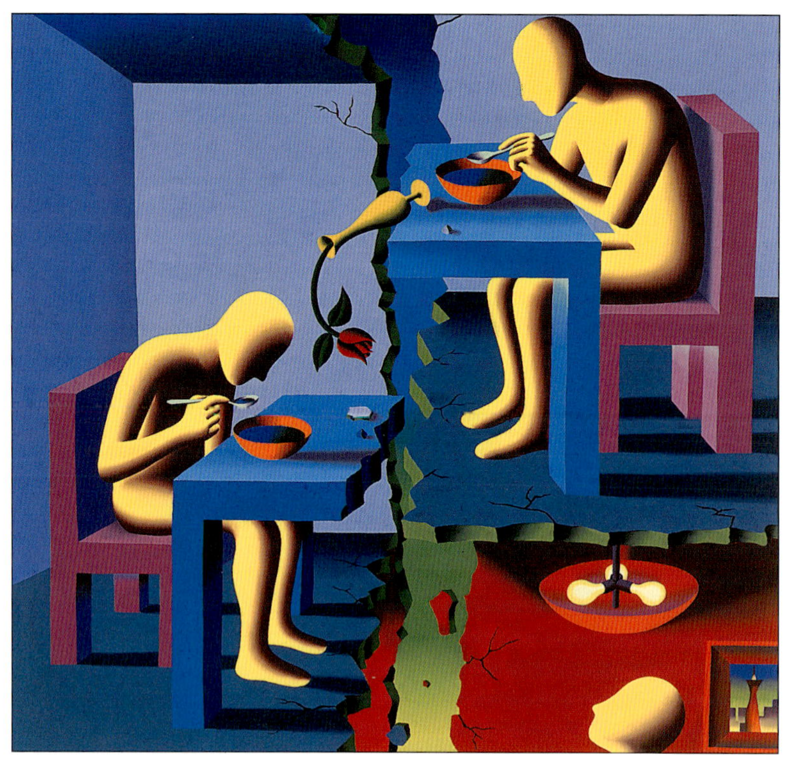

✧ **A Broken Home**
1994
Oil on canvas
49 x 48 inches
Kostabi World

something about it. Carlo McCormick was scheduled to interview me for the *East Village Eye* in early 1984. I made a list of the most common questions that people asked me. I prepared interesting, evocative answers. When Carlo showed up with his tape recorder at my Rivington Street walk-up, lo and behold, he asked the same old questions. I whipped out my notes and began reading the answers. He loved it. He didn't mind that it wasn't spontaneous because it was great material. In the weeks that followed, the *Village Voice*, the *New York Times* and *Art in America* all quoted material from that interview. That was the official birth of my media persona. Soon I began writing self-interviews.

✦ Like this one?

✧ **No, this is a real self-interview. I'm really talking to myself, and it's book-length. The others were short and flippant. Sometimes I hired other people to respond to questions. I would say, "Now how would Kostabi answer this question? If you were a car, what kind would you be?" And the ghostwriter would say "A taxi, because the meter is always running."**

✦ You hired other people to write your self-interview??

✧ **Yes, just like other people paint my self-portraits.**

✦ Are other people writing this self-interview?

✧ **I feel other people in my head are telling me what to say sometimes.**

✦ You're avoiding the question. Did someone else write this self-interview?

✧ **I wrote part of it.**

✦ Who wrote the other part?

✧ **You did.**

✦ I think you're trying to cast doubt about yourself. Even if you did write it all by yourself, you'd like people to be unsure.

My integrity is defined by an ability to stay on the

move between partial, incomplete, and irreconcilable realities. My images are about the media, but my image is a *product* of the media. And I mediate between my images and my image. Life is a collage. Inconsistency is a source of resiliency. We live in an age of fragmentation, disintegration, absence of moral parameters, the demise of the subject, the end of the author, and the impossibility of truth. It is better to be fluid, resilient, and on the move than to be firm, fixed, and settled. Discontinuity is a mirror of reality and a standard for a reasonable life.

✦ It's important for you to be considered important, isn't it?

✧ **Yes.**

✦ Why do you suppose that is?

✧ **I learned that in art school. It's something to aspire toward. Like being good. And I want to be good. I understand the temptation to be bad. Sometimes I feel like eating people. I realize that cannibalism is a natural act, but love tastes better.**

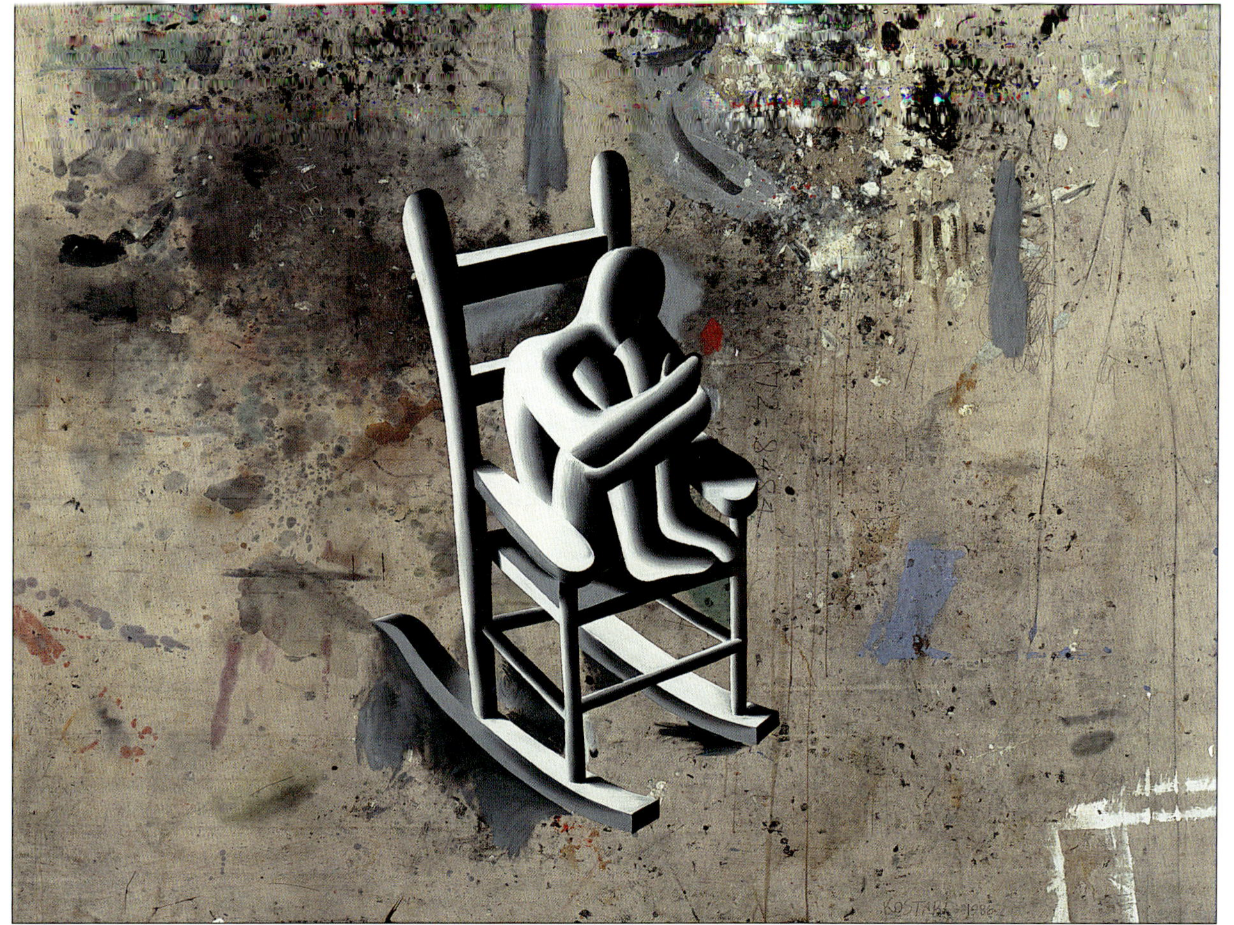

✧ **The Futile Position**

1986

Oil on canvas

68 x 90 inches

Solomon R. Guggenheim Museum, New York

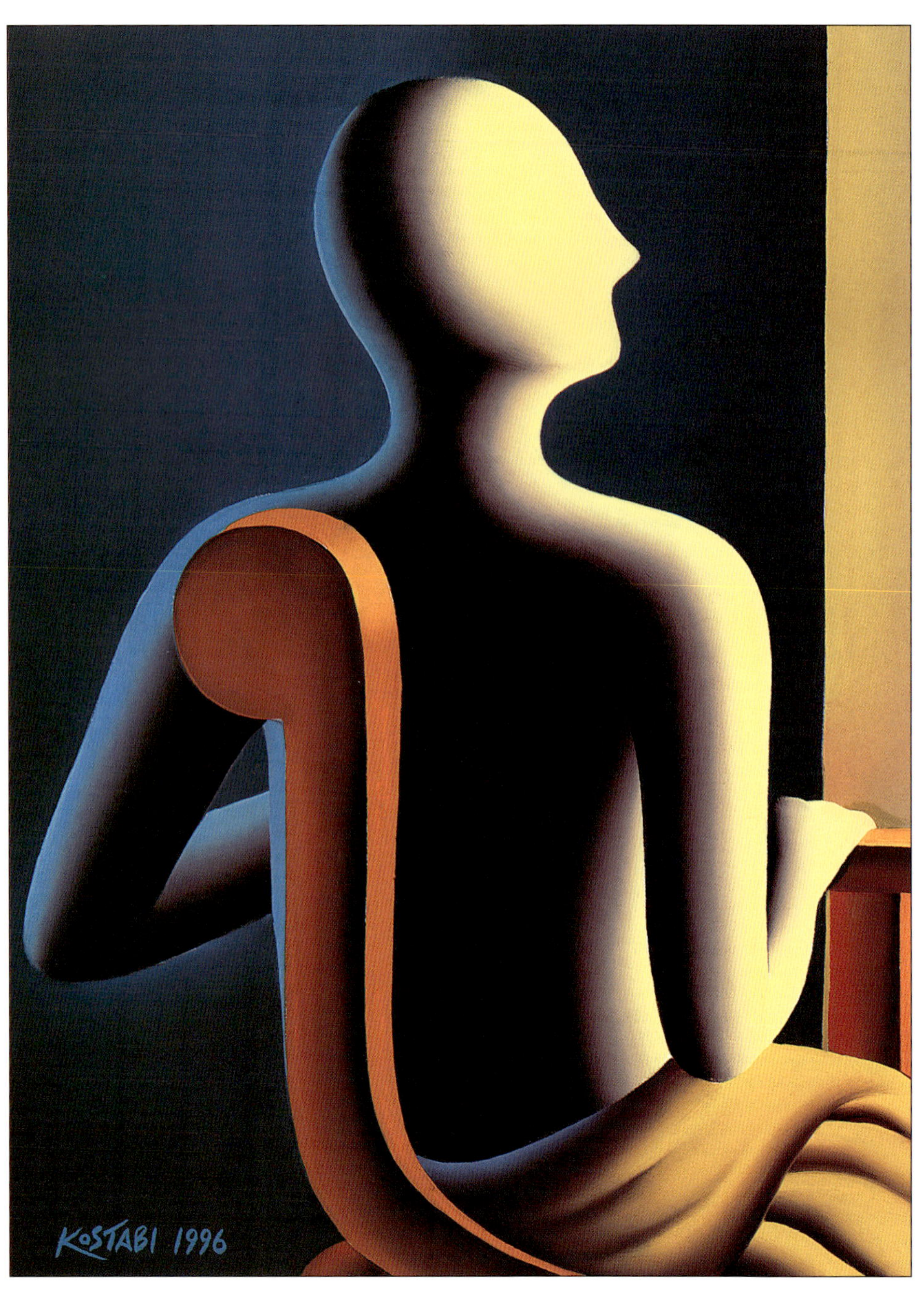
KOSTABI 1996

GET PEOPLE TO WORK FOR YOU

✦ Your sixth and final rule for success is to get people to work for you. Are you talking about hiring assistants?

✧ **Assistants? No. Not necessarily. People are working for you simply by talking about you. Ask for lots of advice. People who give you free advice are working for you. If you have a friend who always raves about you or your work, make sure that he or she is invited to all your events. Surround yourself with positive people. Get negative people out of your life. Don't count on one person for your success or happiness. Above all, believe you deserve success. It doesn't need much explaining. You can do anything you want to do and don't let anyone convince you otherwise.**

✧ page 198:
Sensation
1996
Oil on canvas
24 x 18 inches
Collection of Davide DiMaggio

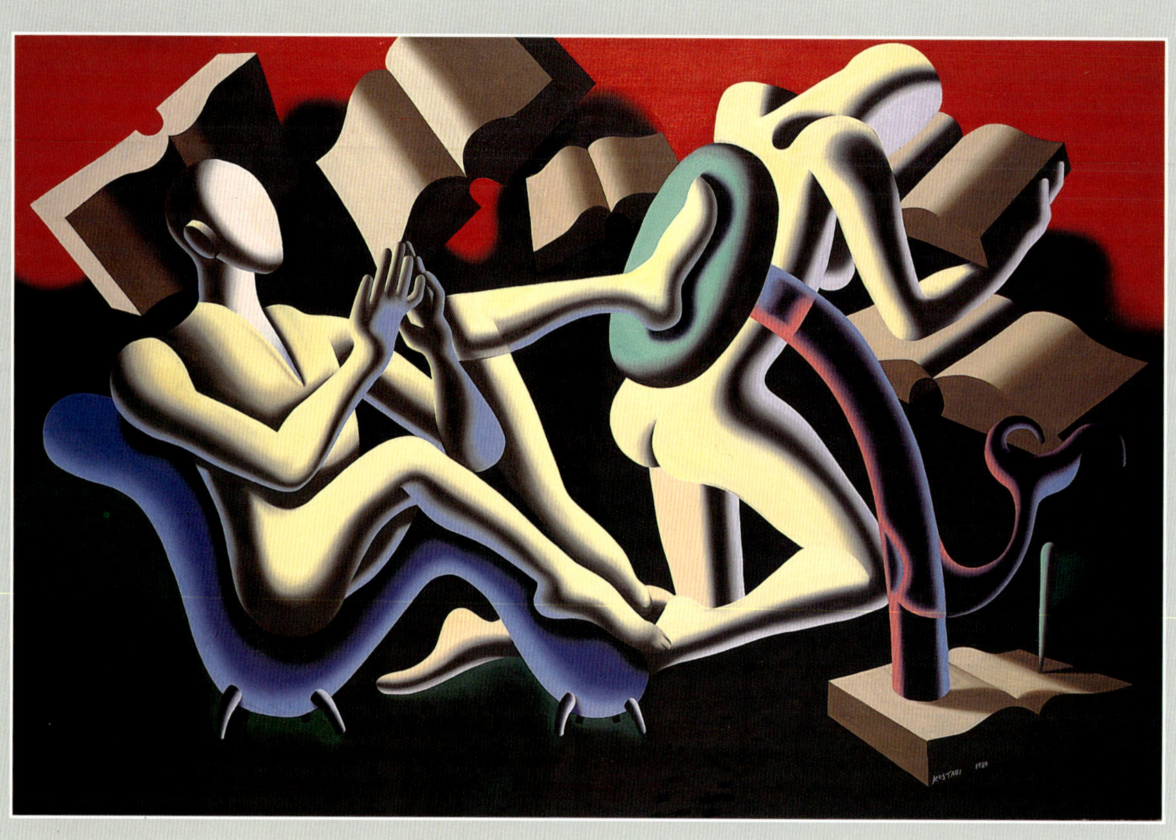

INDEX

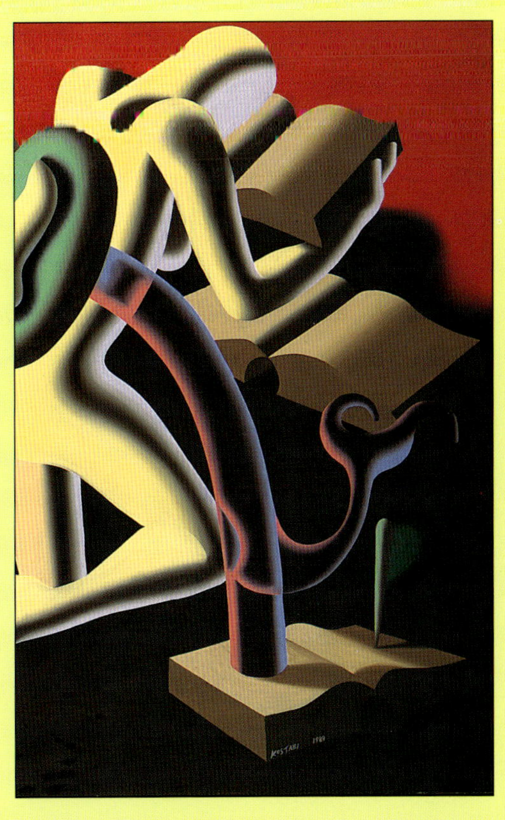

✧ page 200:
Pump up the Volumes
1989
Oil on canvas
60 x 90 inches
Collection of Arthur Bricker

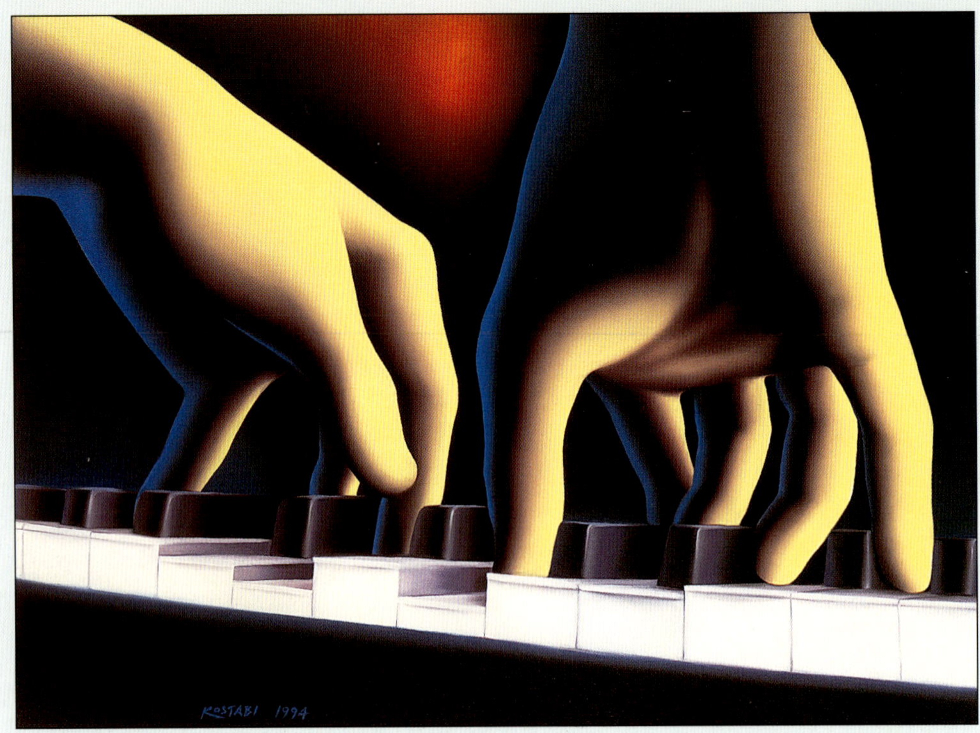

✧ **Polonaise**

1995

Oil on canvas

30 x 40 inches

Collection of the artist

PHOTO CREDITS

Principal photography of Mark Kostabi's paintings by Hiromi Nakano, Paul Kostabi, and D. James Dee.

Daniele Bevacqua

page 102 (top, right)

Peter Serling

page 35, right. Photo copyright © 1996 Peter Serling. All rights reserved. Page reproduced from *People Weekly,* which is a registered trademark of Time Inc. Used with permission.